The U. S. Economy in the 1950's

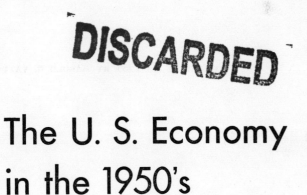

The U. S. Economy in the 1950's

AN ECONOMIC HISTORY

Harold G. Vatter
Carleton College

W · W · NORTON & COMPANY · INC · *New York*

Library of Congress Catalog Card No. 62-12291

PRINTED IN THE UNITED STATES OF AMERICA
FOR THE PUBLISHERS BY THE VAIL-BALLOU PRESS, INC.
234567890

Contents

Charts

Charts

Preface

The present volume reflects the growing recognition that the facts of economic history deserve a more theoretical organization than has been customary. It nonetheless also tries to make available in one small place the essential record of the American economy during the 1950's by examining the economic contours of that decade in contrast to the periods that immediately preceded and followed it. The features which the 1950's share with the past and the present are indeed the key to understanding the decade, for the thought and behavior during any short span of history are best explained by the period's continuity with the years that surround it.

Any history that attempts to rise above the level of sophisticated gossip must be organized around some focus. The focus here, in line with the chief concern of public policy and economic theory today, is on the relative efficacy of the major spending streams as determinants of the rate of economic development. My objective has been to place the history of the 1950's in the long-run context of American economic growth.

The contemporary swing toward theory, particularly growth theory, must of course be careful lest it assume too haughty an attitude toward the human and the humdrum aspects of experience. I am not sure that in my considerable reliance upon contemporary theory I have wholly avoided this danger; but, on the other hand, the long tradition of story-telling that has passed for history needs a stiff antidote.

It is hoped that this review of the 1950's will be useful in college courses in American economic history and the principles of economics. There is also reason to anticipate that it might modestly enlarge the horizon of the interested layman. The book presupposes only that the reader has some familiarity with the elements of economics. The level of technical terminology is introductory, and the few more sophisticated concepts employed are always defined when first presented.

I am much indebted to a number of colleagues and others for their careful reading of various chapters or sections of the manuscript. These include Professor Jesse Burkhead of Syracuse University, Professor Charles Friday of Oregon State University, Professor Virginia Galbraith of Mount Holyoke College, Professor Forest Hill of the University of Texas, Professor Joseph Phillips of the University of Illinois, Professor Jack Thorkelson of the University of Connecticut, Professors Ada Harrison and Robert Will, both of Carleton College, and my wife, Barbara A. Vatter. Although the book is incomparably better than it would have been without their generous help, I bear sole responsibility for errors, weaknesses, and in a few cases, failure to follow advice that has been given.

I wish also to express my appreciation for the careful work of my student research assistant, Mr. Robert Ernest, and for the high sensitivity to good manuscript requirements on the part of my typist, Mrs. Florence Scott.

I am also grateful to the Ford Foundation's Fund for Research in Public Affairs for assistance in pursuing certain aspects of the study.

Harold G. Vatter

Northfield, Minnesota

1 | Identifying Features of the 1950's

Major Distinguishing Characteristics

The Abundant Economy

It became clear to all the world that the United States economy after mid-century was capable of producing enough to provide every man, woman, and child with a minimum-comfort level of living. A rough index of this potential is revealed by the fact that per capita consumption in 1960 was $1,824. Although this is an average, it nevertheless indicates the capacity of the economy at that time to provide all Americans with necessities and some comforts. Moreover, the $329 billion of consumer expenditures still left an enormous margin of output above consumption, for gross national product (GNP) was $504 billion.

The remarkable capacity of the United States economy in 1960 represents the crossing of a great divide in the history of humanity, especially significant in view of the fact that a number of other industrially advanced countries possessed similar capabilities. The full significance for all mankind lies in the possibility that poverty can be eliminated within the foreseeable future. "The poor are always with us" became a dated proposition in the 1950's. The industrial revolution of the eighteenth and nineteenth centuries had made possible a long-run, persistent rise in levels of living in the United States and other Western countries. Extension of the coal-steel-steam power base of that revolution during the

1

twentieth century made conceivable the provision of material necessities for the entire human race, assuming no untoward leaps in the world's population.

The breakthrough on the poverty front led some economists in the 1950's to work with the notion of a distinction between the provision of essentials and the provision of the more affluent kind of consumption found among the upper income strata in the richer economies. This twofold classification of the stream of consumer absorption suggested the desirability of a more refined conception of the economists' traditional law of scarcity, emphasizing the boundlessness of human wants rather than the relationship between available resources and some category of *pressing* wants.

The practical possibility of satisfying pressing wants figured prominently in the development plans of the less developed countries after World War II and became a major issue in the international competition between the great power blocs. It was acknowledged that the rate of growth of production *could* outrun the rate of growth of population by a comfortable margin. The population pessimists in the 1950's placed the race between these two rates high on the list of vital problems that would confront the world during the remainder of the twentieth century. The race would be a crucial problem for the less developed areas in the next decades. It seemed clear, however, that once a country made the leap into a phase of sustained rise in output and living levels, birth rates would probably fall sufficiently to escape for an indefinite period the trap of general poverty. The empirical basis of this hypothesis, of course, was largely the historical experience of the North Atlantic world.

The increasing disparity in contemporary world economy between the wealthy nations and the poor nations brought with it world-wide demands by the underdeveloped countries for a greater share of wealth and income. International aid, which a decade earlier some had disdainfully called "globaloney," became a hallmark of the 1950's.

Aside from the political aspects of these ever more insistent demands by the less developed countries, it became clearer as the 1950's unfolded that the failure of the rich countries to divert substantial portions of their production to the provision of goods to satisfy essential consumer wants, as well as intermediate goods and services for the economically less developed peoples, would at the least generate rather severe feelings of responsibility among many in the rich lands. On the other hand, such aid in the form of gifts appeared to strong opposition elements in the United States and elsewhere to be a wasteful dole. This among other factors lowered the amount of American foreign aid for non-military purposes and limited it for the most part to yearly *ad hoc* programs.

Domestically, the United States came to be considered an "affluent society." The appellation was perhaps new with John Kenneth Galbraith,[1] although the concept of an abundant economy had long been applied to the United States by the institutional school of American economists. Galbraith developed the concept largely in order to contrast the relative affluence of the private sector of the economy with an alleged paucity in the provision of public services; at the same time he brought into focus the fact that the economy of the United States in the 1950's could easily eliminate all poverty within its borders. This had not been the case during the "New Era" of the 1920's, despite much talk at that time of two chickens in every pot and two cars in every garage. Nor was it the case during the depression decade, for at that time the talk was about "poverty in the midst of plenty." The decade of World War II achieved new highs in output, but an economy operating under the forced draft of war cannot claim an equivalent peacetime capacity. Thus it was not until the 1950's that the United States truly became the affluent society. After a dip shortly following the war, real GNP (1954 prices) had again reached its wartime peak by 1950. Real per capita consumption (1960 prices) rose from $1,350 in the last year of the war to the aforementioned $1,824 in 1960. Had capacity been more completely utilized and had the large military budgets of the decade been absent or even substantially reduced, the full-capacity peacetime consumption potential of the American economy would have been even greater.

Of course per capita statistics on consumption are little more than brute indexes. They do not reveal levels of living; neither do they reveal the distribution of the national income. There was much discussion during the 1950's of the low income stratum in the population, of especially disadvantaged groups, and of the so-called depressed areas. With the onset of the 1960's structural unemployment (due to failure of the economy to attain an adequate rate of growth) was added to the growing list of welfare problems.

Theorists of the business cycle had long noted the recurrent tendency exhibited by economies of the American type to ex-

1. See John K. Galbraith, *The Affluent Society* (Boston, Houghton Mifflin, 1958).

pand capacity at a rate in excess of that warranted by the rate of expansion of demand at profitable prices. As a chronic phenomenon this represented, as has been mentioned, one form of abundance. The presence of such pressure of capacity on demand at profitable prices as a *long-run phenomenon* had been noted in the case of agriculture. But, aside from Thorstein Veblen, systematic theoretical recognition of this as a *general* relationship had in the twentieth century broken through the dominant orthodoxy only during the intellectual ferment sparked by the great depression. During the 1950's and at present, great theoretical activity has been centered upon the question whether the rate of growth of aggregate demand can keep pace, at remunerative prices, with the projected potential for sustained growth of total capacity. Such a query is really addressed to a society which is groping for a way to deal with *abundant capacity*.

For those who concerned themselves with United States economic affairs in the 1950's, relative abundance in the sense of both excess capacity and the ability to provide for all pressing wants therefore became a consciously registered fact of economic life and a problem in social control. Why it appeared as a problem in social control, rather than a matter to be handled by a presumed automatic market mechanism, is a phenomenon which can be explained only through an examination of the economy's long-run evolution—an investigation that must go at least as far back as the last quarter of the nineteenth century. More will therefore be said about this later.

Mass Unemployment Eliminated

The central economic goal of the 1930's was the achievement of full employment. The goal was not attained, and unemployment ranged from about 15 per cent to 25 per cent of the civilian labor force between 1931 and 1940. The 1950's escaped such mass unemployment ratios. Average unemployment for the decade was 4.6 per cent of the civilian labor force. Despite various deficiencies in the concept and measurement of unemployment statistics, it seems reasonable to generalize that the postwar decade had at least temporarily solved the major problem that the 1930's had been unable to solve. *How* this was accomplished will soon absorb our attention; at the moment it is sufficient to point out that it was accomplished.

The elimination of mass unemployment by no means left the economy free of any unemployment problem. The lowest unemployment level was recorded during the Korean War of 1950–

1953. In other years the minimum unemployment approached 3 million, which was in excess of 4 per cent of the civilian labor force and an even higher per cent of the nonfarm labor force. Furthermore, as the decade waned the ratios crept upward. Consequently the period was distinguished only by the absence of large-scale unemployment.

To appreciate the achievement of the 1950's in the matter of employment, fruitful comparison may again be made with the 1920's. That decade was generally one of high employment except for the severe postwar contraction of 1920–21. The yearly unemployment ratio reached almost 12 per cent of the civilian labor force in 1921 and was still 7.6 per cent in 1922. These ratios exceed anything experienced in the 1950's. The duration of unemployment in the slump of the early 1920's was also greater than that found in any of the recessions marking the path of change in the 1950's. The contraction of 1920–21 lasted for eighteen months —twice the length of the 1957–58 contraction, the one with the highest unemployment rate in the 1950's. Furthermore, the statistical differences signify more than first meets the eye, for underlying them are notable differences in the structure and behavior of the economy in the two periods.

A Decade of Large Government Budgets

Although it can be argued that an era of large public budgets was inaugurated in the 1920's, with the notable growth of state and local expenditures in that decade, the decade of the New Deal is more generally accepted as the onset of this era. It might well be reasoned, however, that the depression decade was an emergency situation, and that government intervention at that time was a response to the conditions then obtaining rather than the herald of a new era of big government. Public budgets for most of the 1940's were swollen by global war and its aftermath. But the 1950's proved to be the first decade without great depression or global war in which large public budgets were a prominent economic condition.

The ratio of all government purchases to gross private product in real terms (1954 prices) was about .15 in 1950. By 1955 it had risen to .20 (it had been about .11 in 1929 and .17 in 1939), around which figure it hovered each year through 1960. These crude indexes of government's role in the economy certainly suggest a persistent increase over an extended period. They therefore tend to place the burden of argument upon those who would claim that large public budgets are a transitory phenomenon.

Mere statistics do not make for conviction, of course; and a really convincing hypothesis must unfold a theory that would explain why large government budgets, either cold war or welfare, are slated to be an abiding feature of the economy. But for the moment this proposition will simply have to stand as a descriptive statement designed to characterize the 1950's. The groundwork for big government in peacetime had been laid in earlier decades and given legislative sanction by the Employment Act of 1946. (Passed by an overwhelming bipartisan majority, the act declared it to be the continuing policy of the Federal government to promote maximum employment, production, and purchasing power.) But the 1950's completed the establishment of substantial budgets as an abiding "peacetime" phenomenon. This was clearly an identifying feature of the decade, albeit a feature whose long-run significance was beclouded by fluctuations in Federal defense outlays.

Retardation of the Incipient Welfare State

A breakdown of the public budgets according to the level of government and the type of expenditure reveals that the historically high ratios of public expenditures to United States national product in the 1950's were overwhelmingly attributable to military expenditures of the Federal government. This generalization need be qualified only by acknowledging that, as compared with the 1920's, there was a high proportion of Federal transfer payments to persons in the 1950's. Transfer payments are made without reference to current involvement of the recipient, in the sense that he yields nothing currently in exchange for receipt of the payment. Among such payments are old age and survivors insurance (OASI) benefits, unemployment insurance benefits, and veterans' benefits. These payments, despite the fact that they are financed chiefly by regressive payroll taxes, are considered a hallmark of the so-called welfare state as it has emerged in the United States. Since the 1920's they have risen absolutely and relatively to GNP. However, the 1950's failed to reveal any noteworthy rise in the importance of Federal transfer payments as compared to the New Deal days. They accounted for about 4 per cent of GNP in 1939 and 4.4 per cent in 1960. If one adds Federal civilian expenditures to these, then the total of such Federal expenditures plus transfers equaled 7.4 per cent of GNP in 1939 but only 6.0 per cent in 1960. If the combined role of these two components of Federal expenditures is taken as a crude measure of welfarism, the 1950's showed a relative increase since the 1920's but not since the 1930's. The momentum toward a welfare state gained during the great depression decade was largely, although not entirely, dissipated during the 1950's.

The relative importance of all state and local expenditures edged upward slightly during the 1950's, a decade which began with such expenditures accounting for 7.0 per cent of GNP (identical with 1929) and ended with 9.4 per cent. The upward drift was not erratic, but steady and clear. A high proportion of state and local expenditures was in the welfare category, but these expenditures merely kept pace with the growth of GNP. Since these expenditures totaled $47.3 billion in 1960, whereas all Federal civilian expenditures plus transfer payments were only $30.2 billion, it could be contended that the lower levels of government still predominated in the provision of welfare services. Nevertheless, the trend up to 1939 was to raise the ratio of Federal civilian-plus-transfers to total state and local: in 1929 it was $2.3 billion over $7.2 billion, or .32; the New Deal raised the ratio to .82 in 1939. At the end of the 1950's it had fallen back to .64—another indication of the relative retarding of Federal welfarism.

A Decade of Moderate Economic Growth

There has been much concern in the 1960's regarding the rate of growth of total output. Most persons accept the goal of a high rate of economic growth. Indeed, by the mid-1950's many had already substituted the achievement of higher growth rates for mass unemployment as the central problem confronting the economy. Aside from the matter of national pride, together with various domestic economic reasons for rapid growth, the competition with the Soviet Union and the clamor of less developed countries for more aid seemed to call for improved performance in this regard.

Real GNP in 1954 prices exhibited an average annual increment of 2.9 per cent over the period 1950–59.[2] This performance was notably below the 4.7 per cent annual increment for 1921–29 and the 3.72 per cent per year estimated by Raymond Goldsmith for the period 1879–1919.[3] The 1950's seemed to extend a secular, i.e., long-run downward drift in the growth rate of total output.

The 1950's revealed substantial average annual rates of expansion during the first half and weak expansion rates during the second half. The former phase was of course dominated by the Korean War. Real GNP increased at an average annual rate of 4.7 per

2. Boris P. Pesek, "Economic Growth and Its Measurement," in *Economic Development and Cultural Change*, April, 1961, p. 308, Table 2, Method VII.
3. Bert G. Hickman, *Growth and Stability of the Postwar Economy* (Washington, D.C., Brookings Institution, 1960), p. 19, Table I.

cent from 1950 to 1955, but the rate from 1955 to 1959 was only 2.25 per cent.[4] Of the two periods, the latter seems unfortunately the more significant for analytical purposes since no hot war was present.

If 1955 is included in the latter half of the decade and 1960 is added, the analyst has a six-year period to work with. This is quite inadequate for long-range projections, but it is all we have to go by, and the up-to-date student of this period can add the most recent knowledge to provide a richer accumulation of experience. If the annual growth rates of GNP in the first half of the decade are extrapolated and viewed as the potential growth rate applicable to the last half of the decade, the data reveal a substantial and continuous gap between potential and actual GNP from the beginning of 1956 through 1961. Furthermore, each recovery period subsequent to 1953 saw a higher proportion of the civilian labor force unemployed than before.

Looking at the decade as a whole, most persons would judge the growth rate of output as rather sluggish. If the latter part of the decade is made the reference point, the rate would be judged unsatisfactory, particularly when compared with the 1920's or the long-run performance of the economy prior to the great depression of the 1930's. The 1950's were therefore noteworthy for only moderate growth in total production.

The Population Burst

As a unit the 1950's exhibited a reversal of the long-run decline in the rate of population growth since the Civil War. The reversal began with the onset of World War II and was overwhelmingly due to a rise in the birth rate that was caused chiefly by the gains in employment, income, and general economic security associated with war conditions.

The 1950's were distinguished by high absolute rates of population growth exceeding even those of the 1940's, but this trend reached a peak in 1956, after which the rates began to be retarded. This contrast is found both for the absolute rate of increase (number per year) and for percentages. Birth rates per 1,000 of the population showed a similar trend, attaining a high point of 25.2 in 1956–57 and thereafter declining to 23.7 in 1959–60.

It would be sensible to postulate that the rate of economic growth in the late 1950's was insufficient to stimulate population growth rates as high as those obtaining in the early 1950's. The

4. Henry H. Villard, "Some Comments on Growth," *American Economic Review*, March, 1961, p. 123.

highly sensitive marriage rate per 1,000 of population declined
fairly steadily throughout the decade, from 11.1 in 1950 to 8.5
in 1959. Maintenance of an upward drift in births per 1,000 was
sustained until 1957, however, despite the drop in the marriage
rate. The consequence was a rise in the size of the family that also
reversed a long-run downward trend.

Demographic theory has long entertained the hypothesis that
both marriage rates and birth rates in advanced countries are highly
responsive to short-run and intermediate-period economic
changes. This apparently applied to marriage rates in the 1950's;
but it has been suggested that the rise in family size expressed
largely psychological factors, such as the search for psychic
security in an age of alienation through turning inward toward
the family group. Another suggestion has been that babies are
viewed as a consumer durable good expected to yield a stream
of psychic income through time!

One of the interesting aspects of the rise in average family
size was the apparent fact that the middle to higher income strata
exhibited the greater rise. The average family size rose from
3.59 in 1948 to 3.65 in 1957. If this rise is broken down by size
of money income, we get the distribution shown in Table 1-1.

TABLE 1-1

Family Income and Size

Families (ranked according to size of income)	Average size of family		Average number of children under 18 living in family	
	1948	1957	1948	1957
Lowest	3.29	3.27	1.14	1.19
2	3.52	3.60	1.29	1.43
3	3.58	3.75	1.30	1.54
4	3.62	3.80	1.19	1.47
Highest	3.94	3.82	1.03	1.27
TOTAL	3.59	3.65	1.19	1.38

SOURCE: Robert J. Lampman, "The Low Income Population and Economic
Growth," Study Paper No. 12 *Study of Employment, Growth, and Price
Levels,* Joint Economic Committee, 86th Cong., 1st sess. (Washington, D.C.,
U.S. Government Printing Office, December 16, 1959), p. 21, Table 15.

It seems clear that the lowest income category cannot account for
the rise. It is the third and fourth categories—the middle income
strata—that offer the main explanation of the gain in both family

size and average number of children. The data are highly suggestive of a response to the improved economic security enjoyed by
these strata in the 1950's, although psychological factors are certainly not to be ruled negligible. Note also that by 1957 these
same middle classes, not "the poor," have the absolutely largest
average number of children under 18 living in the family.

The baby boom, which could easily run into two generations,
encompassed the 1940's and extended into the 1950's. The babies
of the former decade endowed the 1950's with the consumption,
production, and public-service patterns of a children's influx.
They will endow the 1960's with the economic patterns of a
young adult influx.

Accelerated Technological Advance

The 1950's were a period of rapid technological progress. But
technological progress in a general sense was hardly unique to the
1950's. It was the rate of the advance and the character of the
technological innovations that set the 1950's apart from earlier
decades.

The overall rate of technological progress is a phenomenon
which defies accurate measurement. It is generally necessary to
rely upon indirect results or particular cases, including changes
wrought by specific business innovations, in order to get a "feel"
for the rate of advance. Standard evidence includes estimated
productivity changes associated with the installation of a certain
new piece of equipment. Another approach involves listing a large
number of epochal process or product improvements. This approach is impressionistic, but it is the best means for theorizing
about the overall rate of technological advance. The most plausible hypothesis regarding the overall rate is that it grows un-
evenly but faster as the social cumulation of technology proceeds.
Recognition of this possibility seems to have been what Professor
Charles Frankel had in mind when in 1958 he characterized the
era as outstanding because of the "change in the tempo of
change." [5] The hypothesis that technological progress is an accelerating phenomenon is consistent with the statistics on the
important matter of long-run productivity change in the American economy, which reveal a rising trend since about World War
I.[6] Dr. Solomon Fabricant has called attention to the fact that the

5. Charles Frankel, "Third Great Revolution of Mankind," *New York
Times,* February 9, 1958.
6. Solomon Fabricant, *Basic Facts on Productivity Change* (New York,
National Bureau of Economic Research, Occasional Paper #63, 1958),
pp. 10ff.

long-term pace of advance in output per man-hour increased from 22 per cent per decade during the quarter-century preceding World War I to 35–40 per cent since World War II.[7]

Reference to some of the chief innovations of the decade may yield an appreciation of the contribution of the 1950's to the general progress of the industrial arts. Dating an innovation is of course a hazardous procedure. The 1950's inaugurated the application of nuclear power to harnessed energy production. But nuclear fission and fusion are better dated from World War II, with scientific antecedents that stretch far back in history. The data-processing equipment industry, whose factory sales were $25 million in 1953 and $1 billion in 1960, drew most heavily upon the tiny transistor, which was developed in 1948. Hence, it is best to consider those innovations in production technique that were strongly identified with, although not entirely new in, the 1950's, and alternatively those innovations which were incipient before 1950 and which passed into active use after 1950.

Aside from the lengthy list of new-product technology and certain new organizational techniques, the major innovations in process technology (which in turn were linked with new products and organizational techniques, all types of techniques being interconnected) can be subsumed under three types:

1. An upsurge in the established trend toward substitution of the mechanical direction of operations for direct human supervision. The worker who formerly tended a machine or operation was to a greater extent tending a control, feeder, or handling mechanism. Innovations of this type represented the further spread of automaticity.

2. The incorporation into mechanical control, feeder, and handling equipment of the feedback principle—automation. As illustrated crudely by the household furnace thermostat, automation in the sense here employed means "the introduction of self-regulating devices into the industrial sequence through the feedback principle whereby electronic sensing devices automatically pass information back to earlier parts of the processing machine, correcting for tool wear or other items of control." [8] Automation also brought with it a fantastic increase in the sensitivity and operating speeds of control equipment and a vastly expanded capacity of such equipment to deal with complexity.

7. National Bureau of Economic Research. *Annual Report*, 1959.

8. "Automation and Technological Change," *Report* of the Subcommittee on Economic Stabilization to the Joint Committee on the Economic Report, U.S. Congress, 84th Cong., 1st sess. (Washington, D.C., U.S. Government Printing Office), p. 3.

At least equally significant was the application, introduced by the end of the decade, of feedback technique in the very important job-lot type of production process, as distinguished from the continuous process and the standardized product.[9] This was done by the use of punched tapes, films, or cards.

The great contribution of automation, perhaps the greatest innovation of the 1950's, was the establishment of high speed, precision *self-regulation* in a growing variety of production processes.

Closely associated with the application of automation to economic activity was the enormous growth of the great new industry of the 1950's: electronics. This heterogeneous giant, with factory sales of $9.75 billion in 1960, expanded at the rate of 15 per cent per annum, and had become the nation's fifth largest industry in that year, exceeded only by automobiles, steel, aircraft, and chemicals.

3. Integration of processes, consisting of two general types. One involved the extension of established continuous-flow production methods to encompass and link together more operations, accelerating the rate of flow of the whole. Examples: automatic shuttles to load and transport materials from operation to operation and articulated to provide uninterrupted processing (as in the Chrysler Corporation's Plymouth engine plant which opened on August 1, 1955); also, the continuous-weld pipe mill at the Lorain, Ohio, works of the United States Steel Corporation, which began commercial production in mid-December, 1960. The other process was the combination into a simultaneous action of a number of operations formerly accomplished sequentially. Since sequential operation, either discrete or continuous, was developed historically through specialization, this new form of integration of operations represents a reversal of a long-established trend and is one of the great new technological changes of our time. Examples: a machine for drilling the holes in an automobile crankshaft in one operation that was formerly performed by twenty-nine different machines; also, the fabrication of a complete printed circuit board in one operation instead of by separate hand-wiring in sections. The board itself was "unitized," that is, produced as a single complex item without separable components.

All of these innovations greatly accelerated basic trends already set in motion by the progress of technology; some of them penetrated areas of the economy, like the white-collar occupations, that

9. Edgar Weinberg, "A Review of Automatic Technology," *Monthly Labor Review*, June, 1955, p. 641.

previously had been but lightly touched.

Fundamental to the advance of technology is the production and transmission of power. The great new promise in this field during the 1950's came from nuclear energy. Aside from its extended application to military uses, nuclear energy had a negligible economic impact. Although important for non-energy uses, for example in such fields as radioisotopes and food preservation, the use of nuclear fuels to generate electric power—the chief apparent application in the energy field—was still insignificant in 1960. A number of nuclear powered electric generating stations were constructed by the end of this period, but they were pilot plants that were far from competitive with conventional plants using traditional fuels.

The most dramatic scientific-technological achievement of the 1950's was the launching of artificial satellites, first by the Soviets and then by the United States. However, by the early 1960's the achievement could not yet be considered an innovation (application of an invention). The same may be said of the special new fuels used to launch these artificial satellites. The 1950's were merely the threshold of the space age.

It may seem strange that high rates of technological advance were accompanied by the previously mentioned moderate-to-sluggish growth rate of total output. Moreover, the slowdown in the rate of growth of productivity in the latter years of the 1950's was particularly sharp in the manufacturing sector, where one might expect the productivity effects (output per unit of input) of the striking technological advances to be centered. The puzzle here is essentially imaginary, however. Technological improvements are not the equivalent of output increases. Nor is the application of technological improvements the only factor in average or marginal output per unit of input. Also, aggregate figures often conceal opposing tendencies. For example, firms or sectors which lag in the adoption of innovations may experience constant or decreasing productivity ratios, while others, like the chemicals industry in the 1950's, reveal rapidly rising ratios. Finally, economic activity may shift from more highly productive sectors to those of low productivity, as seemed actually to be the case in the 1950's. One summary generalization is particularly helpful in dealing with the relationship between technological changes, output change, and productivity: increased productivity is positively correlated with increased output, and industries that are growing fast typically reveal higher productivity increases than industries which fail to expand or which expand slowly. In the short run these correlations for labor input might well be dominated by the simple phenomenon of increasing returns with given scale of plant. But in the long run they are more and more likely to be influenced by technological factors. In any case, the retarded growth rate of GNP in the later years of the decade was surely a drag on both the rate of imitation of the newest innovations and the productivity indexes.

Before concluding even an introductory statement about technology in the 1950's, one is under constraint to say something about "research and development." Next to automation, "R & D" was probably the most widespread term in the jargon of technology during that decade, and it retains its prominence today. It seems reasonable to say that R & D was one of the more "blown up" categories of the period. The cold war and the huge Federal government outlays for military and quasi-military research lent a new awesomeness to all kinds of research activity, just as the cold war stimulated educational efforts in science and engineering. Much research, such as the new "motivational research," had little to do with productivity increments, but was thrown into the estimates of rising R & D outlays. These outlays *in toto* rose more rapidly than the national product in the 1950's, reaching $12 billion by the decade's end. About half of total R & D in 1959 was financed by the Federal government, and this was heavily concentrated in the defense category. The overwhelming bulk of unsubsidized R & D was centered in a handful of industries—a characteristic pattern.

Inauguration of an Inflationary Era?

A glance at Chart I shows that as a unit the 1950's were a decade of rising prices. In the case of consumer goods and services, the upward trend of prices is even clearer, for that index lacks the downward sag in the early 1950's which appears in the wholesale index. Also, from the point at which the wholesale index shows a plateau beginning in early 1958 at slightly over 119 per cent of the 1947–49 average, consumer prices continued a steady upward drift into 1961. In March of that year, consumer prices stood at 127.5 per cent of 1947–49.

It is evident from the chart that even the big subgroups of the total wholesale index reveal striking disparities in direction, which must be taken into consideration in any treatment of inflation in the 1950's. With farm products and processed foods omitted, the index for all other commodities traced out the same pattern of price climb after 1955 as it did for consumer prices, for it rose

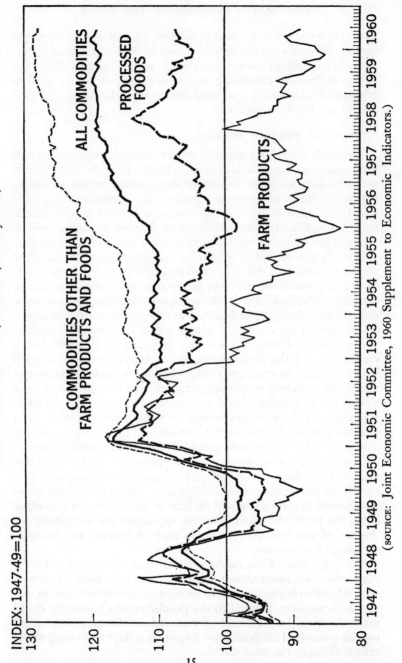

Chart I. Wholesale Prices, 1947–60 (monthly data)

INDEX: 1947-49=100

ALL COMMODITIES

PROCESSED FOODS

COMMODITIES OTHER THAN FARM PRODUCTS AND FOODS

FARM PRODUCTS

(SOURCE: Joint Economic Committee, 1960 Supplement to Economic Indicators.)

15

from 117.0 in 1955 to 128.0 in early 1961. Indeed, this index edged slightly upward even during the slump of 1953–54, so that a continuous upward movement is visible as far back as 1953—an eight-year period containing three recessions. It is this pattern which elicited so much discussion during the 1950's about the possibility of chronic inflation.

Persistence of Moderate Instability

Although the 1950's escaped severe unemployment, they did not avoid some fluctuation in output, employment, income, prices, and a number of other important components in the economic system. Statistics of aggregates traditionally sensitive to the business cycle, such as private investment, corporate profits before taxes, unemployment, and industrial production, generally showed unstable patterns in the three recessions already mentioned as well as in the recession of 1948–49. It gradually became clear that the system was still subject to endogenous forces which continued to generate fluctuations in the private sphere. In addition, the Federal budget, and at one point total exports, were sharply destabilizing forces. The business cycle, although modified, was still present in the economy. The potential severity of these fluctuations in the future was not easy to judge in the early 1960's on the basis of the performance in the 1950's. Economists were aware that certain structural changes had occurred in the economy and its surrounding conditions, changes which promised at least to cushion downswings. And increasing confidence was placed in the power of discretionary action by the government to arrest a possible cumulative downward movement. The recognition that slumps could be contained by both "built-in stabilizers" (such as counter-cyclical changes in transfer payments and certain tax receipts) and discretionary action led widely to the prognosis that even if the private economy could generate severe downward instability, such movement would in fact be moderate. On the other hand, the 1950's did not adequately appreciate the dampening influence of the built-in stabilizers, such as income tax receipts, whenever income rose.

Partly because of the moderation of fluctuations in the 1950's, the focus of attention turned from mass unemployment to growth with high employment. The accretion of unemployment in the recession sequence pointed to the possibility of chronically rising unemployment in a context of retarded, moderately fluctuating output growth. This possibility began to attract increasing theoretical effort in the early 1960's.

New Sensitivity to the Rest of the World

Three major *external* forces in the 1950's significantly raised the sensitivity of the United States to events in the world economy: Soviet-bloc rivalry, increased intervention by less developed countries into international relations, and the rise of powerful competition from Western Europe and Japan.

The "Soviet effect" (by which is meant a direct and often short-sighted countermove in the United States to some initiating Soviet move) penetrated almost every aspect of American economic life —the United States military budget, subsidies to higher education, professional salaries, R & D outlays, tariff policy, foreign aid, and numerous others. In the sphere of United States foreign policy in particular, Soviet-bloc rivalry dominated the magnitude and direction of the government's foreign aid program, totaling almost $73 billion between mid-1945 and the end of 1959. After the Korean War, the Soviet effect was clearly represented in grants and loans to foreign countries: military grants accounted for the bulk of the total, and immediate military-strategic considerations dominated the allocation of all types of grants by area. In the case of the less developed countries, long-run, indigenous developmental considerations were generally subordinated in United States aid policy to more immediate measures designed to insure the recipient against actual or anticipated Soviet influences. Direct Soviet-bloc competition in world markets, however, had only begun to emerge as a significant factor by the early 1960's.

It seemed possible that the 1960's would bring a shift in the nature of the United States response to Soviet-bloc rivalry as it impinged upon the less developed world. The 1950's taught many responsible policy-makers the lesson that the people in less developed countries are most responsive to non-military developmental aid to which no political strings are attached. Whether this lesson will be converted into general practice during the 1960's remains to be seen.

The less developed countries exerted a second external influence, which increased as the decade unfolded, on the American economy and American foreign economic policy during the 1950's. The relations between the less developed economies and the industrially developed nations were in many ways analogous to the "agrarian revolt" that originated as far back as the late nineteenth century against the malfunctioning of the private market mechanism in the United States domestic economy. It was clear, for example, by the end of the 1950's that something closely approximating agricultural price parity in principle would have to be established in the foreseeable future in order to protect the terms of trade of the less developed countries, whose exports consist principally of raw materials. And generally, the emerging nations came to articulate ever more cogently their demands for some form of planned international subsidies from the rich nations. United States sensitivity to those demands was strikingly acknowledged in annual appropriations for foreign aid that in 1960 exceeded $4 billion per year. Toward the end of the decade the United States showed some restiveness at bearing the international burden of aid virtually alone; the Eisenhower administration insisted that the German and other Western governments share in the support given to less developed countries. Upon United States initiative the leading industrial nations of the Western bloc formed early in 1960 a Development Assistance Group to share and accelerate the provision of aid to "countries in the process of development."

The decade was also outstanding for the improvement in the international competitive position of Western Europe and Japan in the commodity markets as these areas recovered, partly with United States aid, from the economic impairment of World War II. The relative position of the United States share in commodity markets did not decline in the aggregate, and it remained high compared to the late 1920's; but the American position showed no enlargement. On the basis of a more general measure of long-run competitive position—the ratio to the trade surplus of net foreign commitments on other than trade account—the United States position definitely deteriorated in the 1950's.[10] Western Europe and Japan got the lion's share of the substantial increase in the volume of world exports during the 1950's, a fact which expressed in one way the improved competitive position of those areas. In the case of Western Europe this improvement was emphasized by the formation (1958) and subsequent economic expansion of the European Economic Community (the Common Market), embracing Belgium, France, West Germany, Italy, Luxembourg, and the Netherlands. This was the third major external factor which trespassed upon the traditional comparative immunity of the United States economy from international changes.

The United States held fairly steadily to about one fifth of the

10. This judgment is based on the discussion of R. N. Cooper, "The Competitive Position of the United States," in S. Harris, ed., *The Dollar in Crisis* (New York, Harcourt, Brace & World, 1961), pp. 137–146 *passim*, and especially Table 1, pp. 140–141.

value of world exports and over one eighth of world imports. The United States overtook the United Kingdom in the 1950's to become the largest single importing nation.

The United States export position is viewed here as being affected highly by external factors, but it clearly reacted also to internal factors. The American share in world markets for goods, services, and funds is affected by American technology, marketing organization, price policies, product characteristics, and a host of other elements. It is a matter of emphasis which set of factors is taken as focal point in any particular period.

Internal factors were at work in the 1950's to change America's role in the world economy and increase its dependence on events in the rest of the world. In the matter of merchandise imports, the elimination of cyclical extremes tended toward stabilization. Aggregate merchandise imports depended chiefly upon the overall growth rate of the system, after 1952 remaining very close to 3 per cent of GNP. Since recessions were comparatively mild, so were the sags in total imports. The likelihood that the American economy might hurt other nations' exports was notably mitigated by the government's commitment to high employment.

From the domestic perspective, the fact that imports followed the level of economic activity as a dog's tail follows the dog attests to the constant functional attachment of the two. But this was not merely a matter of statistical affinity. America's import dependency was not expressed in the ratio of imports to GNP, which was below the 1929 ratio. The vital aspect was the specter of domestic exhaustion of natural resources as they were drawn upon at fantastic rates to feed the more affluent consumer strata and the insatiable demands of the defense program. Import dependence was already particularly heavy in petroleum, iron ore, woodpulp, newsprint, and numerous vital metals—all of which are also produced in some quantity within the United States. Dependence is essentially an economic relationship, of course, which means that the alternatives to dependence on foreign supplies are higher costs, less satisfactory substitutes, and a greater dependence on the nation's ability to provide a flow of research, discovery, and innovation. That innovation has contributed to the supply of alternatives is suggested by the fact that technological progress over the long run has reduced the raw-material input required per unit of output of commodities and created important substitute products such as synthetic rubber.

On the other hand, there was a notable change in the composition of United States imports during the 1950's, indicating an increased preference of American buyers for foreign finished manufactures. This change in the composition of American imports restored finished manufactures to approximately the relative position they had occupied in the late nineteenth century. But more of these items were consumer goods and fewer were capital goods than in the earlier era. Also, the foreign car dominated the upsurge, a trend which collapsed in 1960 as American producers entered the compact car market in strength. The permanence of the changed composition remained in doubt.

The long absolute climb of imports that characterized the 1950's came to an abrupt halt in the latter part of 1959 and continued somewhat below 1959 levels in 1960. It appeared, however, that the cessation was largely a reflection of the slump in domestic activity during 1960 rather than a change of long-run significance.

The increased reliance of the domestic economy on the rest of the world because of internal factors was further represented in (1) the restoration of private capital outflows to proportions resembling the high rates of the 1920's and (2) enormous gifts to foreigners. Both trends helped to offset savings in the form of exports, particularly after mid-decade. These exports served to maintain the rate of economic activity in the home economy at a time when private investment and government domestic outlays were deficient.

Without the government gifts and credits to foreigners and the rising private capital outflow, the United States in the 1950's would most assuredly have experienced on the average an excess of merchandise imports over exports, reversing a trend in its merchandise trade which had obtained since the 1870's.

Because of the assumed importance of net exports for the maintenance of domestic employment, the specter of an import balance on current account (goods and services) haunted avid neomercantilists and other well-intentioned persons toward the end of the decade. Indeed, for one fleeting month—June, 1959—the value of merchandise imports exceeded that of merchandise exports excluding military-aid shipments, after which the former again dropped away. The excess was fleeting, and it was only $22 million, but it seemed to carry a significance far greater than its size would warrant. Americans generally had never accepted the economists' proposition that if a nation is to be a mature creditor it must be prepared to tolerate an import balance. The 1950's foreshadowed to a newly sensitized United States public the prospect of just such a trade pattern.

The squeeze was coming from both the import and the export

sides—the rise of foreign competition due to closing of the technological gap between the United States and a number of other advanced industrial countries, the growing preference of United States buyers for foreign products in the case of certain exhaustible resources and finished manufactures, the partially successful pressure to lower tariffs, the insistence by less developed nations on more favorable terms of trade, and the rise in those components of United States private investment abroad that failed to result in purchases from the United States. If these trends were to continue in the 1960's, only large increases in export-inducing private capital outflow and in the foreign aid program could sustain merchandise exports above the probable rise in imports.

A final notable feature of the 1950's was the much-discussed gold drain during the latter part of the decade. The United States gold stock, which had risen almost steadily from 1929 to an all-time high of $24.4 billion in 1949, dropped to a plateau at around $22–$23 billion between 1950 and 1957, then fell sharply to somewhat less than $18 billion in December, 1960. Associated with the drain after 1957 was a growing deficit in the balance of international payments. All United States payments to foreigners had exceeded all receipts by about $1.5 billion on the average between 1950 and 1956, but these looked moderate at the time. It was also then acknowledged that foreigners should build up their dollar balances. There was a temporary surplus in 1957 because of a bulge in exports resulting from the Egyptian blocking of the Suez Canal subsequent to the British attack on Egypt in November, 1956. Thereafter the deficits in the balance of payments returned, rising to $3.5 billion in 1958 and $3.8 billion in both 1959 and 1960. As is usually the case, there was disagreement among interpreters, based essentially on the question whether the deficits reflected temporary or long-run factors. This question will be examined later, but it is necessary to emphasize here that the development of these deficits lent a dramatically distinct flavor to the changing position of the United States in the world economy during the 1950's.

Older Trends in Contemporary Guise

The 1950's produced a considerable number of "firsts." The more important ones have been mentioned already, and many of the less significant ones will be discussed in later chapters. However, it is plain that a people's chief contribution to any short, non-revolutionary span of history is to give some new shape, add some new emphasis, or infuse some new characteristic into firmly grounded trends. Most of what follows in later chapters will deal with changes of these kinds. However, one interesting example of such older trends which took on new characteristics in the period under consideration was the so-called "metropolitan explosion."

Suburbanization and Urban Sprawl

The industrialization of the United States brought with it the relative decline of agriculture, the rise of the industrial metropolis, and the spread of urban civilization. These trends which were uniquely geared to the expansion of manufacturing, transportation, and public utilities, matured by about 1925. Thereafter, certain new forces began to cause substantial changes in the character of American cities. Superimposed on the older, typical industrial-city framework, these changes reached a high point of development in the 1950's, bringing with them a constellation of economic and other problems that had reached disturbing proportions by the beginning of the 1960's.

Since the United States economy has long been a city economy, the metropolitan explosion and its concomitant problems mirror some of the more important economic changes during the decade. What happened to American cities during the 1950's had a direct relation to such major economic phenomena as the rate of residential construction; the increase in home ownership; the rate of industrial, commercial, and public construction; the level of living of various social strata; the composition of consumption expenditures; the growth of state and local expenditures; and the supply of water for industry. At least equally important is the interesting tendency of metropolitan growth problems to proliferate and accelerate without the coordinate development of measures to deal with them. There is no clearer disparity in the history of a decade replete with disparities than that between problems and measures concerning the "exploding metropolis."

The adjective "exploding" was applied in the 1950's to two developments in the life of the American metropolis. One was the continuation, albeit at a reduced rate, of the long-run tendency of the population of metropolitan areas to grow faster than the total population. The population of all standard metropolitan areas (central cities of 50,000 or more with their surrounding urban areas) increased about 24 per cent between 1950 and 1960, while total population increased about 18 per cent. The contrast would have been even sharper if 1940 were taken as a base—one of the lasting effects of wartime was to accelerate the trend of metropolitan growth. The second component of explosive character in the urbanization process was the greater growth of the metropolitan areas surrounding the central or core city. Here the increase in the 1950's was prominent compared to that in previous decades, the population of the central cities growing by about 8 per cent contrasted with 47 per cent in metropolitan areas outside the central cities (recall that total United States population rose about 18 per cent).[11]

The role of this vast population growth in old and new suburbs and old suburban cities in stimulating economic expansion throughout the whole economy has not been fully appreciated. This growth accounted for enormous outlays for public services; social overhead capital such as power facilities, highways, streets, sewage plants, water systems, schools, etc.; housing; transportation equipment; motor fuel; new investment in private industrial and commercial plant and equipment; and a host of private service, maintenance, and repair activities. Small wonder that city government expenditures jumped 73 per cent between 1952 and 1959 while GNP rose 40 per cent!

Metropolitan "sprawl" was possible largely because of the existence of automobile transportation and the network of highways constructed by all levels of government. A financial crisis grew in metropolitan public transit, despite an inordinate rise in fares, as the automobile became a principal means of transportation within the burgeoning urban areas. The increased use of automobiles within metropolitan areas accounted for a considerable portion of the rise in consumer expenditures on autos, auto parts, gasoline, and oil from 6.5 per cent of total expenditures in 1948 to 9 per cent in 1960. (Private consumer transportation prices rose only moderately faster than all consumer prices.) Metropolitan sprawl also explained in large part increased commuting distances and the rising cost of getting to and from work, as the suburbs spread out to become "exurbs." In the 1950's more and more places of work were located in a widely dispersed pattern through the enlarged metropolitan spaces without any planned relationship to equally dispersed dwelling places. One study showed that in Spokane in the mid-1950's, 73 per cent of the city's workers arrived at work by car, and the median distance they traveled was about $8\frac{1}{2}$ miles.[12]

11. Percentages calculated from Committee for Economic Development, *Guiding Metropolitan Growth*, August, 1960, pp. 46–47, Tables 1 and 2.

12. Leo G. Reeder, "Social Differentials in Mode of Travel, Time and Cost in the Journey to Work," *American Sociological Review*, February, 1956, p. 59.

The increased commuting distances, with their associated human and material costs, were but one aspect of the metropolitan traffic problem as it evolved in the present era of dispersal from the hub. The traffic problem in turn was but one of an extensive list that included urban commercial and residential blight; the decline of the "gray" areas between the hub and the beginning of the vast metropolitan periphery; the haphazard mushrooming of new social service requirements; the erosion of the tax base in the older central city; and the 16,000 local jurisdictions that have been set up to deal with the political and fiscal affairs of 192 standard metropolitan areas (there were 960 governmental units in the Chicago metropolitan area in 1954).

The "sorrows of the cities" led in the 1950's to an enormous amount of ameliorative activity of varying degrees of effectiveness. The editors of *Fortune* published a series of six articles on the exploding metropolis, later published in book form. This series, along with a flood of other technical and popular contributions, did much to call attention to the seriousness of the problems involved. A vast study of the New York Metropolitan Region, begun in 1956, produced a scholarly and comprehensive series of reports on the nation's leading urban constellation. The Congress was asked in May, 1961, to establish a Federal department of urban affairs. Recognition was belatedly being given to a problem which, as has often been the case, had already reached serious proportions.

Depressed Areas

The growing economic problems of metropolitan communities were functionally linked with another development which attracted much attention in the late 1950's and early 1960's as the overall rate of growth in the economy slowed. This was the problem of the so-called "depressed areas."

The incidence of a retarded rate of total growth is uneven in the different economic sectors, industries, and areas. When the economy is growing rapidly, the adjustment to retardation in particular areas is more easily made by means of out-migration, the development of new activities, or the expansion of existing substitute lines. When growth is slow, however, spatial and occupational alternatives are contracted, particularly for labor, in the affected sectors. The metropolitan aspect of substantial and persistent unemployment works primarily through the multiplier effect—a decline in automobile payrolls in Detroit, for example, being transmitted to the urban market-oriented activities in the

Detroit area, such as retail trade and various service lines. This causes disemployment in the latter categories, and soon the community may be a candidate for the "substantial labor surplus" classification—more than 6 per cent of the civilian labor force unemployed. If such a condition persists, the community may become a depressed area. The impact on the whole area is likely to be comprehensive, generating among other things a fiscal crisis and a corresponding crisis in the provision of public services. It is important to realize here that local government employment and payrolls are not as cyclically immune as Federal employment and expenditures. It is likely to be perversely elastic, falling as the community economy contracts.

Twenty major industrial communities and ninety other areas were classified as suffering from substantial and persistent unemployment in May, 1961, many of them with a long-standing unemployment problem. These areas could have been relieved of their problem largely through outward labor mobility and/or the establishment of new activities, processes that would have been facilitated by rapid expansion in the overall economy. The latter would have reduced the problem to one of particular pockets of stagnation or decay, rather than a general one of an inadequate rate of total growth. Incidentally, many of the smaller depressed areas were ones which during the 1950's had lost productive activities to the burgeoning metropolises—the other side of the coin. The organization of thousands of industrial development bodies was one of the striking occurrences in this field during the 1950's. Also during the decade many states sponsored statewide, privately financed development-credit corporations to encourage industrial growth. It is difficult to appraise the total growth impact, if any, of this kind of interstate competition.

It is irresistibly tempting in this connection to draw the analogy between the new, presumably general phenomenon of depressed areas and that most notorious of persistently depressed sectors, agriculture. If the recognition of agriculture as an especially disadvantaged sector requiring Federal intervention is dated from the creation of the Federal Farm Board in 1929, the 1950's brought to a close almost a third of a century of such subsidization. It is notable in connection with what has just been said regarding the aggregate economic growth rate and depressed areas, metropolitan and otherwise, that during World War II the problem of agricultural *manpower* surplus, at least, was "solved." It was solved because there were rapidly expanding employment opportunities in nonfarm activities, with a consequent net decrease in agricultural employment of 1,220,000 between March, 1940, and March, 1945 [13]—in sharp contrast with the early 1930's, when there was rising nonfarm unemployment and a net migration to rural areas.

Many analysts viewed the problems of metropolitan growth and distressed areas as regional matters. The 1950's brought a dramatic upsurge in regional planning and a widespread concern with regional growth, expressing in part the general concern with economic growth and in part the regional competition for new industry, especially in those regions like New England which tended to lag behind others. The new emphasis was reflected in the founding of the Regional Science Association in 1955. A review of the pattern of regional change may be found in Chapter 6.

A Rich Mixture of New and Old

It is clear from this introductory review that the 1950's had produced a rich constellation of distinguishing features—historically relative affluence, the liquidation of mass unemployment, large government budgets reflecting chiefly the chronic cold war, a plateau in the rise of the welfare state, slowed economic growth, the population spurt, accelerated technological advance, persistent inflation, moderate cyclical instability, a new receptivity to the outside world, the urban explosion, the distressed area, and the inauguration of the space age. The list is impressive, yet it is only a preliminary array which needs to be examined in greater detail and supplemented by consideration of other more pedestrian, slowly evolving aspects of economic life. To appreciate these it is necessary to investigate at least briefly the relevant structural and behavioral background of the economy.

13. John R. Graf, *A Survey of the American Economy, 1940–1946* (New York, North River Press, 1947), p. 109.

2 | The Inheritance of the Preceding Decades

The Institutional Setting

The Mature, Mixed Economy

By the end of World War II the American economy had long since been transformed into an advanced industrial system, with its agrarian component reduced to minor proportions. It was an economy rich in technological achievement, possessing a vast stock of durable capital and consumer goods. It was a mature economy of relative abundance. In the phrase of Professor W. W. Rostow, it was well into the age of "high mass-consumption." [1]

The private, nonfinancial sector of the business system that prevailed in the United States was a congeries of market types, with the small, unincorporated businesses numerically predominant and the corporate form economically predominant. For analytical purposes, the range of market structures may be classified into two main types: monopolistically competitive markets and oligopolistic markets. The first type embraced many small firms producing differentiated goods or services and was readily accessible to potential new entrants. Such firms, since each was small relative to the total market, could expect little or no reaction to their business decisions from their competitors. The second type of market—the "dominant-group" industry—was composed of a few large firms, surrounded by a varying number of smaller

1. W. W. Rostow, *The Stages of Economic Growth* (Cambridge, Cambridge University Press, 1960), pp. 10–11.

concerns, the latter accounting for a minor proportion of total sales. Products were typically differentiated. Oligopolistic leaders had to be mindful of the reactions of other leading enterprises to their business decisions but could ignore the policies of individuals in the small-firm fringe. Entry into such markets was difficult in varying degree. It was relatively easy to enter the fringe but not easy to join the leading core.

The private business sector was thus *bifurcated*. Such bifurcation suggests a possible range of behavioral differences associated with the two types of market, and a number of hypotheses built upon the notion of behavioral differences functionally related to the two types will be elaborated in tracing the history of the period under review.

Large organization was less predominant but very important in the labor field by the end of World War II. By 1950 membership in labor unions amounted to about 20 per cent of the total labor force and 29 per cent of total employment in nonagricultural establishments. In terms of membership lists, farmers were probably better organized than wage earners. The organizational revolution had already occurred. In the business sphere the trade association had gotten an early start during the last quarter of the nineteenth century, and this form along with others had matured as far back as the end of the 1920's.

All the major economic groups maintained lobbies at the various government levels, but business and the legal profession had for a very long time enjoyed more subtle connections with the executive and judicial branches, since both branches were typically staffed from these two groups.

Peacetime big government at the Federal level, like big labor, had emerged from the great depression. The "mixed" economy— a combination of the public and the private sectors—had come to stay. *Laissez faire* was as dead as Lord Keynes had proclaimed it to be in the 1920's. (British events in a surprising number of cases seem to have preceded similar developments in the United States by a decade or two.) It is noteworthy, however, that many Americans in the late 1940's failed to see the long-run implications of an economically powerful central government. The view was widely held that the great depression had been the underlying cause of Federal government intervention in the peacetime private economy, and therefore when it had passed, the intervention had also passed.[2] With the publicizing of the "national emergency"

2. This view failed to recognize that the roots of large government reached back at least as far as the beginning of rapid industrialization following the Civil War.

dilemma by the New Deal in connection with most of its interventionist measures came the concept of "emergency" as an antonym to "normal." Many still adhered to this illusion at the end of the war. It took the 1950's to demonstrate that there was to be no return to Mr. Hoover's "normalcy." The great depression ushered in the era of perpetual emergencies of one type or another. Finally, some economists contended that private investment in a mature business system was no longer adequate to sustain growth at satisfactory rates and that rising government budgets would have to fill the deficiency gap thus left.

Whatever the rationale, whatever the ideological resistance, the long-run trend was toward an increasing role for government in the economic life of the country. That was and remains the pattern in all advanced business economies. The maturation of the process was evinced by the passage of the Employment Act of 1946, which represented an abiding commitment to maintain the employment guarantees that had been inaugurated under the New Deal. The Act has been called the Magna Charta of Economic Planning.[3] It was the definitive document of twentieth-century interventionism in the United States.

The bipartisan decision in the Congress that legislated the Employment Act testified to the acceptance of economic reform, for an indefinite period, by American conservatism. However reluctant that acquiescence, it was to become one of the fundamental institutional conditions surrounding the economic system in the coming period. The conservative interventionist economics of Keynes was by 1950 fully incorporated into the legacy of public policy willed to the forthcoming decade. *For the next ten years, at least, the policy issues would be formulated chiefly in terms of a little more or a little less intervention.*

In acknowledging the possibility that trends in the private economy might interfere with national economic goals and in declaring war on economic fluctuations, the Employment Act officially called into question the performance of the private market mechanism. The operation of that mechanism had of course been continually brought under attack from one quarter or another ever since the agrarian revolt of the nineteenth century. There had been a long series of attempts to substitute conscious private group or social controls in place of what had been thought of as the automatically operating private market mechanism.

Soon after the farmers in the 1870's had mounted their attack, big business itself began to reject certain aspects of the private

3. Alvin Hansen, *The American Economy* (New York, McGraw-Hill, 1957), Chapter 5.

market mechanism, notably its tendency to generate price wars. Labor also intruded directly into the markets for its services and indirectly into the judicial and legislative superstructure surrounding industrial relations and the conditions of work. Small business also called for intervention to equate its bargaining power with that of large business. These groups interfered because of what they believed to be failures of the mechanism with respect to competition, use of natural resources, income distribution, industries and products "affected with a public interest," the speculative use of money and credit, or other spheres.

Intervention to correct the cyclical functioning of the mechanism was a later and perhaps more penetrating move than any that had preceded it. It was this objective which underlay the Employment Act. The *guarantee of growth*, which was evolving as a corollary policy of the Federal government during the 1950's, implied the conversion of mere intervention into participation. The commitment to guarantee both stability and growth in an economy in which private, profit-oriented business firms made the basic production decisions meant that the profitability of private business, in the aggregate, had to be guaranteed—not just agricultural business, but large corporate business in general. This was not clearly understood in 1946, and indeed it is by no means fully appreciated even today. However, the economy was more thoroughly "mixed" by 1960 than was envisioned when the Employment Act was passed.

Private Decisions in the Mixed Economy

The dichotomy between the public and the private has deep roots in Western culture. For many purposes it is still quite impossible to proceed analytically without invoking the distinctions between the public and private spheres. Nevertheless, the history of the American economy in the whole modern period has been in part the history of an ever greater infiltration of the public interest into "private" economic affairs. Although it has been easy for people to appreciate this process in terms of the growth of the directly public sphere as represented by government, many failed to understand that this growth did not put the government in business, but rather meant an increase in government regulation and government expenditures for the goods and services of private enterprises.

But the extent to which there has been an infusion of public aspects into private activity, or what was traditionally thought to be private activity, has been even less understood. The growing dissatisfaction with the private market mechanism and the increasing doubts regarding the efficacy of that mechanism's prime mover, private investment, were a fundamental part of that infusion process. It is essential to understand this fact: various decisions by private producers increasingly took on an unfavorable public aspect because those decisions were more and more judged to be socially discordant. First, the decisions resulted in adverse terms of trade for farmers. Then they failed to yield the unorganized employee a competitive wage. Then they resulted in "ruinous" price-cutting. Then they generated enterprise monopoly and a concomitant exclusion of other enterprises from equal opportunity. Next they produced mass unemployment—and so on. In the 1950's they assertedly failed to spur adequate economic growth; reduced the adaptability of price, output, and factor supply (some public decisions did the same); and produced a socially harmful consumption pattern. The point to appreciate here is not whether these views were right or wrong, but that they continued to gain momentum, however moderately, during the 1950's.

All the while the "private" decisions were also becoming more and more the decisions not of individuals, but of large organizations representing interest groups, groups that were thus producing the twentieth-century "organization man." This feature hastened the attrition of the private element in such decisions. By 1950 two particular classes of decisions had come to be actually quasi-public: those made by the managers of financial and nonfinancial firms in the oligopolistic markets and by large labor organizations. This fact received only moderate recognition during the 1950's, however, the dominant notion still being that "public" meant only "pertaining to government." (There is a semantic trap to be avoided here: "the public" is also used legitimately to mean "the people," and sometimes, less legitimately, that portion of the people not involved in a dispute between two parties.) Nevertheless, it will be seen in the subsequent discussion that the 1950's seriously wrestled with the problems raised by this fundamental change.

The new public character with which formerly private decision-making was endowed made the "mixed economy" more than a mere mixture of the government sector and the private sector. In an important sense the mixed economy was a kind of dynamic fusion which was accompanied by a change in the nature of its two components. Analysis of the ways in which the government component has changed and the economic significance of heterogeneity in the private sector will be of concern later.

It was all very well to develop hastily improvised partial substitutes for, and measures to reshape the direction of, the private market mechanism under the imperatives of depression and war. As of 1945 the governmental administrative structure created for these purposes was not thought of as a permanent instrument of control. Neither was it adequately recognized that administrative coordination had to a significant extent replaced atomistic behavior in the system of markets. Consequently the 1950's had to face what appeared to be two rather fresh questions: (1) To the extent that the blindly working forces of "competition" were no longer efficacious, whence was to come a set of criteria to guide decision-makers? (2) Granted that the criteria would be forthcoming (perhaps the performance that would be expected under perfect competition or under workable competition), how could decision-makers be made or induced to adhere to them? Only moderate headway was made in meeting this challenge during the 1950's, as will be seen.

It may well have been a myth that market capitalism endowed human decision-making with a predominantly automatic quality. If myth it was, the experience of the 1930's and 1940's seemed to demand of the 1950's that the myth be laid low. Since the 1950's had to deal with decision-making in the large organization—whether business, government, labor—it was no accident that in that decade economics had to concern itself more and more with social preference functions and also had to combine with psychology and mathematics to create the area of social science known as "decision theory."

Institutionalized Saving-Investment Process

By 1950 the individual saver had already long exerted a subordinate influence in the final decision regarding the disposition of the community's aggregate private saving. Aside from household "capital consumption," the disposition of the bulk of the gross private saving among alternative real investment outlets had for some time been made by business firms. Of gross private savings in 1956 amounting to $64 billion, $43 billion were business savings and only $21 billion were personal savings. Disposition of the former, consisting of undistributed profits and depreciation allowances, was under the direct control of business managers. This was a clear refutation of Keynes' dictum that savings and investment are made by different groups, for the overwhelming bulk of these savings was invested by these same business managers.

Regarding the personal savings, the great bulk found its way into real investment through financial intermediaries such as various types of banks, savings and loan associations, sales finance enterprises, and insurance companies. The mechanisms for linking saving with investment were therefore highly institutionalized by the 1950's.

The capital markets in which the financial intermediaries operated were highly concentrated on both the demand and supply sides. As to the latter, Raymond Goldsmith's study of the asset shares of all financial intermediaries other than investment banks, dealers in securities, and finance companies revealed that in 1922 the group accounted for 34 per cent of all intangible assets, excluding cash and short-term assets, but that this had grown by 1949 to 59 per cent. Their holdings of private fixed long-term intangibles rose from 52 per cent in 1922 to 77 per cent in 1949.[4] Life insurance companies at the end of the 1940's held more than one half of all corporate bonds outstanding and were soon to hold nine tenths of the total outstanding directly placed corporate bonds. By the mid-1950's life insurance companies had raised themselves dramatically, as compared with prewar times, to the dominant factor in the corporate bond market. All this attested to the decline of the individual investor in these types of debt instrument.

On the demand side, the capital markets were drawn upon primarily by the medium-to-large corporation. Hence these markets were characterized by either one borrower and one lender (bilateral monopoly) or one borrower and a few lenders (oligopoly).

Both the "organizational revolution" and the overlapping "managerial revolution" had therefore taken place in the nation's capital markets before the end of World War II. The same question as that posed in other spheres was raised here: What were to be the criteria of allocation (of funds), and who was to assure that the managers would adhere to any given set of criteria? So long as large institutions occupied the commanding position between users and ultimate suppliers of money capital in the external funds flow, possibilities such as bureaucratization, an ultracon-

4. Raymond W. Goldsmith, *The Share of Financial Intermediaries in National Wealth and National Assets, 1900–1949*, Occasional Paper #42 (New York, National Bureau of Economic Research, 1954), p. 4. Goldsmith defines financial intermediaries as institutions "that receive funds from other economic units as creditors, stockholders or trustees, and use these funds to make loans to, or to buy securities of, other economic units which they do not control, rather than to acquire tangible assets for operation as most nonfinancial enterprises do" (p. 19).

servative investment psychology, monopolistic distortions, reduction of the number of alternatives open to users and savers,
and numerous others also arose to complicate the achievement of
an optimum allocation.

The Distribution of Wealth

Although the proposition has been increasingly challenged in
recent times, Americans have traditionally insisted that a wide
dispersion in the control of the nation's tangible wealth is a
requisite for the maintenance of a healthy private enterprise
economy. The dispersion of control over the wealth used in production, it has been generally believed, would guarantee competition, incentive to accumulate, and full-capacity use of resources.
Dispersion of consumer wealth would support American standard-
of-living norms and also assure more markets for mass-produced
goods and services.

The separation of control from ownership of the stock of
producers' wealth, an evolutionary process uniquely connected
with the spread of the large corporation, has made it ever more
imperative to examine the pattern of wealth distribution. Related
to control is the concept of economic power. Like the rate of
technological progress, these notions continuously defy satisfactory quantification. Furthermore, it is not easy to relate control
over the stock of wealth to economic performance.

It is infinitely easier to quantify the flow of income distribution,
even though that task is not without its headaches. Many economists would argue that the distribution of income is a more behavioral and therefore more significant measure of efficiency,
well-being, and economic justice than wealth distribution. Income
distribution, or, more pointedly, redistribution, is more relevant
and amenable to the reformist public policies that have characterized our age, particularly since the New Deal days. Furthermore,
the so-called Keynesian revolution has impelled economic theory
toward a stress upon the flow of money saving and spending, both
types of flow being functionally tied to income distribution and
the related liquidity position of the community in the Keynesian-
type monetary theories. As a result, economists have spent more
effort studying the distribution of income. Since World War II,
investigation of the distribution of the stock of liquid assets has
also been extensively undertaken, since liquid assets not only influence the demand and supply flows of goods but are themselves
the object of demand and supply decisions.

A general panorama of the distribution of wealth in terms of types and sectors in 1948 is of interest. A study by Raymond W. Goldsmith showed that the proportion of national wealth in land declined, as would be expected from the relative decline of agriculture, from about one third in 1916 to one fifth in 1948, the continuation of a long-run trend; that within the aggregate of reproducible tangible assets (structures and equipment), while structures were valued at nearly three times total equipment in 1900, equipment rose in importance to almost one half the value of structures by 1948; that largely because of the automobile and other household durables, consumers' wealth rose relative to business wealth from about three fourths in 1900 to approximate equality in 1948; that government's share of non-military domestic wealth rose moderately from 10 per cent in 1929 to 15 per cent in 1948; and that the share of net private foreign assets in American wealth moved from positive 3 per cent to negative 2 per cent between 1900 and 1948.[5] (This last shift reflected the conversion of the United States from a debtor to a creditor on international capital account.) One should particularly note the change in relative positions of structures and equipment. In the business component of these aggregates, the shift toward producers' durable equipment is one of the most significant secular trends in the pattern of capital formation, as will be discussed more fully later.

One area in which interfirm wealth distribution by size has been examined is the manufacturing sector of the economy. In a study in 1947 regarding the concentration of manufacturing productive facilities, the Federal Trade Commission unfortunately ruled out any attempt to appraise the pattern of wealth controls in terms of the undoubtedly very important "financial interest group" concept. It criticized the results of an earlier study by the National Resources Committee, which had based its findings on interlocking directorates, stock ownership, common banking affiliates, the handling of securities by investment houses, historical intercorporate connections, etc.[6]

Aside from individual industry variation, which was very wide, it is apparent that on the basis of the criterion of *ownership* Amer-

5. Raymond W. Goldsmith, "A Perpetual Inventory of National Wealth," in Conference on Research in Income and Wealth, *Studies in Income and Wealth*, Vol. 14 (New York, National Bureau of Economic Research, 1951), pp. 42–46 *passim*.

6. U.S. Federal Trade Commission, *Report on the Concentration of Productive Facilities*, 1947 (Washington, D.C., U.S. Government Printing Office, 1950), p. 4. The earlier report referred to is U.S. National Resources Committee, *Structure of the American Economy*, Part 1 (Washington, D.C., U.S. Government Printing Office, June, 1939).

ican manufacturing exhibited a high concentration of wealth in 1947. In that year the Commission found that out of about 112,000 active manufacturing corporations and 312,000 firms of all types, the 113 largest owned 46 per cent of the total net capital assets (property, plant, and equipment) for all manufacturing, both corporate and noncorporate. In the same study the Commission cited a 1946 investigation by the Bureau of Internal Revenue which revealed that the 151 largest industrial corporations owned 54.4 per cent of the gross capital assets (gross of depreciation: the larger firms usually allowed relatively greater amounts for depreciation than smaller firms).[7] This distributive pattern could be duplicated, in a very broad sense, for other important sectors of the economy. In some sectors the distribution would of course be much less concentrated, e.g., agriculture, retail trade, and the service industries. On the whole, however, the distribution would exhibit the historic skewed curve of a concentrated population rather than the normal curve of error.

Wealth Distribution among Individuals

Nobody knows for certain, incidentally, whether the concentration of ownership or control of wealth in the whole economy was greater after World War II than it was in 1929 or even earlier. One study by Robert Lampman [8] investigated the share of the largest individual wealth-holders in the wealth of the personal sector of the economy in the 1950's. The personal sector, unfortunately, does not include corporations generally, but only households, farm business, nonfarm noncorporate business, and personal trust funds. Lampman's study concluded that there had been some reduction in the inequality of personal-sector wealth distribution since 1922. However, concentration was nonetheless still very high in the mid-1950's, the share of personal-sector wealth held by the top 0.5 per cent of all individuals being 25.0 per cent. This represented a decline from the 29.8 per cent of 1922, but a noteworthy increase from the secular low of 19.3 per cent to which the share had fallen in 1949. Lampman's summary statement is of considerable interest, partly because of its references to corporate stock holdings by the top group. It reads in part as follows:

Thirty per cent of the assets and equities of the personal sector of the economy in 1953 is assignable to the top wealth-holders, i.e., per-

7. U.S. Federal Trade Commission, *Report on Interlocking Directorates* (Washington, D.C., U.S. Government Printing Office, 1951), pp. 14, 15.

8. Robert J. Lampman, "Changes in the Share of Wealth Held by Top Wealth-Holders, 1922–1956," *The Review of Economics and Statistics*, Harvard University Press, November, 1959.

sons with $60,000 or more of estate tax wealth, who were 1.6 per cent of the total adult population that year. The top group owned at least 80 per cent of the corporate stock held in the personal sector, virtually all of the state and local government bonds, nearly 90 per cent of corporate bonds, and between 10 and 35 per cent of each other type of property held in the personal sector in that year. . . .

The top wealth-holder group, defined according to estate-tax requirements, has varied in number and per cent of the total population over the years. Also, their share of total wealth has varied. It appears, however, that the degree of inequality in wealth-holding increased from 1922 to 1929, fell to below the pre-1929 level in the 1930's, fell still more during the war and to 1949 and increased from 1949 to 1956. However, the degree of inequality was considerably lower in 1956 than in either 1929 or 1922. . . .

A leading exception to the general picture of declining concentration is corporate stock. This particular type of asset appears to have become no less concentrated in ownership over time. . . .[9]

As remarked previously, the confinement of Lampman's investigation to personal-sector wealth prevents derivation of an overall view of wealth distribution or its trend. The exclusions can be appreciated from the fact that the total wealth of the personal sector was in 1952–53 less than half the aggregate value of the nation's economic estate.[10]

It was commented earlier that the postwar years experienced a great interest in the distribution of liquid asset holdings. The Survey Research Center of the University of Michigan in cooperation with the Federal Reserve Board prepared estimates in 1959 and earlier years of such distribution among consumer units for the years 1948 through 1959. The surveys also made estimates for the net worth (both physical and financial assets) of spending units by size. A spending unit was defined as all related persons living together in a household who pool their incomes; thus, corporations were excluded from this survey also. The distribution pattern referred to biological persons (as distinguished from corporate persons) and therefore included from the business sector only the self-employed and the unincorporated firm. Liquid assets included United States government savings bonds, checking accounts, savings accounts in banks, and shares in savings and loan associations and credit unions; currency was excluded. The surveys revealed that the highest 10 per cent of income receivers (before Federal income taxes) held 35 per cent of the total liquid assets in 1950, and the lowest 50 per cent of income receivers held 26 per

9. *Ibid.*, p. 391.
10. *Ibid.*, p. 382.

cent of all liquid assets.[11] The pattern changed but little through the 1950's. In 1950, 47 per cent of the spending units held liquid assets totaling less than $200; in early 1959, 45 per cent held less than $200 of liquid assets.[12] Approximately one unit in four had no liquid assets. Liquid asset distributions were much more skewed than income distributions of spending units.

In terms of net worth (assets minus liabilities), in early 1953 the 11 per cent of spending units worth $25,000 or more accounted for 61 per cent of the aggregate net worth of $641 billion, whereas spending units with net worth less than $5,000, which were over half of all such units, accounted for only 6 per cent of the aggregate.[13] Other and perhaps more refined measures of inequality could be adduced, but they would reveal the same general shape.

The significance of concentration in the ownership of wealth, as distinguished from control of wealth, is a matter that could take one down many interesting bypaths. From the standpoint of the economy's performance, Joseph Schumpeter argued that a considerable concentration is vital to a high rate of technological innovation. But "considerable" is a vague term, and the applicability of Schumpeter's generalization to the existing degrees of concentration in various lines is debatable. Another aspect of the fact of high wealth concentration was the economists' rising theoretical emphasis on oligopolistic markets, with limitation of new entry and of choice among firms and products. The existence of concentration alongside dispersion was also congenial to a model of bifurcated economy, as suggested above; and, too, it underscored the public significance of managerial decisions and corporate stewardship. Finally, concentration in the control over productive facilities became particularly important in the allocation of the rising flood of government orders to private business that was impending on the eve of the 1950's. With the most important portion of those orders on the Federal level destined during the forthcoming decade to consist of defense orders, it was understandable that in President Eisenhower's farewell address in January, 1961, he warned against the formation of a military-industrial elite.

The Size Distribution of Income

Income distribution, as distinguished from wealth distribution, might well be treated as a part of the economic system in the

11. *Federal Reserve Bulletin*, June, 1955, p. 618, Supplementary Table 10.
12. *Ibid.*, March, 1959, p. 252.
13. *Ibid.*, September, 1953, p. 943.

narrower sense, rather than as an element in the institutional setting. But income patterns are so closely linked to the structure of control over wealth that it seems more efficient to treat them together.

The structure of income distribution at the end of the 1940's was well outlined by statisticians, despite many conceptual hurdles. As has long been fully realized, the healthy functioning of the enormously productive American economy depends upon mass consumption of the goods and services to which the major industries gear their production. Mass consumption requires that a substantial family income be assured every major stratum in the population. That an elite class of consumers alone cannot spend enough to absorb the capacity output of the United States economy greatly heightens the importance of the size distribution of income. Although the pattern here too is skewed, there are nonetheless large strata in the population in the middle and upper-middle income brackets whose incomes are large enough to provide an underpinning for a relatively high and a rising volume of standardized products.

Nonetheless, there was at the end of World War II, and there remained at the end of the 1950's, a large segment of the population with insufficient income. In 1947, for example, 36 per cent of all spending units had income before taxes of less than $2,000. This group received only 12 per cent of the total money incomes; and at the prices prevailing in 1947, their incomes after taxes were very low in terms of capacity to support properly a system geared to high mass consumption. This was particularly relevant for the strategic industries producing consumer durable goods. The relative position of the lower strata changed not at all in the 1950's, the 30 per cent in the lowest brackets among spending units receiving 9 per cent of total money income before taxes in 1950 and in 1959.[14] In 1959, 38 per cent of all families and unattached individuals had incomes after personal income taxes of less than $4,000.[15]

One of the more interesting types of income size distribution is the distribution of corporate income. This forms a highly concentrated pattern, which in a fundamental sense both reflects and accentuates the elusive phenomenon of market power. The highly skewed corporate income distribution also implements the notion of market bifurcation, described above, and the hypothesis that "small enterprise" is in a number of ways an especially disadvantaged

14. *Statistical Abstract*, 1961, p. 315, Table 427.
15. *Ibid.*, p. 317, Table 431.

group. Illustrating this income pattern is the fact that, according to the Internal Revenue Service's *Statistics of Income* for 1957–58, of 572,936 corporations reporting some net income for that fiscal year, 29,427 or slightly over 5 per cent received 87.7 per cent of all corporate net income. This ratio was remarkably stable through time, incidentally, for in 1929 the largest 5 per cent (size determined by size of net income) received 84.3 per cent of total corporate net income reported. Turning forward to 1957–58 again, a fuller view of business income concentration may be gleaned from the fact that the largest 574 corporations received the bulk— 52.7 per cent—of the net income of the 572,936 corporate enterprises.

The Functional Distribution of Income

It is desirable to look briefly at the so-called functional distribution of income in order to complete the distributive map of the economy at the beginning of the 1950's and to appreciate the long-run trends of income distribution.

In 1959 Professor Irving Kravis argued, in a definitive examination of functional distribution,[16] that there has been a long-run shift in the distribution of the national income from property to labor and that labor's gain in terms of personal income was larger than it was in terms of national income.[17] Kravis did not deal with GNP, which would have shown a lesser shift away from property income than had taken place in the national income, for depreciation secularly accounted for a rising proportion of GNP. Also, on the national income basis, the exclusion of the compensation of government employees from both total employee compensation and national income resulted in the elimination of much of the increase in labor's share between 1900 and 1957. On such basis the labor share was 70.7 per cent of the total in 1900–09 and 72.2 per cent in 1949–57.[18]

One of the interesting but complicated trends treated by Kravis and others was the secular decline in entrepreneurial income as a proportion of national income from 23.6 per cent in the beginning of the century to 16.4 per cent in 1944–53, followed by a further drop to 13.9 per cent in 1949–57.[19] A major factor in this decline was of course the shrinking position of agriculture.

16. Irving B. Kravis, "Relative Income Shares in Fact and Theory," *American Economic Review*, December, 1959, pp. 917–949.
17. *Ibid.*, p. 917.
18. *Ibid.*, p. 928.
19. *Ibid.*, p. 919, Table 1.

The bulk of the relative secular growth in employee compensation was at the expense of entrepreneurial income. A number of investigators, such as Burkhead,[20] have treated entrepreneurial income (income of unincorporated business, farmers, and the self-employed) as labor income. Burkhead justified this procedure on grounds of the dominant industrial composition of the bulk of unincorporated enterprise. Kravis acknowledged that had he adopted a similar procedure, the relative shares of labor and property in the national income would have remained practically constant since the turn of the century, as many have asserted.

There was also a notable drop in the share going to rent over the long run and a more moderate decrease in the interest share. On the other hand, corporate profits before taxes as percentage of national income increased about 50 per cent in the 1950's over the 1920's, although they hardly changed during 1949–57 as compared with 1944–53.[21] The relative rise in corporate profits after taxes was arrested over the long pull because of the increase in tax liability after the 1920's. Corporate profits after tax, at 6.7 per cent of national income in the 1920's, were almost as high as before-tax profits in 1900–09; and the after-tax ratio remained high at 6.3 per cent in the late 1940's and the 1950's. The corporate tax take, however, rose from 1.7 per cent in the 1920's to 6.3 in 1944–53 and 6.5 in 1949–57. Dividends fell, as corporations retained increasing proportions of their after-tax income, from 5.3 per cent of national income in the 1920's to 3.3 per cent in the 1950's.[22] Unfortunately, all this ignores capital gains.

It may be concluded that the "tax state" was well established by the 1950's. In the private economy, dividends and interest together averaged about 6 per cent of national income. The American economy was therefore hardly supporting a *rentier* society; essentially, on the basis of functional distribution, it was an economy of employees and corporations. Moreover, the historical trend was ever more certainly in that direction. Corporate business accounted for 57.8 per cent of all income originating in business in 1929 and had grown to 62.5 per cent in 1950 (it rose again by 1957, to 65.6 per cent).

Socially, on the other hand, it is necessary to attach more weight to noncorporate enterprise and the self-employed. Although of declining economic importance, the number of noncorporate busi-

20. Jesse Burkhead, "Changes in the Functional Distribution of Income," *Journal of the American Statistical Association*, June, 1953, pp. 195–96.
21. Kravis, *op. cit.*, p. 919, Table 1.
22. *Ibid.*, p. 931, Table 7.

ness firms outside agriculture and the professions, for example, continued to bear a constant long-run ratio of about .034 to total population aged 20 or over since 1929. There were 5,311,000 individually owned businesses outside farming, forestry, and fisheries in 1958. Nevertheless, the overwhelming occupational fact of the mid-twentieth century is that the United States is a nation of employees. The ratio of employees to the total of persons economically engaged rose from 58 per cent in 1870 to 64 per cent around 1900 and stood at approximately 85 per cent in the 1950's.[23]

A recent income and occupational development, one which stood out most sharply as a trend during the 1950's, was the relative decline in the ratio of nonsupervisory or "production" workers to the total. Related thereto was a rise in salaries as proportion of total employee compensation. These changes have to be considered in interpreting long-run trends in "labor's share"; the definition of "labor" may have to be reconsidered. Manual and service workers as a proportion of the total nonagricultural economically active population fell from 62.6 per cent in 1930 to 58.5 per cent in 1950, then dropped farther to 53.7 per cent in March, 1960. It is pertinent to note further that in manufacturing, production worker (nonsupervisory) wages as a proportion of total salaries and wages declined from about three fourths to two thirds in the short period from 1947 to the end of the 1950's. The number of production workers declined absolutely in manufacturing, while the total of all employees rose over the same period. The "managerial revolution," the "research revolution," and the technological advances of the last two decades seem to call for a review of any inclination, when theorizing, to make an easy transition from "employee compensation" to "labor's share."[24]

Examination of the sketch of income distribution presented here, together with other sources, leads to the general conclusion of Robert Solow that there has probably been some "slight but persistent" tendency toward greater equality, but that the United States is by no means "an equalitarian mutation from the polarization" of Europe in an earlier day. Indeed, Solow points out, Great Britain and industrial Western Europe in recent decades have exhibited a contour and direction of income distribution

23. *Ibid.*, p. 921.
24. Professor Kravis by no means identifies the two. However, his treatment of the heterogeneity of employee compensation is addressed chiefly to segregation of the compensation of corporate officers. He also notes that the share of managerial employees below the officer level may be rising.

very similar to the American.[25]

This brief, selective review of certain elements of the institutional setting of the American economic system on the eve of the 1950's and to some degree during the 1950's is designed, like the discussion of identifying features in Chapter 1, to be merely an introduction. Other institutional configurations, together with later changes in those dealt with cursorily at this point, will be examined later in connection with the concrete economic movements during the decade.

Design of the Economic Engine on the Eve of the 1950's

Factor Supplies

The economy of 1946–50 inherited a mixed legacy of protracted depression and wartime exhilaration. Federal spending for war had prevented the private sector from demonstrating its capacity to generate full employment under the generally prevailing economic conditions. *Failure of the private market mechanism, operating in conjunction with a necessarily enlarged public sector, to achieve this goal* prior to the onset of the war left unresolved a number of competing interpretations of the continued mass unemployment and private investment deficiency. After the cessation of hostilities and the initial reconversion adjustment, it was clear that certain liquidity factors, together with physical shortages, would assure a postwar boom and, in the absence of price control, an attendant inflation. It was not at first clear, however, that the ensuing slump in 1948–49 would be as moderate as it was. More important from an historical standpoint, it was not at all evident that the depression specter of protracted stagnation would be dispelled by the new economic configuration that had emerged.

The United States was fortunate to escape war damage from direct enemy attack. It thus fared infinitely better in the immediate postwar period than most of its major allies. This factor had much to do with a United States excess of merchandise exports over imports of about $25 billion in the four years 1946–49 —no small contribution to the expansion of that period. However, the nation's wealth had been consumed without adequate replace-

25. Robert M. Solow, "Income Inequality Since the War," in Ralph E. Freeman, ed., *Postwar Economic Trends in the United States* (New York, Harper, 1960,) pp. 134–35.

ment by fifteen years of depression and war production. Consequently, despite the much "bigger economy" at the war's end, the total national wealth as estimated by Goldsmith had *fallen* from $446 billion in 1929 to $436 billion at the end of 1945.

Not all components had declined, and the declines had been uneven. Some of the more significant decreases were in the nation's residential structures (from $91 billion to $84 billion), nonresidential structures ($57 billion to $45 billion), and private nonfarm land ($61 billion to $43 billion). Both producer and consumer durables increased very slightly for a fifteen-year period, the former by $3.5 billion, the latter by $3.1 billion. All these totals are in 1929 prices and therefore purport to measure real changes in stocks.

How was it possible for the country in the face of a practically constant complement of reproducible tangible wealth (excluding government assets) to raise its real gross private product (1954 prices) from $172 billion in 1929 to $253 billion in 1946? Since there was no significant increase in the quantitative input of real capital in value terms (except for a minor increase in manufacturing equipment), the rise in real product must be attributed chiefly to technological improvement and increase in the quality and quantity of labor (including managerial) input. The productivity increment may be used to express everything but the rise in labor input. Productivity increment may be represented by output per unit of total input, which stood at 144.5 in 1946 on a 1929 base of 100. Productivity increases so measured were about the same for the farm as for the nonfarm sectors during the period referred to, as distinguished sharply from the divergent trends that developed in the 1950's.[26]

In addition to the productivity increment, both the labor force and employment had grown substantially by the end of the war. The civilian labor force had expanded from 49.2 million in 1929 to 57.5 million in 1946, with the unemployment rate in the latter year at 3.9 per cent, only slightly higher than in 1929. In other words, there were 7,620,000 more persons employed in 1946, over 5,000,000 of whom were in the private sector.

Of the total employment of 55,250,000 persons in 1946, agriculture absorbed 8,320,000—a decline from 1929 of 2,130,000.

26. In this and the following discussion, unless otherwise noted the data relating to wealth are taken from U.S. Department of Commerce, *Historical Statistics of the United States, Colonial Times to 1957* (Washington, D.C., U.S. Government Printing Office, 1960), p. 152. Hereafter referred to as *Historical Statistics*.

This absolute reduction process was to continue through the 1950's, extending a trend which on a decennial basis had begun after the census of 1910. By 1960 there were to be only 5,723,000 persons employed in farming. But the out-migration was insufficient to satisfy those who perennially attributed chronic farm surpluses almost exclusively to "too many farmers" rather than to excess capacity.

Manufacturing still accounted for over a third of all employees in nonagricultural establishments at the end of the war and was by far the largest single employing sector, with 14,461,000 wage and salary receivers. Its 38 per cent increase since 1929 compared favorably with the approximately 45 per cent rise over the same period in total wage and salary receivers working in trade, finance, service, and government. Nevertheless, these so-called tertiary employments were destined to gain somewhat more rapidly in the 1950's. In terms of employment, though not in terms of value of product, the tertiary economy was already ascendant. Government civilian employment of 5,595,000, a component of the tertiary category, was particularly noteworthy, because under the conditions then arising it represented a payroll that lent continuing support to the level of income and consumption in the face of economic tendencies making for instability and retardation.

The more or less constant stock of private reproducible business and household wealth at the war's end, as compared to 1929, did not constitute in itself a crying "backlog of need" for a larger stock in any economic sense. That is to say, the existence of the gap between the stock of tangible wealth and the interim growth of output and employment did not alone constitute a prospective *economic* imperative to enlarge the stock (invest). It was chiefly the prospect of a great forthcoming increase in demand, an increase above 1946 levels, which provided the inducement to further increase in investment, output, income, spending, and employment. As it turned out, the major catalyst of the subsequent expansion was a drastic price inflation.

Business Investment Performance

Wartime price controls were effectively removed for most items after the middle of 1946. The main argument for their removal was that the ensuing moderate price rises would quickly stimulate supply increases that would soon thereafter bring prices back down. This turned out to be profoundly false reasoning. The consumer price index jumped from 133.3 in June, 1946, to 153.3 in December. The wholesale index over the same six-month period soared from 112.9 to 140.9. As shown in Chart I,* the whole-sale price climb continued, after a short interruption in mid-1947, into 1948. A number of special factors contributed to this inflation-ary spiral, notably the enormous wartime accumulation of cash and other liquid assets in the hands of firms and consumers, a large increase in bank credit, a rise in consumer credit, the cash-ing of veterans' terminal-leave bonds, the liquidation of dollar balances and sales of gold by foreign countries, the spending by foreigners of United States loans and grants, wage rate increases, administered mark-up pricing by business, and inflationary ex-pectations based on the rising trend itself. A major consequence was a sharp rise in money profits both before and after taxes. The combination was highly conducive to an investment surge; the wave which lasted through 1948 was also supported by rising con-sumption expenditures.

The investment performance for the four years 1946–49 pre-ceding the Korean War is extremely instructive for understanding the subsequent decade. Private investment, beginning with a sharp rise in 1946, did respond to the special stimulants just mentioned, and it was supported by the firm rise in personal consumption expenditures. Wartime bottlenecks in materials and finished industrial goods had been eliminated by late 1948. Yet investment seemed to lack the autonomous power that it should have possessed on the basis of the many years' accumulation of technological possibilities which depression and war had kept on the shelf. The brief spurt of three to four years had raised the stock of capital substantially, as illustrated by the following real changes in the stock of the selected items, estimated by Goldsmith in billions of dollars at 1947–49 prices:

Year	Nonfarm residences	Nonfarm nonresidential structures	Producer durable equipment	Consumer durables
1945	198.5	81.6	61.5	57.5
1949	212.8	88.0	91.9	89.3

Apparently the slow rate of growth of industrial production (there was hardly any rise during the last nine months of 1948) and real aggregate demand played by far the greatest part in halting the surge in aggregate net private investment. Price de-clines for industrial commodities late in 1948 no doubt were also

* A list of charts will be found on p. ix.

influential, however. In technical terms, the net fixed investment (in plant and equipment) function was largely an *induced* investment relationship; i.e., net fixed investment was uniquely responsive to intermediate and short-period income changes, current and expected. And there was no stimulus from a "ratchet" effect in the form of a higher (peacetime) income in the recent past upon which to found expectations. Consequently, as business found itself operating in 1948 at high rates of capacity utilization,[27] early the next year it responded pessimistically to the emerging short-run depressants such as farm and processed food prices, a slight lag in consumption, and the attrition of consumer liquidity from price inflation. Manufacturers, for example, "had not been content to cut back production enough to balance it against new orders. They reduced operations sufficiently to permit a reduction in their inventories each month even while consumer buying continued at high levels." [28] Indeed, in a number of important manufacturing industries, notably nonferrous metals, machinery, electrical machinery, motor vehicles, stone, and chemicals, fixed investment peaked at some time during 1947, although the sales peaks occurred in the last quarter of 1948.

Although the drop in nonfarm inventory investment from plus $3.0 billion in 1948 to minus $2.2 billion in 1949 was the most important component of the investment decline, nevertheless business fixed investment also fell; and it is the behavior of this component that commands attention from the viewpoint of the longer-period characteristics of the investment mechanism. Thus, private purchase of producers' durable equipment fell from $18.9 billion in 1948 to $17.2 billion in 1949; and industrial building construction, which had reached an annual peak of $1.7 billion in both 1946 and 1947, declined to $1.4 billion in 1948 and fell again to $1 billion in 1949.[29]

High rates of capacity utilization are ordinarily considered a positive investment stimulus, whereas in this case they failed to stem the ready pessimism in 1948–49. It seems reasonable to hypothesize, therefore, that the autonomous component of net fixed private investment—that portion which is a response to long-run growth expectations independent of short-run setbacks and to technological opportunities for cost reduction or new product

27. Bert G. Hickman, *op. cit.*, pp. 74–75.
28. Council of Economic Advisers, *The Economic Situation at Midyear 1950*, Report to the President (Washington, D.C. U.S. Government Printing Office, 1950), p. 33.
29. U.S. Joint Economic Committee, *Variability of Private Investment in Plant and Equipment*, Part I, 87th Cong., 1st sess. (Washington, D.C. U.S. Government Printing Office, 1962), pp. 20–23, Tables V and VI.

innovations—was unable to sustain, let alone increase, the rate of capital formation after late 1948.

Chart II, which shows the movement in real GNP and its major components, reveals clearly the sluggish rise from the drop at the end of the war to the recovery after October, 1949. The recovery in gross business fixed investment came in the first half of 1950. The Korean War, it will be recalled, started in June, 1950. The course of real gross private investment for the remainder of the 1950's will be examined later, but Chart II outlines that course

Chart II. Gross National Product in Constant Dollars, 1929–60

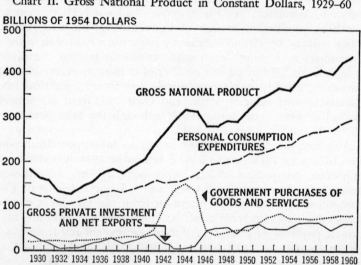

(SOURCE: Board of Governors of the Federal Reserve System, Historical Supplement to Federal Reserve Chart Book, 1961, p. 74.)

clearly. For the moment, attention is called not only to the plateau of real GNP, but also to the steady rise in aggregate real personal consumption expenditures, *a rise which rarely faltered, and on an annual basis never declined, from 1946 through 1961*—a remarkable historical phenomenon.

Noteworthy also was the sluggish ascent of government purchases prior to the American involvement in the Korean War. The general relationship between 1946 and 1950 can therefore apparently be described thus: although consumption and, beginning in 1948, total government expenditures were underpinning the economy and were able to prevent the drop of 1949 from turning into a depression, their joint rate of expansion was insufficient to induce private business investors to continue the expansion of capacity, despite generally high rates of utilization in 1948.

It should be carefully noted that net private investment continues to generate more income through the multiplier effect only when it *increases* from period to period. A constant, continuing rate of net investment will soon carry income up to a ceiling, where it will remain. But such sustained investment continues to add to capacity without any ceiling being reached. Thus, while real gross private domestic investment of all kinds (the net figure is hard to compute) hovered between 38.5 and 49.8 billion during 1946–49, it added almost $100 billion to the nation's stock of reproducible tangible wealth, about $45 billion of which could probably be considered net additions to private business productive capacity. In manufacturing, the real net value (1954 prices) of privately owned structures and equipment rose by $9.7 billion to a total of $70.7 billion in 1949. (This finally raised the stock of manufacturing capital substantially above the $58.7 billion of 1929.)

Residential Construction

Also of high significance for the economic inheritance of the 1950's was the immediate postwar experience in the residential construction field. The American housing establishment was worth less in 1945 than it was sixteen years before—$6.6 billion or about 7 per cent less. In view of the fact that the number of households had risen by 7.9 million or 26 per cent in the interim, there was the usual alleged "pent-up demand" or "backlog." Residential construction has been important not only from the standpoint of the people's level of living, but also because it has usually made up about one fifth to one fourth of aggregate gross private investment. The long cycle in highly volatile residential investment has often significantly influenced the amplitude and duration of the general business cycle. Residential construction powerfully influenced the upward course of total private investment during the upswing of 1946–48, contributed to and later cushioned the downswing of 1949, and sparked to an important extent the subsequent recovery.

But more important for present purposes are two strategic facts about housing in the contemporary economy: First, for various reasons the private housing market, if left strictly private, cannot build housing for the low income groups, and it finds substandard urban rental housing too profitable to scrap; and second, largely because of the first fact plus its interest in stabilizing investment, the government has become heavily committed in the housing market.

The conversion of the private housing industry into a quasi-public activity—that is, a rather more public than private activity—began in a serious way under the New Deal. The New Deal had been anticipated by Republican President Hoover with the passage in 1932 of the Federal Home Loan Bank Act, the major purposes of which were to reduce foreclosures and stimulate residential construction by providing widely dispersed "banks" to extend long-term, low-interest loans payable in moderate installments.

Demoralization of the mortgage market was so serious during the great depression as to constitute one of the many "emergencies" which have since come to permeate the fabric of American life. The New Deal set up the Home Owners' Loan Corporation (HOLC) to take over mortgages in danger of default and the Federal Housing Administration (FHA) to insure the loans of private financial institutions. Then in 1937 the Congress passed the National Housing Act setting up the United States Housing Authority (USHA), which was authorized to extend low-interest loans *with long amortization periods*—the crucial consideration—to local public agencies for slum clearance and low-cost housing projects and to grant subsidies for the purpose of maintaining low rentals in certain public housing projects. The USHA was active during World War II in the construction and operation of defense housing facilities. The Federal National Mortgage Association, which came to be known more popularly as "Fannie Mae," was set up under the Housing Act of 1938 to trade in FHA-insured mortgages on new residences. Fannie Mae was given authority in 1948 to trade in mortgages guaranteed by the Veterans' Administration (VA). The purpose of Fannie Mae was to provide a secondary mortgage market within the nation's home financing system in which this quasi-Federal agency (it was nominally "privatized" in 1954) would take over approved mortgages from lenders. In the late 1940's, given the Treasury-Federal Reserve low-interest rate policy, the Federally underwritten mortgage loan was quite attractive. In effect, by the beginning of the 1950's the whole system of housing credit was substantially underwritten by the government. This was to be an important pillar in the underwritten economy of the coming decade.

Because of the vital part played by Federal underwriting in the home-financing market, the high level of residential construction during 1946–49 must be adjudged a quasi-public performance. The same judgment must be made, in general, about the important role of residential construction throughout the 1950's, for the major emphasis of the Federal programs in the residential financing field has historically been to encourage new construction. This has given the government a powerful weapon for contributing to stabilization or inducing economic growth. According to the midyear economic report of the Council of Economic Advisers for 1950, "Private residential construction accounted for about two-thirds of the increase of about 4 billion dollars in total private investment in new construction from 1946 to 1947. The credit policies and programs of Government played an indispensable part in the expansion of the market demand for homes. This expansion depended on low interest rates, small or nominal down payments, and long periods of amortization. Without public assurances, the policies of private investment institutions could not have been extended far enough to permit this type of financing." [30] Statements of similar general import to this, made at the threshold of the 1950's, could have been, and often were, made in various years during the ensuing decade. The quasi-public nature of the important residential construction component of aggregate investment needs to be recognized and appraised by the acute observer of the private investment mechanism as it operates in our time. It is another aspect of that mechanism which must be incorporated into the previous discussion of the behavior of total private investment during the years 1946–49.

From the standpoint of intermediate and long-term performance of the quasi-private investment mechanism, the strategic components of capital formation that will have to be most carefully analyzed are nonfarm business structures and producers' durable equipment. Historically these, along with residential construction, have made up the essence of private capital formation and have in consequence sparked the growth process in the domestic private economy.

The Structure of Output

Analysis of the private investment mechanism in the 1950's, as well as the examination of all other important changes, must be founded on a clear view of the structure of output, employment, and income. This structure not only tells us what kind of economy we have, but also helps to explain its behavior through time.

30. Council of Economic Advisers, *Midyear Economic Report*, July, 1950, p. 28.

Generally production, employment, and income patterns change only slowly; by first scanning the background years, the 1950's can then be seen as a combination of continuity and discontinuity.

Tables 2-1, 2-2, and 2-3 cover the essential structural aspects of the United States economy. Table 2-1 deals with one kind of output pattern, Table 2-2 with one classification of employment, and Table 2-3 with the income pattern classified by industry or sector of origin.

It will be observed that the data in the tables begin with the year 1929, pass over the great depression and the war decades, and go directly to the 1950's. American economic history did not begin in 1929, but almost all the "consistent" statistical series available do begin there. The year 1929 is fairly satisfactory as a base for many comparisons. It was a year of high-level economic activity. It climaxed the end of *laissez faire* and stood more or less in the midst of the transition period preceding the era of big government and influential labor. It climaxed a "New Era" viewed by most during that period as the optimum in the twentieth-century functioning of the private market and investment mechanisms after World War I. In the 1920's those mechanisms had operated in the most sympathetic of social and political environments. There was, even considering both the speculation and the beginning of the slump, an aura of normality about 1929.

The depression and war years are omitted from these tables because they represent abnormal economic conditions. It would be most distorting to draw conclusions about the 1950's from "trends" in those two periods. The hiatus with which one is left through the use of this procedure is unfortunate but unavoidable. Also unfortunate is the ensuing necessity for a heavy reliance upon the 1950's for estimating what might be typical for a whole epoch.

The data in Tables 2-1, 2-2, and 2-3 are to be used in part as supplements to the discussion so far, as well as aids in understanding the record which follows. The more usual national product accounts, which do not appear in this group of tables, will be examined later, chiefly in connection with discussion of short-run changes. The patterns portrayed in these tables are presented mainly to suggest structural and long-run characteristics of the economy.

A glance at Table 2-1 will yield one view of the nation's product mix and at the same time afford a basis for seeing how data of this sort may be used to construct and illustrate hypotheses about the course of economic history. Since the magnitudes have been de-

TABLE 2-1

Gross National Product, by Major Type of Product, 1929 and 1950–60, in Billions of Constant (1954) Dollars, and Indexes of Manufacturing Production (1947–49 = 100)

	1929	1950	1951	1952	1953	1954	1955	1956	1957	1958	1959	1960
Gross national product	181.8	318.1	341.8	353.5	369.0	363.1	392.7	402.2	407.0	401.0	428.0	439.2
Goods output	95.4	177.6	191.7	196.8	207.7	197.4	216.9	221.5	220.2	211.2	228.3	233.8
Durables	30.8	65.3	74.6	75.1	80.8	71.6	83.1	84.4	83.1	71.5	82.1	83.8
Nondurables	64.7	112.3	117.1	121.8	126.9	125.9	133.8	137.1	137.2	139.7	146.2	150.0
Services	60.3	105.0	114.4	119.8	122.5	124.1	130.2	136.0	141.8	145.3	151.6	157.9
Construction	26.1	35.4	36.0	36.9	38.8	41.6	45.6	44.8	45.0	44.4	48.1	47.5
Percentage Distribution												
Gross national product	100.0	100.0	100.0	100.0	100.0	100.0	100.0	100.0	100.0	100.0	100.0	100.0
Goods output	52.5	56.0	56.1	55.7	56.3	54.4	55.3	55.1	54.1	52.7	53.3	53.2
Durables	16.9	20.7	21.8	21.2	21.9	19.7	21.2	20.9	20.4	17.8	19.2	19.1
Nondurables	35.6	35.3	34.3	34.5	34.4	34.7	34.1	34.1	33.7	34.9	34.1	34.1
Services	33.2	33.0	33.5	33.9	33.2	34.2	33.2	33.8	34.8	36.2	35.4	35.9
Construction	14.4	11.0	10.5	10.4	10.5	11.5	11.6	11.1	11.1	11.1	11.3	10.9
Indexes of Production of Manufactures												
Total	58	114	123	128	139	129	145	150	150	139	158	163
Durables	60	116	130	138	156	138	159	162	162	141	165	169
Nondurables	56	111	115	117	122	122	134	139	141	141	155	160

SOURCES: U.S. Department of Commerce and Federal Reserve Board.

TABLE 2-2

Number of Wage and Salary Workers in Nonagricultural Establishments, 1929 and 1950–60

(Thousands of employees)

	1929	1950	1951	1952	1953	1954	1955	1956	1957	1958	1959	1960
Total wage and salary Workers	31,041	44,738	47,347	48,303	49,681	48,431	50,056	51,766	52,162	50,543	51,975	52,895
Manufacturing	10,534	14,967	16,104	16,334	17,238	15,995	16,563	16,903	16,782	15,468	16,168	16,338
Durable goods	na	8,085	9,080	9,340	10,105	9,122	9,549	9,835	9,821	8,743	9,290	9,432
Nondurable goods	na	6,882	7,024	6,994	7,133	6,873	7,014	7,068	6,961	6,725	6,878	6,906
Production employees	8,445	11,779	12,509	12,706	13,501	12,373	12,957	13,134	12,910	11,658	12,237	12,266
Mining	1,078	889	916	885	852	777	777	807	809	721	676	664
Contract construction	1,497	2,333	2,603	2,634	2,622	2,593	2,759	2,929	2,808	2,648	2,767	2,770
Transportation, communication and public utilities	3,907	3,977	4,166	4,185	4,221	4,009	4,062	4,161	4,151	3,903	3,902	3,901
Wholesale and retail trade*	6,401	9,645	10,012	10,281	10,527	10,520	10,846	11,221	11,302	11,141	11,385	11,645
Finance, insurance, real estate	1,431	1,824	1,892	1,967	2,038	2,122	2,219	2,308	2,348	2,374	2,425	2,485
Service & misc.*	3,127	5,077	5,264	5,411	5,538	5,664	5,916	6,160	6,336	6,395	6,525	6,637
Government (civilian)**	3,066	6,026	6,389	6,609	6,645	6,751	6,914	7,277	7,626	7,893	8,127	8,455
Federal (civilian)	534	1,930	2,270	2,380	2,270	2,170	2,150	2,180	2,200	2,191	2,197	2,236
State & local	2,532	4,100	4,120	4,230	4,370	4,580	4,760	5,100	5,420	5,702	5,930	6,219

TABLE 2-2: Percentage Distribution

	1929	1950	1951	1952	1953	1954	1955	1956	1957	1958	1959	1960
Total wage and salary Workers	100.0	100.0	100.0	100.0	100.0	100.0	100.0	100.0	100.0	100.0	100.0	100.0
Manufacturing	33.9	33.5	34.0	33.8	34.7	33.0	33.1	32.7	32.2	30.6	31.1	30.9
Durable goods	na	18.2	19.3	19.3	20.3	18.8	19.1	19.0	18.8	17.3	17.8	17.8
Nondurable goods	na	15.4	14.8	14.5	14.4	14.2	14.0	13.7	13.3	13.3	13.2	13.0
Production employees	27.2	26.3	26.4	26.3	27.2	25.6	25.9	25.4	24.8	23.1	23.6	23.2
Mining	3.5	2.0	1.9	1.8	1.7	1.6	1.6	1.5	1.6	1.4	1.3	1.3
Contract construction	4.8	5.2	5.5	5.5	5.3	5.4	5.5	5.7	5.4	5.2	5.3	5.2
Transportation, communication and public utilities	12.6	8.9	8.8	8.7	8.5	8.3	8.1	8.0	8.0	7.7	7.5	7.4
Wholesale & retail trade*	20.6	21.6	21.1	21.3	21.2	21.7	21.7	21.7	21.7	22.0	21.9	22.0
Finance, insurance, real estate	4.6	4.1	4.0	4.1	4.1	4.4	4.4	4.5	4.6	4.7	4.7	4.7
Service & misc.*	10.1	11.4	11.2	11.2	11.1	11.7	11.8	11.9	12.1	12.6	12.6	12.5
Government (civilian)	9.9	13.5	13.5	13.7	13.4	13.9	13.8	14.1	14.6	15.6	15.6	16.0
Federal (civilian)	1.7	4.3	4.8	4.9	4.6	4.5	4.3	4.2	4.2	4.3	4.2	4.2
State & local	8.2	9.2	8.7	8.8	8.8	9.5	9.5	9.9	10.4	11.3	11.4	11.8

* After 1929 automotive repair service shifted from trade to service division.

** Totals from Council of Economic Advisers. Breakdowns adjusted according to data from *U.S. Income and Output*, 1958, p. 212.

SOURCES: Department of Labor, Council of Economic Advisers, Statistical Abstract of the United States.

Table 2-3

National Income and Nonagricultural National Income, by Industry Division, 1929 and 1950-60

(Billions of current dollars)

	1929	1950	1951	1952	1953	1954	1955	1956	1957	1958	1959	1960*
National income	87.8	241.9	279.3	292.2	305.6	301.8	330.2	349.4	364.0	367.7	399.6	419.3
Total nonagricultural income **	79.5	224.0	258.8	272.7	288.1	284.9	314.1	333.3	347.8	348.9	382.8	401.7
Manufacturing	21.9	74.4	88.5	90.2	98.0	91.1	104.5	109.9	112.5	104.1	119.4	120.3
Durable goods industries	na	42.6	51.8	53.9	59.9	54.1	63.1	66.4	68.9	60.8	71.0	71.0
Nondurable goods industries	na	31.7	36.7	36.2	38.1	36.9	41.4	43.5	43.6	43.3	48.4	49.3
Wholesale and retail trade	13.4	42.7	47.2	49.0	49.8	50.6	55.0	57.3	59.6	61.1	66.9	69.7
Finance, insurance, real estate	12.7	21.8	23.6	25.6	27.6	29.3	31.0	32.1	34.6	37.4	40.5	42.8
Transportation	6.6	13.3	14.9	15.4	15.8	14.4	15.8	16.8	17.3	16.3	17.5	18.0
Communication and public utilities	2.9	7.2	8.3	9.2	10.1	10.8	11.7	12.5	13.3	14.1	15.3	16.4
Services	10.3	23.1	25.1	27.0	29.2	30.2	33.7	37.0	39.4	41.7	45.1	50.5
Government	5.1	23.5	30.2	34.5	35.3	35.9	37.8	40.3	42.9	46.6	48.8	52.8
Other †	6.7	18.0	21.1	21.9	22.4	22.6	24.8	27.4	28.1	27.5	29.3	31.1
Percentage Distribution in Nonagricultural Income												
Total nonagricultural income	100.0	100.0	100.0	100.0	100.0	100.0	100.0	100.0	100.0	100.0	100.0	100.0
Manufacturing	27.6	33.2	34.2	33.1	34.0	32.0	33.3	33.0	32.4	29.9	31.2	30.0
Durable goods industries	na	19.0	20.0	19.8	20.8	19.0	20.1	19.9	19.8	17.4	18.6	17.7
Nondurable goods industries	na	14.2	14.2	13.3	13.2	13.0	13.2	13.1	12.5	12.4	12.7	12.3
Wholesale and retail trade	16.9	19.1	18.2	18.0	17.3	19.5	17.5	17.2	17.1	17.5	17.5	17.4
Finance, insurance, real estate	16.0	9.7	9.1	9.4	9.6	10.3	9.9	9.6	10.0	10.7	10.6	10.7

56

Transportation	8.3	5.9	5.8	5.6	5.5	5.1	5.0	5.0	5.0	5.0	4.7	4.6	4.5
Communications and public utilities	3.6	3.2	3.2	3.4	3.5	3.8	3.7	3.8	3.8	3.8	4.0	4.0	4.1
Services	12.9	10.3	9.7	9.9	10.1	10.6	10.7	11.2	11.3	11.3	11.9	11.8	12.6
Government	6.4	10.5	11.7	12.7	12.3	12.6	12.0	12.1	12.3	12.3	13.5	12.7	13.1
Other	8.4	8.0	8.1	8.0	7.8	7.9	7.9	8.2	8.1	8.1	7.9	7.7	7.7

* Preliminary.
** Excluding agriculture, forestry, and fisheries.
† Includes mining, contract construction, and rest of the world.
Note.—na means "not available."
SOURCE: Department of Commerce.

57

flated for price changes, they represent crude estimates of physical output changes, just as do, in their own way, the indexes of manufacturing production which have been added at the bottom of the table.

In the past, commodity output and construction have dominated in total production. They have also dominated services in the allocation of consumer expenditures. In the sphere of capital formation, the production of structures and durable producers' goods has dominated the annual flow. However strategic certain types of services may have been for the growth process, the main center of activity has been commodity production. Although so-called "human capital" should not be neglected, the stock of commodity wealth is the primary embodiment of society's technological endowment and the chief distinguishing feature of any advanced economy.

Table 2-1 shows that the 1950's as a whole promoted commodity production to a high position, for the percentages for such production ran consistently higher than the 1929 figure. If it were not for the government component of GNP, i.e., if goods output were related to gross private product, the proportion represented by goods in the 1950's would have been even higher above the 1929 proportion. Moreover, what could be said of goods in general was truer of durable goods. Whereas nondurables revealed no clear trend, the dynamic durables increased in importance as compared with the 1920's—a trend largely dominated, taking the 1950's as a whole, by consumer durables. The commodity-producing industries still seemed to occupy the strategic place in demonstrating the course of economic development, just as they did in the 1920's.

It is noteworthy that construction declined in relative importance compared to the 1920's, although not enough to yield more than a mild upward drift to services, since the rise in goods almost compensated for the construction decline. Hence, the economy was getting slightly, but only slightly, more "tertiary." (In fact, if *government* were removed, the private economy would have been only slightly more tertiary than in the 1920's.)

The decline in the relative importance of construction was an important development for other reasons, however. One reason why the declining trend in construction was so serious a matter is that construction is an activity which has traditionally had a high ratio of direct and indirect employment to value added, and it also sets in motion a large volume of ancillary investment demand per dollar of construction in place.

Other aspects of Table 2-1 are also of interest. For example, it can be seen that the absolute totals for both nondurables and services exhibited both remarkable stability and a steady tendency to rise throughout the 1950's. (The same is true of the index of nondurable manufactures.) Percentagewise, they both showed great stability over the whole period, accounting for about two thirds of real GNP throughout. It is evident that these output activities contributed heavily to placing a solid floor under the economy's expansion during the 1950's. They could not, viewed as aggregates, have played a very dynamic growth role, however, because their growth, although steady, was sluggish.

In the shorter period, it is evident that goods production, and particularly durable-goods production, was during the 1950's the most destabilizing aggregate of those shown. The pattern is found in both the goods output series and the manufacturing production indexes. The main periods of recession during the decade can be clearly discerned from these series: 1954 and 1958. As aggregates, of course, they conceal much, but they are good first approximations.

One of the remarkable series of Table 2-1 is that for construction. The absolute magnitudes in the top panel exhibit a surprisingly stable pattern for construction activity. This is all the more remarkable in view of the great instability of real changes in the residential construction component, as shown by the number of housing starts, for example. However, it might be deduced from the quasi-public character of residential construction in the 1950's as compared with the 1920's that this series would move counter-cyclically in the 1950's. This is precisely what it did in 1954 and 1958 (in current dollars and on an annual basis) —after unfortunately being allowed to decline beforehand, thus contributing to the recession's onset. Public construction also rose moderately in both mild recession years. There are other interesting details within the construction aggregate, but the central fact that seems to emerge is the matter that needs to be put into focus here: the sum of the quasi-public residential plus the "fully public" construction had become economic stabilizers in the 1950's. Furthermore, these two together represented a notably higher proportion of total new construction in the 1950's: about 70 per cent in the construction prosperity year 1955 as compared to 63 per cent in the comparable year 1926. These dominant elements in the construction total had become vital props to both stability and growth in the publicly underwritten business economy of the 1950's.

The Structure of Employment

Major structural features of the economy in terms of the industrial distribution of employees are presented in Table 2-2. The reference is to wage and salary workers, not labor force, in private and government sectors. The 44.7 million nonagricultural employees shown in the table for 1950 represented about 86 per cent of the total experienced, nonagricultural, civilian labor force. The use of nonagricultural totals should always proceed, of course, with the context of declining farm employment in mind.

Table 2-2 reveals the high degree of stability in the proportion of manufacturing to all nonagricultural workers. Comparison of 1929 with the 1950's is best made by selecting a year of high level activity in the 1950's, such as 1955 or 1956. The employee distribution data reinforce the conclusions reached above on the continuing importance of goods production based on the output pattern. Manufacturing employees have for over thirty years accounted for about one third of the total. Production workers, however, have shown a distinct decline, most of it in the short period since the Korean War. This is an abiding structural change.

A second structural feature of employee allocation is the rising proportion shown by all civilian government employees, from about 10 per cent in 1929 to 13.5 per cent in 1950. This upward shift is also an abiding one. It continues through the ensuing decade. It reduces, *ceteris paribus*, the relative positions of all the other employments. The data pinpoint what was said in Chapter 1 regarding the failure of the Federal government non-military component to grow during the 1950's. It is also notable that state and local employees *did not* increase significantly as a proportion of the total between 1929 and the early 1950's. It was the later years of the decade that showed a clear absolute and proportional upward swing in this series. The state and local employment rise and the expenditures connected therewith were an additional prop to both stability and growth in the publicly underwritten economy of the 1950's. It will be noted that by 1960 this category was approaching the point at which one out of every eight nonagricultural wage and salary workers was a state or local government employee.

Great contemporary interest is centered upon our alleged tertiary economy. It was shown above that so far as output was concerned in the total economy, and particularly in the private economy, the tertiary lines did not exhibit any clear substantive rise. In terms of employees, however, there has been a definite

THE INHERITANCE OF THE PRECEDING DECADES

rise. If tertiary is represented by wholesale and retail trade, finance–insurance–real estate, and service activities, and if the total of these is related to total nonagricultural employees excluding government, then the tertiary employments rose from 40 per cent of the whole in 1929 to 46.6 per cent in 1960. This seems to be a pretty clear trend in the private economy and is very sharp if civilian government wage and salary workers are included in both totals. The discrepancy between the output ratios and the employee ratios may be attributed chiefly to the smaller gain in the productivity of employees in the tertiary lines than in certain other important industries such as manufacturing. From such differential productivity gains it follows that, ignoring price differentials, the tertiary industries would not improve their relative output position as much as they increased their relative importance in terms of employment (as represented in Table 2-2 by number of employees attached to the given activities).

The declining position of transportation, communication, and public utilities conceals opposing trends in its components. The major reason for the aggregate fall was the secular decline in railroad transport in the United States. Railroad employment fell from about 1,700,000 in 1929 to some 1,200,000 in 1950, then dropped again drastically to around 800,000 in 1960. The absolute numbers of employees in both communication and public utilities, on the other hand, rose between 1950 and 1960. The decline shown for the mining industries is the continuation of a long-term trend. The series for contract construction shows the same general stability in relative position that was noted regarding output in Table 2-1. It can also be observed for income in Table 2-3, since contract construction dominates and offsets the mining reduction in the "Other" category of that table.

The Industrial Structure of Income

A panorama of economic structure has been brought into view, and some functional aspects of that structure have been observed. Table 2-3 fills in the panorama with more detail. Where the categories in Tables 2-2 and 2-3 are comparable it will be seen that shares of the total number of wage and salary workers are roughly equal to shares of the national nonagricultural income. A striking exception is finance, insurance, and real estate, in which case the income share is far above the employee proportion. Apparently this sector is able to command an inordinate portion of the social dividend as compared to other groups. It is apparent also that this differential capability was substantially reduced in the 1950's as compared to 1929. Wholesale and retail trade, on the other hand, consistently extracts a smaller portion of income than it accounts for in terms of wage and salary workers. Unlike the financial sectors, it somewhat enlarged its power to command a share of the social dividend in the 1950's as compared with 1929.

It should be recognized that comparisons of income-share with number of employees are fraught with danger, since there are other claimants on income besides employees. In that connection it is interesting to remember that wholesale and retail trade, especially the latter, is the homeland of small business. Out of the income, or net value added measured at factor cost, as shown in Table 2-3 for this sector there were in 1956, for example, almost 2,000,000 proprietors and partnerships in addition to the 11,221,000 wage and salary workers who were presumed claimants against that income (there were also about 263,000 corporations). In finance, insurance, and real estate, on the other hand, there were only about 107,000 proprietors and partnerships (265,000 corporations) in addition to the 2,308,000 employees. Appropriate calculations would show that after deductions of the total wage and salary bills for the two sectors, residual claimants of all types would have had title to $14 billion in trade and $22.5 billion in the finance group in 1956. It is impossible to determine the extent to which these totals express competitively determined rates of yield to persons controlling nonlabor factors or express the exercise of noncompetitive market power.

The chief further use of Tables 2-1, 2-2, and 2-3 will be to formulate additional hypotheses about the performance of the economic system, hypotheses founded upon the structural characteristics represented in them. Other structural features will also need examination, but the main ones have already been mentioned, and these will prove to be a necessary framework for understanding the contours of economic change in the 1950's.

3

Contours of Change in the 1950's: Korean War and the First Recession

The Economy on the Eve of the Korean War

Economic historians are concerned with short-period change primarily because it may offer a clue to general characteristics and long-run movements. The contours of economic change from the recession of 1949 through the Korean period and post-Korean slump to the recovery in late 1954 offer a rich source of laboratory material for this purpose. But the material can be utilized only if frequent reference is made to what followed in the later years of the decade. A convenient division of the discussion is provided by the differences between the two parts into which the decade falls. But recognition of this division will not be allowed to obscure the essential continuities of the whole period. The carry-forward and carry-back device will continue to serve the present purpose, just as it did in Chapters 1 and 2.

Even a cursory glance at the performance of the United States economy in the 1950's suggests two broad hypotheses under which many seemingly disparate facts can be gathered. The first hypothesis was already touched upon in the previous chapter in connection with the discussion of the apparently induced nature of the great bulk of private net investment as revealed, for example, during 1948: it postulates that personal consumption expenditures play a heightened role in the economy—a more strategic role in growth and retardation than in the late nineteenth and perhaps early twentieth century. Furthermore, consumption is presumed

63

to contribute most heavily to setting both a ceiling on the rate of growth and a high floor under the recessions. Consumption change can be viewed, therefore, as a more dynamic and autonomous force than it is in those theories, like the Keynesian, that make it a passive influence dependent largely upon income change (which in turn is viewed as dependent upon "volatile" investment). Without accepting the rigorous connections of the famous acceleration principle, this hypothesis does posit the primacy of consumption, and, more particularly, changes in consumption.

A second broad hypothesis to be gleaned from the experience of the American economy in the 1950's, is that government budgets in the contemporary economic atmosphere must rise if growth at full employment is to be assured. Although deficits are not precluded, the proposition refers to balanced budgets—except for recessions, where the immediate requirement is more for stability than for growth. Certainly surpluses are to be avoided except possibly as a temporary anti-inflationary measure. If, as typical, the Federal budget should come into balance in a cyclical upswing at noticeably less than full employment, then it should be kept in balance by raising expenditures until maximum employment is attained. With such a policy there would be deficits only in the slumps, which will probably be mild; hence the debt will not, in all probability, rise as fast as a satisfactorily growing income. One corollary is that the debt could not be reduced, a proposition that in any case came to be generally accepted in the 1950's.

A part of the dynamic role thus assigned to public budgets has to do with the indirect impact of these budgets on other spending streams—consumption, domestic investment, net foreign investment. The other part is, of course, the direct impact: a wholly tax-financed increase in government spending (G) raises income initially, through the combined effect of expenditures and tax multipliers, by the amount of the increase in G.

Private Long-Term Investment before Korea

In its annual economic review in January, 1949, the President's Council of Economic Advisers, which had been set up under the Employment Act of 1946, declared:

The high investment outlays of business during the past two years have contributed an unusually large portion of the total flow of spending. This has been a natural aftermath of the wartime deferral of most lines of facilities expansion and improvement, accompanied by acute depletion of inventories. To undertake this investment, business emerged from the war with large accumulated reserves of liquid assets, elaborate postwar plans, and a relatively reduced burden of debt charges.

In many fields, including nearly all nondurable goods lines, the expansion of capacity to catch up with postwar markets, the replenishment of inventories, and the reduction of order backlogs to reasonably normal proportions has now been accomplished; further investment will take largely the form of cost-cutting improvements and new products. In a few important industries, expansion of facilities and inventories has still not overtaken obvious current needs.[1]

If 1929 is used as a norm, the brute aggregates do not confirm the Council's appraisal very well. Except for inventory investment, 1948 was the year of highest private investment activity by far during 1946–49. Yet in that year gross nonfarm producers' plant and equipment investment was 9.6 per cent of gross private product—close to the 1929 performance of 9.5 per cent. The fixed investment rate in 1948 was therefore good but not as spectacular as the "backlog" theory would have required.

Expansion of the nation's capital stock up to 1949 seems to have left the ratio of capital to output below "normal proportions" if 1929 is taken as an appropriate norm. According to *Historical Statistics of the United States*,[2] the value of the stock of nonfarm, nonresidential structures plus producers' durable equipment relative to gross private product in 1949 and 1929 was as follows:

Year	Stock	GPP	Ratio Stock to GPP
1929	95.9	100.1	.958
1949	179.9	238.7	.754

This is a type of *actual* capital-output (K/Q) ratio. If we did not know that there has been a secular tendency for the K/Q ratio to fall, a factor qualifying the use of 1929 as a norm, it might easily be concluded that the "backlogs" were far from being overcome. All that can be ventured, on the basis of what is known about the trend in the K/Q ratio in various sectors and for the total economy, is that the drop shown in these figures is probably too large to represent the long-run tendency alone: the depression and wartime deferrals therefore had in all probability not been made up by the time of the cyclical drop in business plant and equip-

1. Council of Economic Advisers, *Annual Report*, January, 1949, p. 17.
2. *Historical Statistics*, p. 152.

ment outlays from $23.5 billion in 1948 to an annual rate in the cyclical trough—the fourth quarter of 1949—of $21.6 billion.

It must be recognized, on the other hand, that the value of the stock of capital does not simply translate into *productive capacity* over time. In fact, most theorists accept the generalization that a constant dollar's worth of plant and equipment in the contemporary economy has a higher rated capacity, or capacity at normal operating rates, than such a dollar of capital in, say, 1929. In other words, the improved quality of equipment and the rationalization of plant layout have made investment more capital-saving, which is only another way of saying that the capital-output ratio has secularly fallen. This trend is fundamental to understanding the role and the operation of the investment mechanism in the total system, as will be elaborated later.

One important detail needs to be noted here, however. The secular fall in the actual ratio (as distinguished from the full-capacity ratio on which the concept is based) of privately owned stock of plant and equipment to real gross private product (1959 prices), although apparently arrested during the 1950's, concealed during that decade two contrary movements. The actual ratio for plant continued to decline, but that for equipment drifted slightly upward.[3] The equipment ratio may have reflected special influences, a major emphasis on cost-saving innovations together with a strong expansion in commercial equipment.

As the economy moved upward into 1950, having passed the cyclical trough in either August or October, 1949, business expenditures for new plant and equipment began to climb. However, it is not certain that they would have exerted a continued stimulating influence during the rest of the year had it not been for the Korean War. A survey in early 1950 indicated moderate planned reductions in such expenditures for the last half of the year.[4] The onset of the Korean War precluded a test at that time of the efficacy of the peacetime private long-term investment mechanism.

The Pre-Korean Slump

The decline of 1949 has gone down in the record as an inventory recession largely because the disinvestment in inventory was greater than the decline in GNP and because the recession did

3. Machinery and Allied Products Institute, *Capital Goods Review*, September, 1959. Cited in Hickman, *op. cit.*, p. 188.
4. *Survey of Current Business*, April, 1950. Cited in Robert A. Gordon, *Business Fluctuations* (New York, Harper, 1952), pp. 444, 24.

not culminate in a depression. But major inventory shifts such as that of 1949 are usually but proximate expressions of more under-lying imbalances. At any rate, the drop was brief and moderate on the whole, as can be seen, for example, from Chart III. GNP in this chart is plotted from current dollars and therefore shows the mild recessions of the 1950's more clearly than the curve of real GNP in Chart II. So far as the recession of 1948–49 is con-cerned, Chart II shows merely a flat section for GNP, since real GNP on an annual basis hardly fell.

Chart III. Gross National Product 1929–60 (Department of Commerce estimates; quarterly figures adjusted for seasonal variation)

BILLIONS OF DOLLARS (annual rates)

ANNUALLY 1929-1938
QUARTERLY 1939-1960

GROSS NATIONAL PRODUCT

PERSONAL CONSUMPTION EXPENDITURES

GOVERNMENT PURCHASES OF GOODS AND SERVICES

GROSS PRIVATE INVESTMENT AND NET EXPORTS

(SOURCE: Board of Governors of the Federal Reserve System, Histori-cal Supplement to Federal Reserve Chart Book, September, 1960.)

In one important respect the recession was not so mild as it appeared to be in other respects: the unemployment rate. About 7.6 per cent of the civilian labor force—4,684,000 persons—were unemployed at the peak of unemployment in February, 1950. This was after the recovery in the fall of 1949. The average rate for the year 1949 was 5.9 per cent, not reached again until the recession of 1958. The drop in farm income was also very sharp.

The mildness of the recession in major regards may be attrib-uted, in approximate order of importance, to the following incomplete list of factors, many of which are somewhat overlapping or quite directly connected. (1) Total consumption rose through the recession year. (2) In contrast to a Federal cash surplus of $8.3 billion in 1948, there was in 1949 an excess of Federal, state, and local government cash payments to the public over cash receipts of $2.5 billion (chiefly through the operation of the "built-in stabilizers": automatic declines in tax receipts, increase in transfer payments such as unemployment compensation, and farm price supports). (3) There was a powerful upward surge in new housing starts beginning in March, 1949. (4) The abolition of consumer credit controls during the first half of 1949 elicited a jump in total consumer installment credit from $8.3 billion in February to $10.9 billion in December. (5) The moderate decline in the prices of commodities other than farm products and foods (Chart I), and the stickiness of wage rates, insulated the recession against the consequences of a cumulative downward price spiral. (6) The availability of automobiles increased. (7) There was a notable absence of speculative excesses in either the preceding boom or the recession.

Monetary policy played a minor, neutral role, much as during the preceding expansion years. The money supply fell very slightly, leaving the bulk of the fall in spending to be absorbed by a decrease in income velocity of about 2.5 per cent. Member-bank reserve requirements were lowered, but an offsetting reduction in the Federal Reserve System's holdings of government securities produced on balance an unorthodox decrease in member-bank reserves. Rates of interest—already kept low, in line with the Treasury policy, in effect since the New Deal days, of supporting the price of government securities to keep down the cost of servicing the Federal debt—slipped somewhat lower during the year.

From all this the general and the long-lasting factors which contained the downswing must be derived. Among the likely candidates is first of all the comparative immunity of consumption, which rose against the tide of declining disposable income. This immunity was no doubt generated in part by union wage stability and in part by the built-in stabilizers, some of which were lasting factors of increasing importance as the decade evolved. Disposable income did not yet display the degree of immunity from decreases in GNP that it came to show later. As can be seen from Table 3-1, disposable income, in seasonally adjusted annual rates, declined $4.7 billion between the peak and the trough quarters. This amount of decline was over half the amount of drop in GNP of

TABLE 3-1

Personal Income, Consumption, and Saving, 1948–49 Recession
(Amounts in seasonally adjusted annual rates in billions of dollars)

	Pre-recession peak (Oct., Nov., Dec., 1948)	Trough (Oct., Nov., Dec., 1949)	Change Amount	Per cent
Wage and salary disbursements	138.7	133.2	−5.5	−4.0
Private	118.7	112.2	−6.5	−5.5
Government	20.0	21.0	+1.0	+5.0
Transfer payments	10.7	12.6	+1.9	+17.8
Proprietors' income	40.4	35.0	−5.4	−13.4
Business and professional	23.1	22.3	−0.8	−3.5
Farm	17.3	12.7	−4.6	−26.6
Property income	24.0	26.1	+2.1	+8.8
Rents	7.6	8.7	+1.1	+14.5
Dividends	7.6	7.8	+0.2	+2.6
Interest	8.8	9.6	+0.8	+9.1
Other income	0.6	1.0	+0.4	+66.7
Total personal income	214.4	207.9	−6.5	−3.0
Less: Personal tax and nontax payments	20.4	18.6	−1.8	−8.8
Equals: Disposable income	194.0	189.3	−4.7	−2.4
Less: Personal consumption expenditures	180.8	184.0	+3.2	+1.8
Equals: Personal saving	13.2	5.3	−7.9	−59.8

SOURCE: Federal Reserve Bank of St. Louis, *Monthly Review*, December, 1958, p. 148.

$8.9 billion. One can appreciate the comparatively high elasticity of this response in the light of the fact that in the mild recession of 1953–54, disposable income *increased* between the peak and the trough quarters; and in the more severe slump of 1957–58 it fell only $1.2 billion concomitantly with a GNP decline of $16.6 billion.

How much immunity was this? One can only estimate that *some* of the sluggishness reflected the new props emanating directly or indirectly from the government sphere. Consumption no doubt expressed the large decrease in the rate of saving (59.8 per cent) out of current consumer income, plus the dishoarding of funds derived from converted liquid assets. Personal liquid asset holdings, which had risen to equal disposable personal income in 1946 and 1947, were still only moderately below it by 1949. However, many liquid asset holdings were destined to be dissipated rapidly under the blows of the Korean War inflation, soon to occur. It is noteworthy that as the 1950's waned, the economy's liquid assets rose more slowly than GNP.

The table illustrates certain sources of strength supporting disposable income and consumption expenditures. These include the increase in government wages and salaries, a characteristic of all three postwar recessions during the 1950's. The short-run rise in transfer payments was helpful though not yet impressive. (It is doubtful that social security transfer payments are a *long-run* growth factor, however, since they are regressively financed.) The increase in rental income was episodic. The drop in personal tax payments about matched the increase in transfers, functioning as an equivalently mild booster. Hence it may be concluded that the dynamic role of consumption in determining the mildness of the slump and, as in the mild recessions of the 1920's, sparking the recovery that followed was in this case not yet strongly shaped by the new features of the economy and its institutional integument.

Other candidates for new and more permanent influences are readily discernible and have been suggested in the earlier discussion. These are the nonautomatic features of the public budgets, residential construction, and the downward inflexibility of many strategic commodity prices and factor prices such as union wage rates. These types of influences will be examined more carefully later, when their potency in the context of subsequent recessions, together with the added weight of the recognition that they had become lasting elements, can be more fully appreciated.

The Long Expansion

Pre-Korean Recovery

The recovery inaugurated a long upswing which faltered only once in the path of its trajectory to a high point in the second quarter of 1953. That recovery began before the Korean War. Yet the expansion path cannot be disengaged from the economic stimulus derived from the war. The question whether private long-term investment could provide, in the contemporary economic atmosphere, the main driving force for a sustained expansion was again doomed to be unresolved, as in 1939.

There can be no doubt that the recovery of 1949–50 was

sparked overwhelmingly by the private economy, despite the role of government in the housing market, the payment of over $2 billion of National Service Life Insurance dividends to veterans in early 1950, and the props under consumption. In fact, these props were offset in part by a drop in Federal cash payments to the public of $4.5 billion between 1949 and the first half of 1950 (in turn offset partly by an increase in state and local cash payments).

Although lacking the stimulus of a strong price rise in the pre-Korean months, private business showed itself still capable of a lusty recovery power in such areas as manufacturers' new orders, industrial production, and private nonresidential construction. Steel was pressing against capacity limits soon after the settlement of the autumn, 1949, strike. Automobile production also increased rapidly in early 1950, despite a strike at Chrysler that began in January. But the main component of the private investment increase was, as in many past cyclical recoveries, inventory investment—$7.7 billion out of $12.8 billion between the fourth quarter of 1949 and the second quarter of 1950. Long-run business investment in plant and equipment, traditionally a laggard in recoveries, ran true to form. The McGraw-Hill survey of leading corporations' capital spending plans, although reversing its gloomy January results in a May, 1950, report, still found that "even on the basis of revised plans, it looks as though outlays in the second half of 1950 will be somewhat below the second half of 1949. . . ." [5] This was the last McGraw-Hill report before Korea. A June forecast by the Commerce Department and the Securities and Exchange Commission was slightly more optimistic. No one knows, however, what would have happened without Korea.

One of the more interesting aspects of the investment expansion during the period was the contrast between very large business and the total business sector. The Federal Reserve Board reported that, on the basis of a representative sample of large corporations studied, the outlays for plant and equipment by large nonfinancial firms as a group "continued to decline slightly in 1950 and did not reflect the post-Korean wave of expansion until the following year, while total plant and equipment expenditures increased in 1950." [6] The large corporations in the Board's study accounted for 50 per cent of total manufacturing plant and equipment out-

5. *Business Week,* May 20, 1950, p. 19.

6. *Federal Reserve Bulletin,* July, 1953, p. 710. The manufacturing corporations included in the study accounted, with three exceptions, for more than 50 per cent of their respective industry assets and sales.

lays in 1950, for 52 per cent in 1951, and for 60 per cent in 1952. Aside from the impressive proportions recorded by only 202 corporations, their growing relative importance as time passed seems consistent with the proposition that they were slower to make fixed investment commitments than the rest of the manufacturing business population. Possibly detailed study might show that the large firms had higher rates of excess capacity in the early recovery phase.

The New Role of the Military Budget

Even before Korea the structure of anticipations in the American economy had been changed by the onset of the cold war following the United States Senate endorsement of the Truman doctrine calling for the containment of world Communism in March, 1947. From that time on, a secular rise in the Federal military budget appeared as a built-in feature of the nation's spending stream. About two months prior to the outbreak of the American phase of the Korean War, *Business Week* declared:

Pressure for more government spending is mounting. And the prospect is that Congress will give in—a little more now, then more by next year.

The reason is a combination of concern over tense Russian relations, and a growing fear of a rising level of unemployment here at home.[7]

Aside from the lasting change in the structure of anticipations data represented in persistently large military budgets, it is extremely important to appreciate the concomitant introduction of a powerful new discretionary stabilizer (or destabilizer): the rate of disbursement of already appropriated funds. As the cold war evolved, the Federal spending agencies always operated with a huge fund of authorized defense monies—obligational authority —the disbursement rate and allocation of which were subject to a considerable degree of discretion. It was noticed, particularly after the onset of the 1957–58 recession, that the discretion could be exercised to influence the level of economic activity. By changing the rate of actual disbursement out of the large backlog of unspent appropriations, the executive could very greatly influence the course of the economy in the short and intermediate period. Such discretionary power increased, of course, as the magnitude of authorized defense monies mounted toward the end of the decade. In fiscal 1959, for instance, approximately $74 billion was available for defense expenditure. From this, some $42 billion was

7. *Business Week*, April 15, 1950, p. 15.

expended during the year, leaving an unexpended balance of about $32 billion.

In addition to the open-ended shape of the prospects for military spending at any time, toward the end of the decade it became gradually clearer that "fear of a rising level of unemployment" would also prevent any drastic reductions in the Federal budget. As one editorial writer stated in 1960, the nation had gotten to the point at which nothing would be permitted to go down except unemployment.

The connection between the public budget and unemployment was not made clearer at any time during the decade than it was after the commitment of American forces in Korea (see Chart IV, Unemployment). The unemployment rate had remained te-

Chart IV. Unemployment as Per Cent of Civilian Labor Force, 1947–60

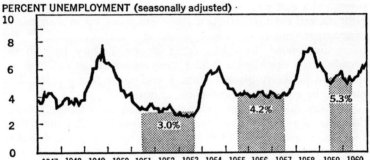

(SOURCE: National Association of Manufacturers, *Unemployment, Its Causes and Cures*, April, 1961, p. 1.)

naciously high, though falling under the recovery impetus, through June, 1950, at which time it was still 5.2 per cent of the civilian labor force (3.4 million). Thereafter it continued to drop almost precipitously until it reached around 3 per cent early in 1951. Continued exhilaration under the spending waves in all major sectors pulled the rate down farther until it touched *bottom for the decade*, on a monthly basis, in October, 1953. At that time there were only 1,162,000 unemployed, or 1.8 per cent of the civilian labor force.

Federal cash payments to the public for military services increased $3.3 billion in the second half of 1950 as compared with the first half. However, the increase failed to offset decreases in other components. It was not until 1951 that the large increases came in the military cash payments—from $15 billion in the last half of 1950 to $24 billion in the first half of 1951. Still, the government ran a budgetary surplus of $3.5 billion in the fiscal year ending June 30, 1951, largely because of higher tax rates that became effective in the latter part of calendar 1950 and because of rising prices and incomes after the onset of the war.

The outbreak of war did not, therefore, bring about a boom because of a large immediate stimulus emanating directly from a big deficit-financed increase in the Federal budget. It was the immediate impact of *expectations* of such a war-induced budgetary change that no doubt provided the driving force of the expansion. According to the *Economic Report of the President* for January, 1951, ". . . the effect upon business operations of the anticipated increase in the military program more than offset any counter-inflationary impact of the cash surplus." [8] Expectations prompted a vast wave of buying in nearly all sectors. Consumers, business, and even government rushed to stock up in anticipation of shortages and rising prices, producing of course precisely the result anticipated. In milder form the community later in the decade often exhibited a similar "announcement effect" [9] in response to publicity given Federal spending or taxing plans. This came to be a part of the economic atmosphere.

The expenditure spree and its associated "demand-pull" inflation ran up the GNP by almost $29 billion between the second and fourth quarters of 1950. About $10 billion of this was consumption spending, almost $8 billion government purchases, and most of the rest inventory accumulations. But plant and equipment investment was still not exhibiting any dramatic rise. Prices accounted for much of the increase in all components of the GNP, the wholesale index of all prices other than farm products and foods climbing from 148.7 in June to 166.7 in December. Real GNP (first half of 1951 prices) rose $14 billion.

The inflationary movement was strongly encouraged by a large expansion in bank credit, as mentioned before. The discount rate was raised only slightly in August, and reserve requirements were not raised until January, 1951. The money supply expanded by almost $7 billion during the last six months of 1950.

8. *Economic Report of the President,* January, 1951, p. 250.
9. I first encountered this term in M. L. Weidenbaum, "The Government Spending Process and Economic Activity," *American Journal of Economics and Sociology,* January, 1961, pp. 174–75.

Monetary Policy vs. Debt Management

It was this short-run inflationary role of the monetary system which precipitated final action to put a stop to the long-established low interest policy of the Treasury and resolve the conflict between it and the Reserve authorities that had been building up for some years.

Understanding the issue involved in this policy controversy requires recognition of two basic relationships. The first is the interconnection, on competitive assumptions and with various time lags, of all the different types of interest rates, such as the rates on mortgages, industrial bonds, and government securities: asset holders will shift from one type of paper to another depending on risk-yield ratios. The second is the fact that with a given amount of income, or yield, on a paper asset, its price varies inversely with the going rate of interest in the market for paper of that type. In other words,

$$\text{Present price of asset} = \frac{\text{amount of yield per period}}{\text{going rate of interest}}$$

or, $P = \frac{a}{r}$. For example, if r is 4 per cent, and the amount of yield per annum is \$2, the present price that under competitive conditions in the money or capital markets would be paid for a paper claim would be \$50. Hence, with the "coupon rate" of \$2 for a bond being given, the present price will vary inversely with changes in the interest rate, or discount rate, r. Of course, P can also be changed by changes in the demand for and supply of such claims, just as any commodity price is influenced by supply-demand conditions.

As remarked earlier, since the New Deal days the Federal Reserve authorities had cooperated with the Treasury to assure a ready market for government securities at all times by standing ready to buy at par any quantity of government securities not taken by the commercial banks or the general public. Such a policy of assured demand pegged the price at par or better. With the coupon rate given, this meant that r could not rise. Keeping down r on government securities meant keeping down the annual interest cost of the rising Federal debt and also exerting a downward pressure on the whole structure of interest rates in the economy. This latter policy was of course excellent during the depression, since low interest rates generally tend, if other conditions are favorable, to stimulate borrowing by business to finance capital formation and in turn to foster economic expansion. Also, pegged interest rates helped maintain the community's liquidity, for they made long-term government securities highly liquid by virtue of their immunity from the risk of price decline.

The Federal Reserve Board's commitment to buy government securities had also been necessary during World War II in order to assure a ready market. World War II was financed mainly by deficits. Hence the Federal Reserve Banks acquired $22 billion of governments between the end of 1941 and the end of 1945, giving the Treasury deposit credits in return, against which the Treasury wrote government checks. These checks went to persons selling goods or services to the government and were then deposited in the commercial banks, whence they went to the Federal Reserve banks, thus being converted into commercial bank reserves. Such reserves became the basis for multiple expansion in the money supply, which more than doubled between 1941 and the end of the war.

If the Federal Reserve Board is committed to *buying* government securities, then it may not be able to engage in open market *selling* in order to tighten credit conditions. Since open market sales and rising interest rates are a part of any consistent anti-inflationary, credit-tightening policy, the hands of the Federal Reserve Board were tied in this regard by its historic commitment to the Treasury when, in the post-World War II years, the central problem for the Board became how to control inflationary pressures. The Board became increasingly resentful of its captive status and received influential support for its pleas for independence in a report of the Subcommittee on Monetary, Credit, and Fiscal Policies of the Joint Committee on the Economic Report (Douglas Committee Report) issued in January, 1950. The inflationary crisis subsequent to the outbreak of hostilities in Korea brought the matter to a head in August, 1950, when the Federal Reserve Board raised the discount rate to $1\frac{3}{4}$ per cent and at the same time was forced to buy almost $8 billion of a maturing government issue because private persons refused to absorb these securities at a lower rate of discount. Convinced that further support of the government bond market would generate intolerable inflationary pressures, the Federal Reserve Board won its freedom after considerable behind-the-scenes sparring, in an Accord of March, 1951. The Board was released from its historic commitment to peg government securities and could pursue appropriate monetary policies, presumably in the interest of economic stability. The Treasury thereafter had to adjust its debt management policies to the more flexible interest policies of the Federal Reserve Board. The price risks ordinarily associated with participation in the bond market were restored to government securities; and government short- and intermediate-maturity paper was deprived of its former resemblance to interest-bearing cash. Its liquidity was thus appreciably reduced. The Federal Reserve Board took advantage of its new power to exercise restriction by raising the discount rate again, to 2 per cent in January, 1953, in the face of rising consumer prices and certain wholesale prices (Chart I).

The history of the Federal Reserve-Treasury conflict and the March, 1951, Accord, which "solved" the problem only at the expense of certain debt-management goals, illustrated a general phenomenon: the emergence of conflicting economic objectives within the vast Federal organization itself. The development of such conflicts is characteristic of all large organizations in an economy of conflicting vested interests. It is characteristic of metropolitan government, of the large private corporation, of big labor. It is an accompaniment of the "organizational revolution."

Price Trends in the Korean Expansion

Chart I shows that the second great wave of price increases after World War II took place in 1950 and was essentially completed by early 1951. These increases had less to do with the quantity of money than with a sharp rise in money velocity. The second wave, like the first, was steep and covered a narrow period of time. Both were overwhelmingly the product of a ground swell of demand, primarily consumer and inventory demand. Together they account for the bulk of the deterioration in the value of the dollar since World War II. On a 1947–49 base, the index of wholesale prices of all commodities except farm products and processed foods rose 37.6 percentage points between 1946 and 1951, over three fourths of the total rise of 49.7 points for the whole period 1946 to 1961. A lesser pyramiding of price inflation in the early postwar era took place with respect to consumer prices. The chief immediate responsibility for permitting these concerted attacks upon the value of money must be borne by the Congress and the respective Federal administrations, who were in a better position to pursue rational policies than were the profit-maximizing marketers in private households and businesses. Because of this time shape of the price trend and because the upward trend after 1953 represents a different configuration of determinants, it is desirable for most purposes to drop out, wherever convenient, 1950 data when tracing economic magnitudes, calculated at market prices, for the Korean War expansion period.

Despite the fact that military pressures on the economy were initiated at a time when production and spending had already reached moderately high levels relative to existing capacity in most lines, the major emphasis in public policy was to elicit greater military production through a system of wage and price incentives. The belated Defense Production Act was not passed until September 8, and its attached powers, vested in the President, to impose general wage and price controls were not applied until the end of January, 1951, long after the Chinese had crossed the Yalu River on October 26, 1950. While the surge of expectationally induced, inflationary spending, superimposed upon an economy already well on the way to recovery, was running up prices at a startling rate, stabilization measures were confined chiefly to selective controls, a savings bond campaign, and moderate tax increases. The selective controls, effective in particular cases though discriminatory in their more severe impact on the low income groups, required larger down payments and shorter payment periods in automobiles and other consumer durables. The rise of consumer installment credit was rather effectively slowed during the vital last half of 1950. Selective restrictions in the housing field under Regulation X, plus materials priorities, brought to an end the great housing boom that had contributed importantly to the pre-Korean recovery (Chart V). The decline in *value* of new housing construction put in place lagged behind the decrease in housing starts, shown in the chart, so that total outlays did not fall until October. Priorities, allocations, and materials controls, on the other hand, tended to feed the inflationary fires by leaving less to be scrambled for by eager business buyers driven by the fear of shortages.

In the area of direct stimulation to the expansion of capacity in key industries, the Federal government inaugurated two main kinds of assistance to private enterprise: accelerated amortization of outlays for plant and equipment, and long-term loans (under the Defense Production Act). In addition, the government itself directly constructed some facilities in cases where private business failed to respond to the special inducements. The procurement of critical materials was expedited through Federal subsidies to exploration and development, loans, and foreign economic aid programs.

Chart V. Housing Starts and Gross National Product, January 1, 1946, to March 1, 1961

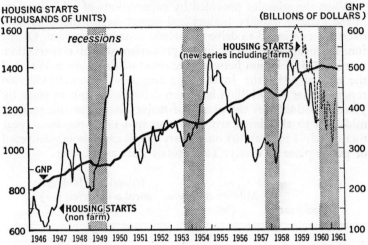

HOUSING STARTS
(THOUSANDS OF UNITS)

GNP
(BILLIONS OF DOLLARS)

(SOURCE: *Monthly Review*, Federal Reserve Bank of Minneapolis, June, 1961, p. 3.)

The inflationary surge was arrested in the spring of 1951 by the subsidence of scare buying associated with the large consumer and business inventory accumulations, the decline in purchasing power of consumer incomes, increase in civilian supplies, higher taxes, the aforementioned selective credit restraints, and the belated application of price and wage controls. Thenceforth the semi-war economy would develop within a more or less stable price framework.

Consumer prices continued to rise, although more gradually, during 1951, then leveled off until 1956. Wholesale prices declined somewhat during the Korean War and thereafter gradually rose until mid-1955 (Chart I). Price behavior in the year 1951 was therefore rather striking, in that consumer prices rose while wholesale prices fell. However, this disparity was perhaps a correction movement, since wholesale prices had risen proportionately more than consumer prices between June, 1950, and the General Ceiling Price Regulation late in January, 1951. By November, 1951, the former index (other than farm products and foods) had risen 12.1 per cent over June, 1950, while the latter had risen 10.8 per cent.

The Military Budget

When the stimulus provided by expectations of a big increase in the Federal military budget had passed, actual increases took over and continued to drive the whole economy upward. Of the funds appropriated for military procurement and construction, totaling $155.1 billion between the onset of the Korean War and the end of 1954, the Joint Committee on Defense Production reported that $92.9 billion had been delivered or put in place by June 30, 1954. Since the period of major interest at this point is mid-1950 to the downturn following mid-1953, the fiscal year totals (July 1 to June 30) on military goods and services delivered or put in place fit neatly. These totals were as follows:

Fiscal year	Military deliveries (billions)	federal cash budget surplus or deficit (−) (billions)
1951	9.0	7.59
1952	23.6	.05
1953	31.4	−5.27

The surplus or deficit of cash receipts and payments for the *whole* Federal budget has been added to the conventional budget to show more fully the total impact of the budget. The data indicate that the fiscal 1951 budget impact, though considerable, was moderate compared with 1952 and 1953.[10] Chart VI shows the tremendous rise in total Federal expenditures for the period on a calendar year basis. The state and local total has been included for comparison with respect to the relation of government spending to economic stability, to growth, and to the 1953 downturn.

The increase in military expenditures during the initial phase of the buildup was concentrated in items subject to rapid expansion, such as military payrolls, food, and clothing. The armed forces rose by about 1 3/4 million during the first year of the war effort— about four fifths of the ultimate total increase. National security outlays rose from 6 per cent to 11 per cent of GNP.[11]

The expansion of private plant and equipment got underway in earnest after mid-1951. Because of the great overlap between de-

10. U.S. Joint Committee on Defense Production, *Fourth Annual Report* (Washington, D.C., U.S. Government Printing Office, 1955), p. 1.
11. U.S. Department of Commerce, *National Income*, 1954 edn., p. 25.

Chart VI. Government Expenditures for Goods and Services

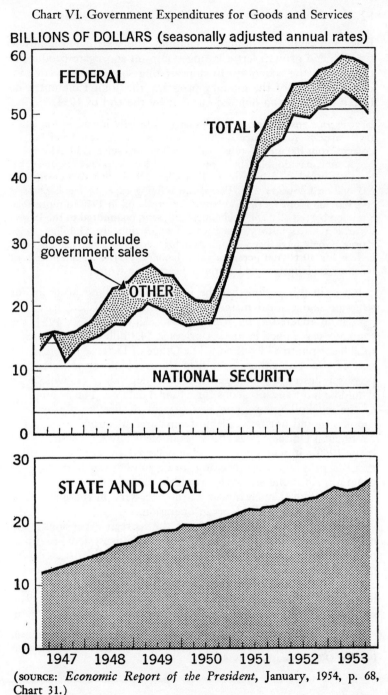

BILLIONS OF DOLLARS (seasonally adjusted annual rates)

FEDERAL

TOTAL ▶

does not include
government sales

OTHER

NATIONAL SECURITY

STATE AND LOCAL

1947 1948 1949 1950 1951 1952 1953

(SOURCE: *Economic Report of the President,* January, 1954, p. 68,
Chart 31.)

81

fense and civilian production facilities, the wartime stimulus to fixed capital growth left a lasting stamp on aggregate productive capacity in the economy. In summarizing some of the major industrial effects of the military program, the Joint Committee on Defense Production pointed out that by the end of 1954,

large expansions in basic industries have materially increased the country's capacity to produce both for war and for peace. Steel has increased from 100 million tons to 124 million tons since 1950. Aluminum production has doubled in 3 years. . . . Electric power capacity has been expanded . . . from 69 million kilowatts in 1950, to an estimated 103 million kilowatts. . . . Petroleum refining capacity has kept pace, too, moving from 5.4 million barrels of crude oil in 1950 to more than 8 million barrels. . . . The chemical industry, committed to the largest expansion in its history, has invested approximately $5 billion since Korea. Goals have been established for about 60 chemical materials calling for 50 to 100 per cent over January 1951. . . . Shipments of machine tools quadrupled in the 3 years after Korea. . . .[12]

It was in this period that the material stockpiling program for strategic and critical materials was firmly established, based on legislation enacted as far back as 1946. As of June 30, 1954, the stockpile was valued in market prices at $4.3 billion. (By 1960 this total had risen to $7.9 billion.) The Office of Defense Mobilization was empowered either to hold in the stockpile or to release to private industry the acquired materials, depending on whichever would be most advantageous for national defense. The assumption of the stockpiling program was that in the event of war such supplies would not be available from foreign sources outside the continental United States and areas immediately accessible. In the early 1960's it was publicly acknowledged by the government that this program had turned out to be another big price-support program, since the stockpile would be practically useless in the event of a global nuclear war and unnecessary in the event of a limited war such as the Korean operation.

The Committee pointed out that the Korean expansions were effected almost entirely through "private" investment, meaning not in government-owned facilities. But it also added that "government incentives such as rapid tax amortizations, loans, guaranties, and supply contracts have done much to encourage industry to complete these goals." Through September 15, 1954, some $18 billion or 60 per cent of all the applications for new

12. Joint Committee on Defense Production, *Fourth Annual Report*, 84th Cong., 1st sess., House Report No. 1 (Washington, D.C., U.S. Government Printing Office, January 5, 1955), p. 2.

defense-production facilities, were certified for rapid tax amortization.[13] It is important to recognize the connections between the Federal budget in the Korean period and these facility expansions, partly for the light they throw upon the pattern of business plant and equipment expenditures (and capacity growth) in the period and partly for understanding the evolution of certain major industries in the decade. This will be elaborated in Chapter 6.

Turning back to aggregate developments, it may be seen from Table 3-2 that national security expenditures of the Federal government, which had been running at a quarterly rate of rather less than $4.5 billion during the first three quarters of 1950, had jumped sharply to almost double that by the second quarter of 1951, not allowing for price changes. The rise was fairly steady through the war period up to the quarterly peak rate of $13.6 billion in 1953 II, although the amount of rise per quarter declined after 1952 II. The year 1952 was the high point of stimulation given the economy from quarterly *increases* in Federal military spending. In its National Financial and Business Review on January 5, 1953, the *New York Times* emphasized past cuts in Presidential appropriations requests by Congress, an expected cut in the Federal budget for the forthcoming fiscal year, and the reduction of the economic impact of the arms budget associated with both the Congressional cuts and the fifty-five-day steel strike in mid-1952. It also pointed up the new President's proposal to make sharp cuts in military expenditures.[14] The adverse effect of these prospects on business expectations in 1953 must be considered in appraising the course of events during that year.

Comparisons of the magnitude of national security expenditures with other spending streams further emphasize the economic role of the military budget. For example, national security expenditures in 1951 I at $6.9 billion were still running less than private investment of $8.5 billion in "other" construction (public utility, farm, and miscellaneous) plus producers' durable equipment during the same quarter. But by the third quarter the former already exceeded the latter, and thereafter national security expenditures remained persistently larger than business plant and equipment expenditures throughout the whole period. Indeed, after the military buildup got rolling, the defense expenditures approximated all gross private domestic investment in magnitude (Table 3-2). In the important durable goods category, government pur-

13. *Ibid.*, pp. 2–5 *passim*.
14. *New York Times*, National Financial and Business Review, January 5, 1953, pp. 49, 80.

Table 3-2

Gross National Product or Expenditure, Quarterly, 1951–53
(Billions of dollars)

	1951					1952					1953				
	I	II	III	IV	Year	I	II	III	IV	Year	I	II	III	IV	Year
Gross national product	77.9	80.6	82.3	87.4	328.2	83.1	84.6	85.1	93.3	346.1	88.5	91.5	91.1	93.8	364.9
Personal consumption expenditures	49.8	50.7	50.7	57.1	208.3	50.5	53.9	53.2	60.7	218.4	54.4	57.4	56.7	61.6	230.1
Durable goods	6.8	6.6	6.3	7.4	27.1	5.7	6.8	6.1	8.2	26.8	6.8	7.7	7.4	7.8	29.7
Nondurable goods	25.8	26.6	26.9	31.7	111.1	26.3	28.2	28.3	33.1	116.0	27.6	29.3	28.9	33.1	118.9
Services	17.2	17.5	17.4	18.0	70.1	18.6	18.8	18.8	19.4	75.6	20.0	20.4	20.3	20.7	81.4
Gross private domestic investment	16.1	14.7	14.6	11.5	56.9	14.0	10.9	13.0	12.8	50.7	14.3	12.8	13.6	10.7	51.4
New construction	5.2	5.9	6.4	5.8	23.3	5.0	5.9	6.5	6.2	23.7	5.4	6.5	7.1	6.6	25.5
Residential nonfarm	2.6	2.8	2.9	2.7	11.0	2.2	2.8	3.1	3.0	11.1	2.4	3.1	3.3	3.1	11.9
Other	2.6	3.1	3.5	3.1	12.4	2.9	3.2	3.4	3.2	12.6	2.9	3.4	3.7	3.5	13.6
Producers' durable equipment	5.9	6.1	5.4	5.8	23.2	5.9	6.4	5.3	5.6	23.3	6.0	6.5	6.0	6.0	24.4
Change in nonfarm business inventories	4.7	2.3	2.5	−.5	9.0	2.7	−1.7	1.1	.9	3.0	3.1	.1	.8	−1.7	2.2
Net foreign investment	−.7	.0	.2	.8	.2	.6	.1	−.6	−.2	−.2	−.5	−.6	−.7	−.1	−1.9
Government purchases of goods and services	12.7	15.2	16.9	18.0	62.8	18.1	19.6	19.4	20.0	77.2	20.3	21.8	21.5	21.6	85.2
Federal	7.7	9.7	11.3	12.3	41.0	12.7	13.8	13.5	13.9	54.0	14.5	15.5	15.1	15.0	60.1
National security	6.9	8.8	10.4	11.2	37.3	11.6	12.5	12.0	12.8	48.5	12.7	13.6	13.1	12.6	52.0
Other	.9	1.0	1.1	1.2	4.2	1.3	1.4	1.7	1.5	5.8	1.9	2.1	2.1	2.4	8.5
State and local	5.0	5.5	5.6	5.7	21.8	5.3	5.9	5.9	6.1	23.2	5.8	6.2	6.4	6.7	25.1

source: Department of Commerce, *National Income,* 1954 edn., p. 223, Table 44.

chases in 1952, overwhelmingly military in character, exactly matched the total output of producers' durable equipment—$21.3 billion. That was 28 per cent of all durable goods produced in the economy during the year. National security expenditures were by far the most rapidly growing of all major spending aggregates. There can be no doubt that they were the most dynamic determinant of the rate of economic growth in the years 1950–53, years which provided the highest growth rate of real GNP for the entire decade.

Private Investment in the Korean Expansion

In appraising the performance of private investment it is desirable to treat residential construction separately, because the determinants and behavior of this investment category are quite different from those of other categories. As for inventory investment, economic history deals with it chiefly to the extent that *short-run* events are under consideration. What is decisive for the long-run course of capital formation, and of the economy therefore, is business investment in structure and equipment. These can be read in a rough way from Table 3–2 by combining "other" construction with producers' durable equipment, as was done above. But more carefully delineated series are available in Department of Commerce sources. Within the total of all business, the data for manufacturing are sufficiently representative for general purposes. These data show, as revealed in Table 3-3 for manufacturing, in billions of dollars, that the investment expansion during and after the Korean War period was considerable. The first column gives the gross flow in current dollars. The middle set of three columns shows net additions in real terms. The last set shows the growth in the stock of fixed manufacturing capital. The sustained investment performance brought continued net additions to the sector's stock of capital which reduced its average age from over ten years to about nine in 1955, after which the average age increased again. Both the economy in the aggregate and the manufacturing total of gross fixed investment displayed remarkable stability, on an annual basis, from 1951 through 1955. Toward the end of the eight-year span preceding the 1957–58 recession there was a noteworthy rise in gross manufacturing fixed investment.

The last set of three columns illustrates an important structural change in the composition of fixed investment in the manufacturing sector that holds generally through the nonfarm business economy: the rise of equipment to a dominant proportion

TABLE 3-3

Expenditures on New Plant and Equipment, All Manufacturing
Industries, 1950–1960
(Billions of dollars)

Year	Expenditures on new plant and equipment (current dollars)	Net formation of private structure and equipment capital (1954 dollars)			Real net value of private structures and equipment (1954 dollars)		
		Structures	Equipment	Total	Structures	Equipment	Total
1950	7.5	—.1	1.9	1.8	38.8	33.7	72.5
1951	10.9	.7	2.2	2.9	39.5	35.9	75.3
1952	11.6	.6	2.1	2.7	40.0	38.0	78.0
1953	11.9	.5	2.0	2.5	40.6	40.1	80.6
1954	11.0	.4	1.2	1.6	41.0	41.3	82.2
1955	11.4	1.0	.9	1.9	41.9	42.2	84.1
1956	15.0	1.0	2.3	3.7	43.0	44.9	87.9
1957	16.0	1.1	2.4	3.5	44.1	41.6	91.4
1958	11.4	.6	.3	.9	44.7	47.6	92.3
1959	12.1	.6	.4	1.0	45.4	48.0	93.4
1960	14.5	1.2	1.5	2.7	46.6	49.5	96.1

sources: *Statistical Abstract*, 1961, p. 794, Table 1095; Department of Commerce, *U.S. Income and Output*, 1958, p. 197, Table V-14.

of the stock of fixed capital. The stock of equipment (column 6) began the decade valued at less than structures (column 5) but ended the period with a greater value. This completed a phase of a secular trend that began many decades earlier, a trend adverse to the construction industry and favorable to manufacturing. Also, as has been mentioned, it is a trend which probably reduces, other things equal, the capacity of the system to absorb labor and savings. This will be examined in more detail later.

Although the volume of long-term investment was sustained and stable in the years of Korea and immediately after, it was not outstanding as a proportion of total output. It is difficult to know what is "normal" in this case as in the case of most other magnitudes. If one turns again to 1929 in the search for a basis of comparison, one finds the performance below "normal." Private nonagricultural plant and equipment expenditures were 12.4 per cent of GNP in 1929, but in no year of the 1950's did the total approach such a percentage. The highest percentage for the decade was 9.9, in 1956. The average for the decade was 9.2 per cent.

Early in 1954 the Machinery and Allied Products Institute published a study of the demand for manufacturing and non-manufacturing plant and equipment in the postwar period. The study concluded:

Postwar plant and equipment expenditures combined have accounted for no more than a normal percentage of the gross private product. In view of the low level of these expenditures in the preceding depression and war, and the backlog of deferred demand accumulated during this period, this is obviously much less than might seem to be called for. Certainly there is no suggestion in these combined figures of any excessive investment since the war, nor is there any indication that the recent rate is not sustainable in the future.[15]

This conclusion is consistent with the data presented here. The aggregates for manufacturing naturally conceal wide component dispersion. They also omit substantial and rising records of fixed investment in other lines, for example, in public utilities and communications. But the general pattern is as represented.

It seems reasonable, therefore, to conclude that the long-term investment performance in the Korean period supports the generalizations made earlier with respect to the behavior of such investment in the years between 1946 and the Korean War. Long-term investment did not exhibit dynamic, independent power to carry the economy upward. After the initial, war-induced jump in 1951, long-term investment in the strategic producers' durable equipment category, though fairly well sustained, hovered tenaciously between 6 and 7 per cent of real gross private product for seven years. A glance at Table 3-3 showing net formation of privately owned manufacturing equipment capital in real terms shows a plateau with rough terrain. The only notable aspect of the long-term investment performance for this category in the period was its stable and sustained character. Modernization and gradual expansion in capacity were proceeding, apparently under the stimulus of high and rising consumption and government spending.

Inventory investment during the years 1951–53 displayed its usual erratic short-run orientation, sometimes sparking an upward oscillation in spending, at other times precipitating downward fluctuation. The pattern may be discerned from scrutiny of

15. Cited in the *Bulletin*, National City Bank of New York, October, 1954, p. 112.

Table 3-2. The connection between the downward oscillation of the economy in the third quarter of 1952 and the quarterly non-farm inventory movements preceding it can readily be seen. From a net investment rate of $2.7 billion in 1952 I, there was a drop to a net disinvestment rate of $1.7 billion in 1952 II—in other words, a total decrease of $4.4 billion. Of course, this change was only a proximate cause of the downward fluctuation in other magnitudes in the third quarter. For example, spending on both consumer durables and nondurables had declined from the fourth quarter of 1951; so had net foreign investment. Also, several large strike actions ran up a post-1946 record of idle man-days. There was a brief strike in steel during April and May followed by another in June and July, the latter directly involving about 560,000 workers.

Planned inventory accumulation sparked to an important degree the upward movement beginning in the fourth quarter of 1952. This boomlet was also furthered by numerous other factors, not the least of which was a dramatic upward shift in weekly man-ufacturing earnings and in the consumption function. (Regarding the consumption function, disposable income between the third and fourth quarters rose $4.7 billion but, as Table 3-2 shows, consumption rose in a most un-Keynesian manner by $7.5 billion.)

What of residential construction? It may be seen at once from Chart V that a mild decline in the rate of family formation and, more significant for the short run, the tightened credit terms under Regulation X plus the Federal Reserve Board's restrictive mone-tary policy, were effectively keeping down the number of new housing starts. The weak upward crawl from mid-1951 to early 1953 was only slightly faster than the rise in GNP. Housing was to exert a more dynamic expansionary influence only with the onset of the 1953–54 recession.

Consumption in the Korean Expansion

Careful scrutiny of Chart III shows which of the major spend-ing streams were chiefly responsible for carrying the GNP up-ward from an annual rate of $319.3 billion in the first quarter of 1951 to $369.9 billion in 1953 II. The dynamic spending streams, those with continual positive multiplier potentials, were govern-ment purchases, *which rose every quarter from 1951 I to 1953 II*, and personal consumption expenditures. Consumption expendi-tures, seasonally adjusted, increased every quarter from 1951 III to 1953 III. The dynamic force of private investment *increases*, active briefly in late 1950 and early 1951, had spent itself by the end of the second quarter 1951.

The two jogs in the consumption line of Chart III show the two panic buying sprees of consumers, the first following the United States commitment in Korea on June 27, 1950, the second after the Chinese counteroffensive against United Nations troops in the Yalu Valley. The responding inventory investment jogs could be neatly fitted into these. The consumption jogs do not, of course, show up in the annual data plotted on Chart II. This chart of real growth shows the steady rise in consumption perhaps more lucidly.

In appraising the general pattern of consumption in this whole period from 1950 through 1953, it is well to remember that there was considerable dispersion in the price movements of items comprising the consumer price index. For example, prices of services-including-rent (and especially transportation) rose substantially, prices of consumer durables tended to fall after the late 1950-early 1951 ascent, and prices of nondurables-excluding-food drifted very gradually upward along with the total. Consequently, the current dollar figures in Table 3-2, since they embody these divergent trends, may present a misleading overall view. A truer view is given by the price-deflated series in Table 3-4.

TABLE 3-4

Personal Consumption Expenditures by Major Spending Categories,
1950–1955
(In billions of 1954 dollars)

	1950	1951	1952	1953	1954	1955
Personal consumption	216.8	218.5	224.2	235.1	238.0	256.0
Durables	32.1	29.2	28.5	33.1	32.4	39.6
Nondurables	109.2	111.2	115.0	118.3	119.3	125.4
Services	75.5	78.2	80.8	83.7	86.3	91.0

SOURCE: *Economic Report of the President*, January, 1962, p. 210.

These data show clearly that it was nondurables and services that carried the upswing onward during the Korean expansion from 1950 through 1953 from the consumer side of the market. The performance of services was all the more remarkable in that they rose substantially despite the considerable price increases. It will also be observed that these spending streams were quite thoroughly insulated against the 1954 recession (as were nondurables to a much lesser degree). The indifferent trend in consumer durables until 1955 reflected the reaction following the bulge in spending for these items in 1950, the retardation of the postwar growth curve of stocks of durables per household, and the restrictions on consumer credit (these restrictions—the so-called Regulation W —were removed in May, 1952). Average monthly domestic sales of passenger cars, for example, did not reach their 1950 peak of 543,000 again until 1955.

The pedestrian record of consumer durables during the Korean War years, except for a jump of short-run significance in 1953, meant that the average age of existing stocks was beginning to rise, a trend which continued and accelerated thereafter throughout the decade. Future increases in consumer incomes, the release of restrictions on consumer credit, and the aforementioned aging of stocks, would combine to create favorable conditions for a boom in consumer durable expenditures later on.

The Recession of 1953–54

There were apparently two chief causes for the downturn following the cyclical peak in the second quarter of 1953. The first was the slowdown, and in some important lines the absolute drop, in retail sales early in 1953. The second was "the reduced military production rates in prospect." [16] Basically, the cause was atrophy of the stimulus that had been provided by national security expenditures.

The clue to the course of events was given by a crucial indicator of changes in economic activity: average weekly hours of production workers in manufacturing, which began to fall in the first months of 1953. Total retail sales barely rose subsequent to the third quarter of 1952. The "accelerator effect" was no doubt thereby set in motion: cessation of absolute growth at the retail level set the stage for an absolute decline in investment following the appearance of unexpected inventory accumulations. Unplanned manufactures and wholesale and retail inventories mounted beginning in the fall of 1952. Wholesalers' inventory-sales ratios began to drift upward after mid-1952. The annual rate of nonfarm inventory investment rose from $4 billion in 1953 I to $7 billion in the next quarter, the highest accumulations occurring in a few vital durable goods lines, such as motor vehicles and primary metals.[17]

Monetary Policy

The Federal Reserve Board, as so often in the past, was forced to proceed in a "damned if you do and damned if you don't" direction. That is to say, it tightened credit prior to a slump,

16. *Economic Report of the President*, January, 1954, p. 22.
17. *Ibid.*, p. 21.

exposing itself to the naive criticism that it was responsible for the slump. Actually, the Board displayed traditional rationality, whether intended to anticipate the professed high interest program of the new Republican administration or not, by raising the discount rate from 1¾ to 2 per cent in January, 1953. The Board saw a serious inflationary threat in the three years of moderate, steady growth of the money supply; a sharp increase in business loans from banks in the closing months of 1952; an upward drift in wholesale prices of industrial goods; and the aforementioned price climb in consumer services, such as decontrolled rents, medical care, and transportation. The Federal Reserve Board therefore sold government securities on the open market in order to put pressure on member-bank reserves.[18] Thereafter it apparently decided to pursue a policy of watchful waiting, not wishing to create too stringent conditions surrounding the availability of credit.[19]

This cautious policy was rather rudely disturbed when the Treasury announced in April, and threw onto the market for cash in May, $1.2 billion of long-term 3¼ per cent bonds. The issue represented an avowed Treasury policy of lengthening debt maturities and embracing a higher interest rate structure. The 3¼ per cent was carrying out the latter with inordinate determination, for the yield on long-term government securities had reached only 2.87 per cent in early March, 1953.[20] The resulting further upward pressure on the interest rate structure apparently seemed to the Federal Reserve authorities to create the possibility of an overly stringent credit policy in view of economic conditions by the second quarter of the year. The Board therefore reversed itself, entering the open market to make purchases in May and June and reducing reserve requirements in July. (The discount rate was not cut until February, 1954, however.) The Board's action was propitious, much more propitious than the Treasury's.

One of the more intriguing aspects of the 1953 interlude was the reversal of roles in the historic Federal Reserve-Treasury

18. I am indebted for this summary of monetary-debt events to the Joint Economic Committee, *Staff Report on Employment, Growth and Price Levels* (Washington, D.C., U.S. Government Printing Office, December 24, 1959), p. 329. The report will hereafter be referred to as the *Eckstein Report*, after Otto Eckstein, Technical Director of the study.

19. The reader is referred to the excellent and cautious analysis of monetary policy at this time by Earl C. Hald in his discussion of the paper by Kenneth D. Roose, "Business Fluctuations in the United States since 1951," in the American Economic Association, *Papers and Proceedings*, Vol. XLV, No. 2, of the *American Economic Review*, May, 1955, pp. 384–387.

20. Ralph E. Freeman, "Postwar Monetary Policy," in *Postwar Economic Trends in the United States* (New York, Harper, 1960), p. 70.

controversy over the Treasury's policy of pegging the price (maintaining a ceiling on interest rates) of government securities. In May and June it was the Treasury whose bond-selling actions were tightening credit, while the Federal Reserve was working toward greater monetary ease.

The mild irony of the Federal Reserve's open market purchases in May and after, taken to exert a downward pressure on interest rates, is enhanced by the fact that the System had announced in April, 1953, its now famous policy of "bills only." That policy declared that the Reserve authorities would thereafter confine their open market operations to transactions in Treasury bills only, in order, among other things, to allay the persistent skepticism of the market regarding their proposed policy, pursuant to the Accord of March, 1951, no longer to peg the price (keep down interest rates) of government securities—"and most certainly not those on intermediate- and long-term securities." [21] It is probable that the direct impact of "bills only" on interest rates was incidental; but the policy did, like any open market activity, influence the *availability* of credit, i.e., the position of the supply curve of credit.

The recession reached its trough in the third quarter of 1954. The downswing verified the business community's worst expectations regarding the trend of national security purchases, which plummeted from an annual rate of $53.0 billion in the peak quarter, 1953 II, to $41.9 billion in 1954 III, a decline of about 21 per cent. Additionally, a decline in Federal non-defense expenditures added to the total drop from peak to trough another $2.5 billion. The drop in Federal expenditures did not abate until early in 1955. The accompanying rise in state and local government expenditures, so typical of the whole decade, was $3.9 billion, leaving a net for all levels of government expenditure (transfer payments excluded) equal to minus $9.7 billion.

Income, Consumption, and Prices

The center of interest for economic history in the mild 1953–54 recession lies chiefly in the behavior of income, consumption, and prices. The decline of $13.3 billion, the sum of the drop in government purchases and gross private investment, would probably have taken place from peak to trough even if the other major spending streams had been constant. But since net foreign investment rose (by $1.1 billion) and consumption also rose (by $5.4 billion), the net fall in GNP was held to only $6.8 billion, a

21. "Federal Reserve Operations in Perspective," *Federal Reserve Bulletin*, March, 1961, p. 276.

mere 1.8 per cent. In GNP terms this was the mildest recession of the three between 1950 and 1959. It was also the most moderate in terms of the unemployment rate (Chart IV).

The fortunate boost in net foreign investment was due primarily to a slight rise in exports, excluding military grants-in-aid, combined with a decline in imports. Reversal about mid-1953 of an export decline that had persisted since early 1951 has been attributed for the most part to the industrial expansion of Western Europe and the United Kingdom in 1953 and 1954.

The performance of disposable income and consumption constituted the primary explanation, from the standpoint of expenditure flows, of the recession's mildness and, together with housebuilding, the ensuing recovery. Table 3-5 shows the magnitude of

TABLE 3-5

Personal Income, Consumption and Saving, 1953–54 Recession
(amounts in seasonally adjusted annual rates in billions of dollars)

	Pre-recession peak (Apr., May, June, 1953)	Trough (July, Aug., Sept., 1954)	Change Amount	Per cent
Wage and salary disbursements	198.8	195.4	−3.4	−1.7
Private	164.8	160.8	−4.0	−2.4
Government	34.0	34.6	+0.6	+1.8
Transfer payments	14.1	16.5	+2.4	+17.0
Proprietors' income	40.7	40.9	+0.2	+0.5
Business and professional	27.5	27.8	+0.3	+1.1
Farm	13.2	13.1	−0.1	−0.8
Property income	33.2	35.3	+2.1	+6.3
Rents	10.5	10.9	+0.4	+3.8
Dividends	9.4	9.7	+0.3	+3.2
Interest	13.3	14.7	+1.4	+10.5
Other income	1.9	1.6	−0.3	−15.8
Total personal income	288.7	289.7	+1.0	+0.3
Less: Personal tax and nontax payments	35.9	32.9	−3.0	−8.4
Equals: Disposable income	252.8	256.8	+4.0	+1.6
Less: Personal consumption expenditures	233.3	238.7	+5.4	+2.3
Equals: Personal saving	19.6	18.0	−1.6	−8.2

SOURCE: Federal Reserve Bank of St. Louis, *Monthly Review*, December, 1958, p. 148.

the increase in consumption along with the immediate explanations for it. While GNP fell from a $369 billion annual rate in the peak quarter to $362 in the trough, consumption rose, thus clearly demonstrating the dynamism and the autonomy from GNP that characterized consumption in the 1950's. Of course, autonomy with respect to GNP does not mean autonomy from all income considerations. It was chiefly, though not entirely, because of the rise in *disposable* income that consumption rose. And new institutional features of the economic environment had much to do with the autonomy of disposable income as compared to GNP changes.

Although private wage and salary disbursements declined as would be expected (1,779,000 of the total of 1,960,000 nonagricultural disemployment being concentrated in manufacturing), the rise in government payrolls (largely state and local), property income, and transfer payments provided important offsets. The decrease in personal tax and nontax payments and in personal saving accomplished most of the rest that was necessary to raise consumer expenditures in the face of the slump. It will be observed that consumption rose *more* than disposable income.

It is important to aggregate the role of government in bolstering disposable personal incomes. This is simply done. Practically all the transfer payments are attributable to government. To these must be added the reduction in tax payments and the increase in government payrolls. This gives:

Increase in transfer payments	$2.4 billion
Reduction in personal taxes	3.0 "
Increase in government payrolls	0.6 "
	$6.0 "

Given the moderation of the slump, it seems clear on the basis of this crude tabulation that government was also providing vital recession props to consumer incomes and therefore to personal consumption expenditures. It should be recalled, however, that in the 1953–54 recession the *Federal* government's role was in part contrary to the standard counter-cyclical prescriptions, for it reduced both national security and other purchases of goods and services. On the other hand, the Federal government did run a slight cash deficit in fiscal 1954 ($200,000,000—exactly equal to the state and local government deficit).

Long-Term Investment

Business long-term investment, though slightly sensitive to the recession, rode it out with only a moderate decline. Expenditures for new plant and equipment fell from a peak of $28.8 billion in 1953 III to a trough of $25.7 billion in 1955 I. The decline was widely diffused, the commercial and public utilities sectors being among the least affected. It has previously been noted that the major item in the recession drop of private investment was the usual culprit—inventories. There was a fall of only about 6 per cent from peak to trough in producers' durable equipment outlays.

Why was the decline in long-term investment not more severe? The answer may lie in a combination of the mildness and brevity of the recession drop in total spending, the stickiness of prices, the favorable sales prospects that emerged from the virile performance of total consumption and housing, and the strength of the corporate financial position.

Business investment was also much encouraged by satisfactory profits and cash flow (depreciation and depletion allowances plus retained income). The Korean excess profits tax expired in January, 1954. Offsetting the fall of corporate profits in 1954 was a decrease in corporate tax liabilities (one of the built-in stabilizers of the new era). The tax decrease completely absorbed the decline of $4.3 billion in corporate profits before taxes between 1953 and 1954; and aggregate corporate profits after taxes in both years were higher than in 1952. The new institutional features of the economic environment therefore acted not only to bolster disposable income, but also to cushion the effect of contraction on business profits. Furthermore, the 1954 Internal Revenue Code provided for more liberal depreciation allowances, thus bolstering cash flow in 1955. Profits rose by some $9 billion before taxes and $4.5 billion after taxes in 1955.

Table 3-6 shows one important view of the changing profit position of manufacturing corporations in 1953 and the first three quarters of 1954, which includes the trough quarter in 1954. The rate of profits after taxes on stockholders' equity, for the larger firms at least, showed no significant sensitivity to the 1954 recession. It is also worth while to note the record of the total cash flow for all corporations, except banks and insurance companies, for the whole period under review, as shown in Table 3-7.

It is widely hypothesized by economists that the total cash flow, or gross business savings, is highly important in determining fluctuations in long-term investment. In a study of the years 1947–60, it has been shown that capital expenditures on new plant and equipment in a given quarter are closely correlated to the level of cash flow in the preceding two quarters.[22]

22. Chase Manhattan Bank, *Business in Brief*, May–June, 1960.

TABLE 3-6

Ratio of Profits after Taxes to Stockholders' Equity,
Private Manufacturing Corporations, by Asset Size Class
Quarterly at annual rates, 1953 I–1954 III

Asset size class (thousands of dollars)	Year 1953	1953				1954		
		I	II	III	IV	I	II	III
All asset sizes	10.4	10.7	11.2	10.5	9.5	9.4	10.4	9.3
Under 250	7.3	7.0	13.2	11.0	−4.2	0.1	8.1	8.0
250–999	7.3	7.9	10.3	8.1	2.2	4.6	8.1	8.1
1,000–4,999	7.5	8.9	8.8	7.4	5.0	5.3	6.1	5.6
5,000–99,999	9.5	10.3	10.6	9.5	8.1	8.1	8.8	8.1
100,000 and over	11.8	11.8	12.1	11.9	12.5	11.7	12.3	10.8

SOURCE: *Economic Report of the President,* January, 1955, p. 192, Table D-51.

TABLE 3-7

Total Corporate Cash Flow and Its Major Components, 1950–55
(In billions of dollars)

Year	Total cash flow	Retained profits and depletion allowances	Depreciation and amortization allowances
1950	$20.8	$13.0	$ 7.8
1951	19.0	10.0	9.0
1952	17.8	7.4	10.4
1953	19.7	7.9	11.8
1954	19.8	6.3	13.5
1955	26.6	10.9	15.7

SOURCE: *Economic Report of the President,* January, 1962, p. 283.

As already pointed out, investment in housing played an important part in cushioning the recession of 1953–54. As is clearly shown in Chart V, the line of new housing starts moved sharply upward throughout the slump. This experience with residential construction showed decisively the extent to which activity in housing is responsive to public policy in the credit sphere. The weakness of the real forces underlying the demand for housing in 1954–55 emphasizes the efficacy of credit conditions as a factor. In addition to the general easing of credit early in 1953, VA-insured mortgages were permitted an increase in the interest rate ceiling from 4 to 4½ per cent; thus they became much more attractive to lending institutions, particularly so because rates of return on many other types of investment were less attractive. No-down-payment loans rose from 11 per cent of the total in 1953 to 48 per cent in 1955, and thirty-year loans increased from 5 per cent of the total to 44 per cent over the same period. It may be surmised that the greater portion of the increase in housing starts shown in Chart V was the product of appropriate public policy in the field of housing credit. Indeed for the decade as a whole, conventional housing starts displayed a pattern of relative stability with steady growth, the counter-cyclical bulges, especially in 1953–54, being largely attributable to FHA and VA starts. There were other factors, of course, one of which was continued urbanization and suburbanization.

The magnitude of the stimulus to general expansion derived from residential nonfarm building may be appreciated by noting that in value terms the total rose from its pre-recession level of $11.1 billion in 1952 to its next peak annual rate of $17.2 billion in August, 1955. For comparative purposes it may be observed that although total expenditures on plant and equipment in *all manufacturing* in 1952 were $11.6 billion, they had risen to only $12 billion in the third quarter of 1955. In the high investment year 1956, housing accounted for 30 per cent of total nonfarm investment excluding inventories. The capacity of housing investment to induce economic expansion would be hard to overestimate.

The 1953–54 recession occurred without price declines in either the general wholesale price index (the index of all industrial prices) or the general consumer price index. Only the prices of farm products continued the march down from their 1951 heights, a march that by 1955 was turning into a rout (Chart I). Among the consumer group, both rent and services-excluding-rent continued their climb in the attempt to catch up (from a prewar base, 1939) with other consumer prices. On a 1947–49 base, the consumer services and rent were far above commodity prices and above the general consumer price index. On this base, commodity prices in the consumer index did fall during 1954. This was the only price group in the index that indicated there was a recession taking place.

It will be seen from Chart I that the price plateau of the 1953–54 slump was approaching the point at which the terrain would again begin to rise. Indeed the next phase in the decade's price history would create many more problems of interpretation than had the first phase from 1950 to 1955.

4

Contours of Change in the 1950's: Mid-decade Rise to the Recession of 1957-58

A study of industrial growth by the Midwest Research Institute published in 1957 declared that "military demand has been the major and almost exclusive dynamic growth factor in recent years." [1] The brief survey of the economy from 1949 through the end of the Korean War period has suggested that the conclusion of the Institute does seem consistent with those portions of economic reality selected for the purposes of that survey. The present historical study highlights the role of both government budgets and consumption in the growth process of the contemporary economy. Government military spending was undoubtedly the most important general growth factor until the end of the Korean War expansion. Furthermore, it was the major growth factor in most, though not all, of certain large rapidly growing industries throughout the whole decade, as will be shown in Chapter 6. Finally, the slowdown in military spending during the later years of the decade was unaccompanied by an offsetting increase in Federal welfare expenditures, shunting the responsibility for growth to other spending streams that failed to rise sufficiently to fill the vacuum thus left. The general retardation in the later years may be attributed in part to this slowdown in overall Federal spending, even as particular growth industries continued to

1. Stefan H. Robock, *Changing Regional Economics* (Midwest Research Institute, MRI—252, 1957), p. 4, as cited in Murray L. Weidenbaum, "Some Economic Aspects of Military Procurement," *Current Economic Comment*, November, 1960, p. 10.

expand under the stimulus of portions of that Federal expenditure stream.

The steady growth of consumer spending, on the other hand, assured continued general growth after the Korean War. Although the rate of increase of consumer spending was insufficient to assure a satisfactory general growth rate, rising consumer expenditures were nevertheless the most important single determinant of general economic growth during the later years of the decade.

The Expansion Period after 1954

The Government Budgets

The year 1954 found the economy operating with declining government cash payments to the public. The combined cash budgets of all levels, after running a small deficit in fiscal 1954 (covering the 1953–54 recession), produced a sizable deficit of $4 billion in fiscal 1955, then ran surpluses in both fiscal 1956 and 1957. The fiscal 1956 cash surplus was substantial: $4.1 billion. The shift to surpluses was entirely due to the Federal cash budget, since the state and local governments continued to incur small cash deficits through fiscal 1958. The Federal surplus was $4.5 billion in fiscal 1956 and over $2 billion in 1957. This depressive aspect of the Federal budgetary situation was the result of continuing efforts of the Federal government after 1953 to bring the budget into balance. Despite Federal tax rate reductions, effective in 1954, that cut into cash receipts in fiscal 1955, there was a jump of about $9 billion in receipts in the next fiscal year and still another jump of $5 billion in fiscal 1957. These were traceable chiefly to persistent surpluses in the trust fund accounts— Unemployment Trust Fund in 1956 and the Old-Age and Survivors Insurance (OASI) Trust Fund for all the years through fiscal 1957; the postponement of reductions in corporation and excise taxes scheduled first for April, 1955, and then for April, 1956; and larger revenues flowing from higher incomes in the economy. On the expenditure side, Federal cash payments to the public were held between $70.5 billion and $72.6 billion during fiscal 1954–56. When these rose in fiscal 1957, cash receipts also rose to remain above them. In consequence of these and certain other changes, the Federal debt was decreased slightly in fiscal 1956 and 1957—two notably exceptional years in the decade's public debt history. The debt stood at $276.3 billion at the end of the fiscal year ended June 30, 1958. (This was about 62 per cent of GNP, a substantial drop in the ratio, which had stood at 90 per cent in 1950.) The Federal cash budget was thus not a stimulant during the years from the end of the 1953–54 recession to the end of fiscal 1957. Indeed, it may well have been a depressant.

Federal government purchases of goods and services declined in real terms (1954 prices) from calendar 1953 through 1956 and thereafter rose slightly to a plateau at about 10 per cent of real GNP for the remainder of the decade. These expenditures could bolster a slump; but they could not, at their approximately constant real aggregate amount, stimulate long-run expansion. Stimuli from the Federal budget in the late 1950's had to come from rising transfer payments and from cash deficits ("net income-generating expenditures"). There were deficits in fiscal 1958 and 1959, the latter very large—over $13 billion in the cash budget; but a small surplus again appeared in 1960.

Meanwhile, state and local expenditures and total government transfer payments were busily growing. It will be seen from Table 4-1 that both these categories, given the mild cash deficits

TABLE 4-1

State and Local Government Purchases and All Government
Transfer Payments to Persons

Year	State and local purchases	Transfer payments to persons
1954	27.7	16.2
1955	30.3	17.5
1956	33.2	18.8
1957	36.8	21.9
1958	40.8	26.3
1959	43.6	27.2
1960	47.2	29.1

SOURCE: *Economic Report of the President*, January, 1962, pp. 207, 225.

in the expanding state and local budgets and the short-run consumption-inducing impact of transfer payments, tended to stimulate economic recovery. GNP rose about 39 per cent over the period shown. But state and local government purchases rose 71 per cent and transfer payments 79 per cent.

The first series in the table rose $4 billion in the slump year 1958, and the transfer income series rose $4.5 billion. These were important cyclical rectifiers. Gone in the 1950's was the "cyclical perversity" of state and local budgets that had featured the business cycle of an earlier day—a relationship involving simultaneously declining national income and state and local expenditures.

State and local government expenditures, typically financed in association with small cash budget deficits, proceeded throughout the decade at the steady upward pace shown in Chart VI. There was no essential deviation from this path during 1955–57. These expenditures, despite the regressive tax structures associated with them, bolstered and helped to stabilize total spending.

One study by the Department of Commerce has shown, however, that the real average rate (1954 dollars) of growth of *all* government purchases of goods and services for *all* levels of government combined fell from 5.1 per cent per year for the whole period 1948–60 to 2.4 per cent per year for the period 1955–60 (Table 4-2).[2] The latter rate, *which is pulled down because of the*

TABLE 4-2

Postwar Growth Rates and Average Deviations from Trend of Major Components of Real Gross National Product
(Per cent)

	Average annual rate of growth	Average deviation from trend
Gross national product	3.4	2.6
Personal consumption expenditures	3.4	1.0
Durable goods	4.1	5.6
Nondurable goods	2.7	.7
Services	4.2	.7
Producers' durable equipment and private nonresidential construction	1.5	4.7
New private nonfarm residential construction	3.9	7.5
Government purchases of goods and services (Federal, state, local)		
1948–60	5.1	12.0
1955–60	2.4	1.4

Note.—Rates of growth are based on linear logarithmic regressions using data in 1954 dollars for the period 1948–60.
SOURCE: U.S. Department of Commerce, Office of Business Economics.

Federal component, was far below the 3.4 per cent average annual rate for real GNP shown by the same study for the whole period

2. Louis J. Paradiso and Mabel A. Smith, "Developments in the Consumer Market," *Survey of Current Business,* January, 1961, p. 19.

1948–60; it rather approximates the 2.25 per cent rate for real GNP referred to in Chapter I for the period 1955–59.

Consumption

The steady rise of personal consumption expenditures in the whole decade can be clearly seen by referring back to both Chart II and Chart III. The major exception to the steady pattern is the Korean War jogs which were noted earlier. Chart III shows best the greater stability of consumption as compared with money GNP. Of course stability has always been a feature of aggregate consumption as compared to GNP and gross private product, and historically the propensity to consume has shifted counter-cyclically. What is striking about consumption in the 1950's is its almost unremitting rise, the decline in GNP and gross private product being associated with merely arrested increases in personal consumption expenditures. On an annual basis, aggregate consumption never fell between 1950 and 1960, although there were absolute declines in GNP once and in gross private product twice. Thus was demonstrated the short-run autonomy of consumption with respect to gross current income. This independence, however, did not exist so strikingly with respect to current disposable personal income, which was insulated to a great degree against changes in GNP and gross private product, a fact which largely explains the short-run independence of consumption with respect to gross current income changes. The residual source of autonomy may be explained by the "permanent income" hypothesis of Milton Friedman (i.e., that current consumption on other than durables is dependent upon expected average or normal income over a long period).

Consumption and GNP in real terms grew at the same rate from 1948 to 1960, as shown in Table 4-2. The table also shows that aggregate consumption was the most stable of all major spending streams, with an average deviation from trend of only 1.0 per cent. *There was no drop in the rate of growth of aggregate real consumption in the latter part of the decade, as there was in the GNP and the all government purchases series.*

Since the overall growth rate dropped far below 3.4 per cent in the later years, while aggregate consumption did not, it seems plausible that trends were present within the consumption aggregate that adversely affected the GNP rate. In the first place, the growth rate in nondurable goods for the whole period, as well as for the latter half, was comparatively low. The sustained but low 2.7 per cent rate in an expenditure category that accounted for

46.5 per cent of all consumer purchases in 1960 must have exerted a drag on the GNP rate.

The real culprit, however, was consumer durables. The 4.1 per cent average annual growth rate of expenditures on consumer durables shown in Table 4-2 unfortunately conceals the very sharp contrast in the early and late years of the postwar period. Real consumption expenditures on durables in 1954 dollars rose at an average annual rate of 6.6 per cent between 1947 II and 1955 IV, but the rate was only .9 per cent between 1955 IV and 1959 II.[3]

Expenditure on services, on the other hand, was well sustained, the rate of growth even rising slightly in the later years. At a 4.2 per cent rate this purchase category, accounting for 40 per cent of total consumer outlays in 1960, may be credited with a strongly buoyant influence—limited, however, by two related developments: first, this sector was growing at the expense of consumer durables; second, the service sector had historically been a comparatively low income (low productivity) sector. The service lines not only remained a low income area, but they also failed to keep pace during the decade with the increase of annual earnings per worker and of productivity in most commodity-producing industries. The shift in spending to the service lines tended to retard the rate of growth of productivity in the economy, despite the comparatively rapid growth of the service sector. (It will be recalled that large productivity increases are associated with high growth rates as a general rule.) The shift to services also tended to retard expansion in plant and equipment output because of the comparatively low investment in fixed capital per worker or per man-hour in the service industries.[4]

What was true of consumer durables was true of expenditures for all durables, which increased 5 per cent per year during 1946–55 but only .5 per cent from 1955 to 1960.[5] The slowdown can easily be seen in Table 2-1, wherein it is shown that the production index of durable manufactures rose 43 percentage points from 1950 to 1955; but in a period of equal length during the last half of the decade, 1955–60, the index rose only 10 percentage points.

3. *Eckstein Report*, p. 78.
4. See George Stigler, *Trends in Employment in the Service Industries* (New York, National Bureau of Economic Research, 1956), p. 158.
5. Chase Manhattan Bank, *Business in Brief*, May–June, 1961).

Consumption and Growth

Since the shift in consumer expenditures toward services contributed to the general decline in the rate of increase of durable goods production, it must be concluded that the shift also contributed to the retardation in the rate of economic growth.

What about the other side of the coin—the shift away from durables? Here can be found another explanation for retarded growth, because the production of consumer durable goods is more capital-intensive, because depressing the rate of expansion in durables, *ceteris paribus*, would be expected to dampen the rate of productivity rise in the economy as a whole, and because the total primary wage and salary effects of a dollar of consumer expenditure on durables is probably substantially higher than a dollar of expenditure on services. On the last-named point, one study based on a 190-sector, input-output technical matrix of the United States economy for 1947 showed that the direct plus indirect labor requirements generated in producing $1,000 of materials and services in the case of consumer durable expenditure was $610, whereas it was only $517 in the case of services excluding rentals.[6]

It may be presumed that the consumer market for durables was "stocked up" by mid-decade, and there was a decline in the rate of growth of wants for these items. This is a possibility. However, the slowdown in the rate of household durable goods absorption for such a lengthy period is puzzling. The simple satiation hypothesis is also placed in doubt by the sharp rise after 1955 in the age of consumer durables, as measured by the ratio of gross to net stocks. Hence it seems reasonable to examine alternative interpretations. One hypothesis [7] is that the retarded growth of disposable income after 1955, coupled with the differential rise in prices of services, many of which (e.g., rent, utilities, cleaning and laundry, auto repair and operations, household and auto insurance, medical and hospital care) are in the nature of family fixed costs, compelled the deflection away from durables. After all, many durables are purchased out of discretionary income.

The price trends since 1956 are shown in Chart VII. On conventional theoretical grounds the durables were falling in price relative to services and therefore should have been substituted for

6. Alan M. Strout, "Primary Employment Effects of Alternative Spending Programs," *Review of Economics and Statistics*, Harvard University Press, November, 1958, p. 326, Table 4.

7. U.S. Senate, Special Committee on Unemployment Problems, *The Impact of Unemployment in the 1958 Recession*, Committee Print, 86th Cong., 2d sess. (Washington, D.C., U.S. Government Printing Office, 1960), p. 4.

Chart VII. Consumer Prices

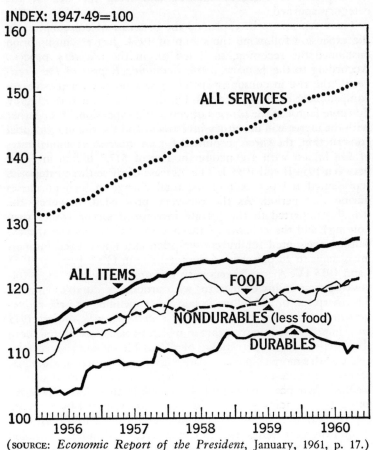

INDEX: 1947-49=100

(SOURCE: *Economic Report of the President*, January, 1961, p. 17.)

the increasingly more high-priced services. But this did not happen; and the fact of income retardation, together with the fixed-cost and discretionary-income hypothesis regarding the structure of consumer preferences, seems to be the most plausible preliminary explanation of the determinants of consumer allocations between durables and services in that period.

The conclusion seems to be that changes in the composition of consumer expenditures after the middle 1950's may explain in part the drop in GNP growth rate below that for aggregate consumption. This depressive impact operated both from the side of the expenditure category favored and from the side of the category spurned.

There remains to be explained the behavior of consumption in the expansion following the slump of 1954. Just as consumption cushioned the recession, so it led off in the recovery process. According to the January, 1956, *Economic Report of the President*, "the rise in consumer spending was not . . . a passive accompaniment of rising incomes. On the contrary, it was a highly dynamic factor in the process of economic expansion." [8] Together with the increase in inventory investment and the rise in residential construction, the three accounted for an increase at annual rates of $18 billion with a concomitant rise of $17.7 billion in GNP between 1954 II and 1955 I. The increase of these three categories represented 102 per cent of the total change in final purchases during that period. As the recovery proceeded, however, the stimulus imparted to the private investment sector (other than housing) and the collapse of the housing boom reduced the expansion accounted for by consumption and raised fixed business investment to 28 per cent of the total rise in GNP between 1955 I and 1955 IV. After the recovery was under way in 1955, it followed a time-hallowed pattern, with producers' durables lagging. The sharp rise of $16 billion in consumer spending *and the reduction in personal saving below 1954 recession levels* during 1955 (making three successive years in which personal saving fell, both absolutely and as a percentage of disposable income) were associated with a more than coordinate rise in expenditures on durables, particularly automobiles. Annual factory sales of passenger cars reached their peak for the whole decade in that year—7,920,000 units. The spending surge in durables was expedited by a record expansion of $6.1 billion of consumer credit compared with $600 million the year before and an annual average of about $3 billion during the earlier postwar years. The great bulk of the rise in 1955 was installment credit.

The consumer durable boom came to an end in 1955 for automobiles and in 1956 for other durables. In both real and money terms personal consumption expenditures on durables fell in 1956 compared with the previous year, a drop for which automobiles and parts were chiefly responsible. This should not becloud the fact that the stagnation in *all* consumer durable demand had already set in, however.

8. *Economic Report of the President*, January, 1956, p. 23.

Private Domestic Investment

In the previous chapter the decline in business expenditures on new plant and equipment in the 1953–54 recession was shown to have conformed to the general mildness of that experience and the financial condition of the corporate sector to have remained relatively firm.

Under the stimulus of rising consumption in general and consumption of durables in particular, of the publicly stimulated residential construction boom, and of the associated favorable sales prospects, the amplitude of induced business fixed investment that followed was certainly the most impressive of the decade. By the end of 1957 about $9 billion had been added to the real net value of privately owned structures and equipment in manufacturing since 1954. This exceeded by about $1 billion the additions between 1950 and 1953 (see Chapter 3).

The investment wave of 1955–56, perhaps the strongest of the decade, generated a reciprocal interaction with other spending streams. This mutual reinforcement carried the economy upward toward its peak real GNP of $409.3 billion (1954 dollars) in the second quarter of 1957. The expansion resembled, in the strong reciprocally expansive role of rising business fixed investment and consumption, the traditional cyclical expansion process. Yet neither expenditure stream rose with sufficient power to *sustain* a substantial rate of rise in real GNP. The absolute rise in 1955 GNP over 1954 was $29.6 billion, or 8 per cent: this was the one year prior to the 1957–58 recession that had a large increase. The rise in real GNP in 1956 over 1955 was only $9.5 billion, or 2.4 per cent. The rise in 1957 over 1956 was only $4.8 billion, or 1.2 per cent. The rate of increase in investment was, like that for consumption, insufficient even to sustain a constant absolute increase in real GNP. And the declining absolute rate of increase of GNP set the stage for an absolute decrease in investment, as the accelerator relationship would suggest.

Some of the major aspects of the investment expansion during 1955 and 1956 are shown in Table 4-3. The data are extended through 1960 where available or of special interest. The most significant columns are the first two, which together comprise business fixed investment. These data are presented in constant dollars because of the sharp rise in capital goods prices in 1955 and 1956 and because it is desirable to envision not only the pattern of the cyclical expansion but also the extent to which real capital was forthcoming. These price-deflated aggregates are

TABLE 4-3

Selected Aspects of Private Investment Activity at Selected Annual and Quarterly Rates, 1953–1960
(quarterly data at annual rates)

| Year and quarter | Producers' durable equipment (billons of 1954 dollars) | New private construction * (billions of 1954 dollars) | Index of industrial equipment output** (1957 = 100) | Index of commercial equipment output** (1957 = 100) | Defense orders for hard goods (billions of dollars for fiscal year ending June 30) | Corporate retained profits† (billions of dollars) | Corporate cash flow‡ (billions of dollars) | Unincorporated enterprise income (billions of dollars) | | |
| | | | | | | | | Manufacturing | Services | All industries |
	(1)	(2)	(3)	(4)	(5)	(6)	(7)	(8)	(9)	(10)
1953	22.5	14.0	97.2	77.1		8.9	19.7	1.72	7.99	40.9
1954	20.8	14.3	87.4	72.5	18.2	7.0	19.8	1.54	8.13	40.5
1955	22.5	15.7	91.5	81.8	14.2	11.8	26.6	1.63	9.88	42.3
1955 I	20.3	15.2	86.5	75.7		11.1				
1955 II	21.7	15.5	91.3	79.0		11.5				
1955 III	23.7	16.0	91.2	83.6		13.0				
1955 IV	24.4	16.1	94.0	88.3		12.8				
1956	24.8	16.1	104.4	94.9	13.2	11.3	27.8	1.59	9.87	42.9
1956 I	24.4	16.3	98.9	91.0		11.7				
1956 II	24.6	16.4	106.3	93.2		10.7				
1956 III	24.9	16.6	104.6	95.4		10.2				

Year										
1956 IV	25.1	16.5	106.4	101.3		11.9				
1957	*24.1*	*16.5*	*100.0*	*100.0*	*14.6*	*9.7*	*28.0*	*1.39*	*10.38*	*43.3*
1957 I	*25.2*	*16.9*	*105.6*	*104.5*		*10.6*				
1957 II	*24.3*	*16.9*	*101.9*	*101.7*		*9.2*				
1957 III	*24.0*	*16.9*	*98.4*	*99.4*		*9.4*				
1957 IV	*22.7*	*16.6*	*91.9*	*95.2*		*8.0*				
1958	*19.4*	*14.8*	*82.3*	*88.0*	*15.3*	*6.4*	*26.3*	*1.27*	*10.89*	*46.3*
1959	*21.3*	*14.8*	*97.0*	*104.0*	*15.5*	*10.3*	*30.6*			*50.5*
1960	*22.7*	*16.0*	*102.0*	*118.0*		*8.6*	*29.5*			*47.9*

SOURCE: Department of Commerce, Federal Reserve Board, Council of Economic Advisers, *Eckstein Report, Statistical Abstract.* *Excluding residential nonfarm. **The mid-month of the quarter is recorded for the quarterly totals, since quarterly data are not available. †Profits after Federal corporate income taxes minus dividends. ‡Retained profits, depletion allowances, and depreciation.

rather sobering. For example, they yield a more unimpassioned interpretation of the record than the statement in the *Economic Report of the President* in January, 1958, that "the increase in business outlays on plant and equipment from the first quarter of 1955 to the third quarter of 1957 was of boom proportions, amounting to almost 50 per cent." [9] Table 4-3 does show a rather dramatic real rise in a shorter time span than that just quoted—a 24 per cent rise between 1955 I and 1956 IV in producers' durable equipment.

Inclusion of the construction series in the second column does little to assist the rate of rise. Indeed it would substantially reduce the percentage increase for the shorter time span. The striking thing about the construction component of fixed investment is its very slow upward crawl, in real terms, over the three years of relatively high level activity shown. This record is consistent with what was noted earlier about the decline in proportion of investment in structures during the contemporary era. New private business construction did much to maintain employment and income for a time, but it was not dynamic in the sense of raising them by substantive increments from period to period. It is the *increment* to investment that raises income and employment, not continuation at some given level. *The average annual rate of growth of real outlays for plant and equipment between 1948 and 1960 was the smallest of all major spending streams*—about 1½ per cent.

Residential construction (Chart V), although contributing mildly to the recovery phase, turned downward after early 1955, and from then on exerted a negative influence on the expansion. As pointed out above, the responsibility for this kind of housing performance lay, under the existing conditions, in the hands of the public authorities. They were more concerned with the danger of inflation than with the rate of economic expansion.

In the more dynamic producers' durable equipment series it will be observed that the period of significant increases terminated at the end of the first year, 1955. Thereafter the contour was that of a very slight, gentle rise to 1957 I, following which it dropped off to slump levels. We are thus left with one year of brisk expansion in this category of investment activity—an expansion neither powerful enough nor sufficiently long-lived to give the economy the boost it needed to achieve a period of sustained and vigorous growth. This was a clear case, after the fourth quarter of 1955, of continual additions to capacity without any significant

9. *Ibid.*, January, 1958, p. 12.

Chart VIII. Manufacturing Capacity and Production

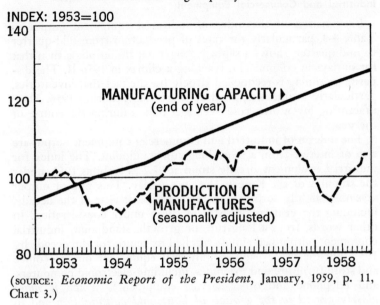

INDEX: 1953=100

(SOURCE: *Economic Report of the President*, January, 1959, p. 11, Chart 3.)

additions to income. (We do not know the amount of the additions to capacity—*net* investment—from these figures since they are *gross* purchases of producers' durable equipment.) The resulting discrepancy which developed between capacity and output (or sales), shown strikingly for manufacturing in Chart VIII, which is reproduced from the January, 1959, *Economic Report of the President*, goes far to explain why the expansion in output was not sustained.

Throughout the period of this investment wave the Secretary of the Treasury was calling for ever more investment and urging tax reforms to achieve that end. It has been seen that for the long pull in the 1950's the average annual rate of growth of the value of fixed investment was anemic, and perhaps Secretary Humphrey was unconsciously oriented toward this fact. However, in the short run he was probably wrong in failing to see the need to raise the other spending streams to warrant the growth in capacity that was occurring. It would have taken an almost phenomenal investment rise and a high expenditures multiplier to raise income and spending during the later 1950's to rates sufficient both to absorb existing excess capacity and to warrant such investment.

Industrial and Commercial Equipment

Examination of the index of industrial equipment output in Table 4-3, particularly the rates of production from mid-quarter to mid-quarter, shows a slightly longer expansion phase than that for outlays in column (1), reaching a climax in 1956 II. The disparity in timing is reconciled largely by the fact that inventories, particularly in durables, piled up increasingly during 1956. Manufacturing inventories rose over $5.5 billion during the course of the year.

The indexes of industrial and commercial equipment output are also of interest from a more long-run standpoint. The index for industrial equipment already stood at 97.2 as early as 1953, under the stimulus of the Korean War prosperity. This rate of output was only slightly surpassed in any subsequent year of the decade, including the years of investment surge under consideration. In other words, from a long-run, or growth, standpoint, industrial equipment output had almost reached its zenith for the decade by 1953. On the other hand, commercial equipment output (office and store furniture and machines, including electronic computers, and telephone and other service equipment), *which is more closely geared to the growth of household consumption* and to the service industries, had not reached nearly such heights by 1953 as had industrial equipment. By the same token, there was still plenty of growth potential left in the series at that date. The consequent more rapid rise in this series between 1955 I and 1957 II endowed it with a greater income-stimulating capacity than that associated with the increase of industrial equipment production. The same differential held for the upswing from 1958 through 1960.

The fiscal year series on defense orders for hard goods—Table 4-3, column (5)—shows that these orders, which directly stimulated the durable goods and investment goods industries, were not a factor in the 1955 expansion. The moderate rise in fiscal 1957 reintroduced Federal spending into the expansion path of the economy to a degree.

Corporate Financial Position

The financial condition of the strategic corporate sector in the aggregate, insofar as represented by retained profits and total cash flow, is shown in Table 4-3 to have been quite favorable. The jump in the internal sources of funds for investment in 1955 was gratifying. There was certainly no apparent abatement in the flow prior to the downturn in 1957. The subsequent fraying of the corporate financial position therefore came from sources external to the cash flow—at least external to the *ex post* flow. It may be noted that the total cash flow, on an annual basis, weathered the 1957–58 recession very well, although the retained profits component suffered considerably in 1958, partly because dividend payments in 1958 were as large as in 1957.

These short-run developments should not be permitted to obscure a long-run trend of considerable significance in the design of corporate internal financing: the rise of depreciation charges to become the leading source of corporate capital financing. Depreciation funds which provided about one fourth of total investment financing requirement in 1950, had risen to about one half at the end of the decade. The chief factor underlying the growth of depreciation allowances was of course the increase in the asset base. Of secondary but nonetheless considerable and rising importance after mid-decade was the effect of the depreciation provisions in the 1954 Revenue Code. These permitted the consistent use of alternatives to straight-line depreciation, so that about two thirds of the purchase costs of a durable asset could be written off during the first half of the estimated useful life of the asset.

A more complete analysis of corporate financial condition would have to point out that corporate cash flow (internally available funds) failed to keep pace with the expansion of investment in plant, equipment, and inventory, during 1956 particularly. This is not apparent in Table 4-3, partly because inventory investment is not shown, but also and more important because the investment and output series in the table are in real rather than in current dollar terms. The demands made by investment expansion were substantially in excess of the internal cash flow. Two results followed. Corporations from the end of 1955 had to reduce their liquid asset holdings (cash and United States government securities) to maintain their investment programs. This reduction process, fed by rising credit extensions to consumers and other businesses, continued at a rapid rate in 1956, reaching a low point in 1957. The second result was an increased reliance on external fund sources—a characteristic pattern in the course of a general investment wave. One such source was the commercial banking system: there was an increase of $5.5 billion in the total of commercial bank loans to business during 1956. A second source was new corporate security issues, especially bonds and notes. New funds from this source totaled $9.6 billion in 1956, an increase of

$1.7 billion above 1955. In both channels the borrowers confronted a rising trend of interest rates reflecting not only short-run demand-supply disequilibrium but also the influence of the Federal administration's set policy of monetary stringency, in effect since early 1955. With the Federal cash budget surplus of $5.5 billion in calendar 1956—the largest in the decade—neither the monetary nor the fiscal environment was very favorable.

It is difficult, therefore, to appraise the net effect of the cross currents operating on the financial condition of the corporate sector—even the few mentioned here. One is tempted to find the factor that ultimately tipped the scales against continuation of the investment wave in the growing discrepancy shown in Chart VIII between capacity and output. Behind that was the fall in the rate of increase in spending, particularly consumer spending. As has been mentioned, this experience was quite consistent with the general notion of the accelerator: a decrease in the absolute rate of increase of spending induces an absolute fall in investment.

The last three columns of Table 4-3 provide contrast and, at the same time, a deeper understanding of the 1955–57 expansion. They show that the income base of the expansion was narrower than might otherwise be surmised, and they further reveal that the noncorporate business sector shared but slightly in the expansion. This is true even if agriculture were deleted from the total. The record for manufacturing "small business" was particularly dismal. The service component, linked as it is closely to consumption, came off rather better than manufacturing. On the whole, however, the income position of this important segment was too drear for it to have contributed much but restraint upon the upward course of the economy.

The rise in unincorporated enterprise income during the slump year 1958 may be attributed almost entirely to agriculture, forestry, and fisheries. This development was primarily due to good weather, increased crop production, and an 11 per cent rise in livestock prices.

In summary, the investment wave of 1955–57 made an important contribution to the moderate expansion in real GNP (Chart II). The rise in GNP was substantial in the concentrated expansion period from early 1955 to about mid-1956.

The weaknesses in the upswing are pinpointed by the fact that the rate of increase in nonagricultural employment slowed down markedly after mid-1956, average hours worked in manufacturing having turned downward even earlier. The curve of manufacturing employment described a flat plateau through 1956. Unemployment, after declining moderately to mid-1955, hovered at 4.2 per cent of the civilian labor force for almost two years without any further decline and thereafter rose sharply (Chart IV).

Net Foreign Investment

The expansion was favored in the crucial year 1956 and early 1957 by a jump in exports. The increase in total merchandise exports in 1956 was about $3.5 billion over 1955, raising net foreign investment (defined at that time as exports of goods and services minus imports of goods and services) by about $2 billion. Had this trend continued, it might have cushioned the impending slump, though its magnitude was insufficient in 1956 to do much more than compensate for the negative net changes in business inventories that were taking place. The export jump was nonrecurrent, however, being largely a result of the disruption of normal shipping that followed the closing of the Suez Canal after the abortive invasion of Egypt by British, French, and Israeli forces. The added export demand was heavily concentrated in petroleum.

The Recession of 1957–58

A glance at Chart III or Chart IV will show the slump of 1957–58, encompassing the period from 1957 III to 1958 II. Further study of Chart I will show that, so far as all wholesale prices or industrial prices were concerned, there was no such slump. Chart VII shows the same intransigence for consumer prices. This depression insensitivity of so many important price series, coming as it did on top of a prior sharp rise which had accompanied a 4.2 per cent unemployment rate and only moderately rising aggregate money demand, gave birth to a new set of questions regarding the nature of price inflation under contemporary conditions.

Before dealing in detail with these developments, however, it will be desirable to trace briefly the contours of the 1957–58 recession.

Contours of the Recession

Following the pattern of decline that would be expected, private investment fell the most in percentage terms. Because of the recession resistance of consumption and government purchases, however, the fall in GNP was smaller than the drop in gross gross private investment. This had also been true in 1948–49, but not in 1953–54 because the largest amount of decline in that recession was in government purchases. It may be clearly seen, then, that the 1957–58 slump was registered as a wholly private investment slump. As usual for the decade, inventory disinvestment accounted for the bulk of the latter, followed in relative importance by producers' durable equipment, which fell by $5.7 billion. The drop in producers' plant was only $1 billion from peak to trough on a quarterly basis.

TABLE 4-4

Decline in Major Spending Streams, Recession of 1957–58

Spending streams	Change from peak to trough	
	Billions of dollars	Per cent
Consumption	0	0
Private investment	−17.5	−26.2
Government purchases	3.9	4.5
Net foreign investment	−3.1	−86.0
GNP	−16.6	−3.7

SOURCE: Computed from Commerce Department national product accounts.

The recession fall in plant and equipment outlays on an annual basis was of course concentrated in manufacturing, and within manufacturing it was centered in the durable goods industries. Public utilities and communications hardly responded. Neither did the commercial activities—trade, service, finance, and construction. The stability of consumer spending for nondurables and services had scored again.

Table 4-5, showing the recession changes in personal income, consumption, and saving, indicates as did the similar tables for the earlier recessions the operation of the new depression resistants. The big task for the resistants was to offset as much as possible the impact of the drop in private wage and salary disbursements. Within the latter total it is significant that the major culprit again was the commodity-producing industries, wherein the total of such disbursements fell from $103.4 billion in June, 1957, to $95.0 billion in April, 1958. In the distributive activities the decline made hardly a ripple, and in the service trades there was no decline.

It will be seen that in combination the increase in government wages and salaries (chiefly state and local in this case) and transfer payments plus the decrease in personal tax and nontax payments, totaling $7 billion, offset the great bulk of the drop in private wage and salary disbursements. With sticky wages and other prices in vital areas contributing importantly to the prevention of downward cumulation, nothing shows more clearly than this tripartite combination the new role of government in arresting a recession before it could develop into a depression. To be sure, the combination is no *guarantee* against depression. The combination is largely non-discretionary, and its efficacy would be doubt-

TABLE 4-5

Personal Income, Consumption, and Saving, 1953–54 Recession
(Amounts in seasonally adjusted annual rates, in billions of dollars)

	Pre-recession peak, July–Aug.–Sept., 1957	Trough Apr.–May–June, 1958	Change Amount	Per cent
Wage and salary disbursements	240.5	233.6	−6.9	−2.9
Private	199.9	191.8	−8.1	−4.1
Government	40.6	41.8	+1.2	+3.0
Transfer payments	21.6	26.2	+4.6	+21.3
Proprietors' income	43.5	44.1	+0.6	+1.4
Business and professional	31.7	30.7	−1.0	−3.2
Farm	11.8	13.4	+1.6	+13.6
Property income	43.8	43.8	0.0	0.0
Rents	12.0	12.1	+0.1	+0.8
Dividends	12.7	12.4	−0.3	−2.4
Interest	19.1	19.3	+0.2	+1.0
Other income	2.4	2.2	−0.2	−8.3
Total personal income	351.8	349.8	−2.0	−0.6
Less: personal tax and nontax payments	43.1	42.3	−0.8	−1.9
Equals: Disposable income	308.7	307.5	−1.2	−0.4
Less: Personal consumption expenditures	288.3	288.3	0.0	0.0
Equals: Personal savings	20.4	19.2	−1.2	−5.9

SOURCE: Federal Reserve Bank of St. Louis, *Monthly Review*, December, 1958, p. 148.

ful in the event of more serious declines in private economic activity. Only major discretionary moves by the Federal government could deal with severe depression.

From the standpoint of easing the slump, it was fortunate that in fiscal 1958 payments from the OASI trust fund exceeded receipts *for the first time* and benefits from the state unemployment funds exceeded tax receipts by over $1.4 billion.

But it must also be realized that automatic stabilizers not only tend to put a floor under recessions. They generally put a ceiling on expansions. "When economic activity quickens after a slump, the rise in Federal revenues begins immediately and slows the recovery in employment and incomes," pointed out the January, 1962, *Economic Report of the President*.[10] Thus in the recovery period embracing 1958–60, receipts into the state unemployment trust fund accounts rose $666 million while withdrawals for compensation payments fell by $560 million. Similarly, while national income rose some 12 per cent between calendar 1958 and 1960, Federal personal tax and nontax receipts climbed 18 per cent and corporate profits tax accruals 20 per cent. Meanwhile, the Federal cash budget switched from a deficit of $7.3 billion in calendar 1958 to a surplus of $3.6 billion in 1960. The cash budget was close to balance in fiscal 1960, at a time when there were almost 4 million unemployed—about 5.6 per cent of the civilian labor force. Many authorities pointed out that the built-in features of the Federal budget therefore yielded economically restraining budget surpluses long before full employment was achieved. From this a corollary policy conclusion was drawn that certain discretionary budget measures would ordinarily have to be taken during expansion to offset the budget's automatic restraints. It also followed that the monetary authorities should not be too hasty in putting on the brakes during economic recoveries.

It will be observed from further examination of Table 4-5 that in the 1957–58 slump the drop in personal tax and nontax payments—one of the built-in stabilizers—was of negligible magnitude. This stabilizer was not very effective. This is no particular reflection on its ultimate stabilizing capacity, of course, because the mildness of the decline in total personal income prevented the emergence of a significant change in personal taxes. The relationship is underscored by the contrasting experience in the case of highly volatile corporate profits. The drop in profits was $12.2 billion, but the offsetting decrease in tax liabilities of $5.7 billion reduced the decline to $6.4 billion, resulting in a 29 per cent fall in corporate profits after taxes from peak to trough.

It has been said that the parity programs for agriculture also acted like built-in stabilizers. They indeed tended to stabilize

10. *Ibid.*, January, 1962, p. 71.

prices. The operation of the program in the 1957–58 recession occurred in the surprising context of a record crop output, rising farm prices, a continued strong domestic demand for food, and only a slight drop in exports. Consequently the stabilizing role of the price support program took the form of absorption of a portion of the large crop that otherwise might have depressed prices and therefore farm incomes.

The insulation of consumption in the downturn is again perhaps the most notable feature of 1957–58. Despite the presence of some possibly nonrecurrent elements in the situation, such as the rise in farm income, it seems safe to conclude that this insulation had become a characteristic of the economy as now constructed. The insulation referred to is the inelasticity of response to changes in money GNP. In the recession phase of the great depression, i.e., between 1929 and 1930, GNP fell $12.7 billion and consumption $10.1 billion. This is a marginal C/GNP ratio of .80. In the 1937–38 recession on an annual basis the ratio was .48. In both 1948–49 and 1953–54 consumption rose while GNP declined between peak and trough quarters. In 1957–58, on a peak-to-trough-quarter basis at annual rates GNP fell $16.6 billion while consumption fell not at all.

Employment and Unemployment

In estimating the degree of permanence that may be attached to this vital stabilizing relationship, it is well to bear in mind the discussion in Chapter 2 regarding the structural changes in the industrial distribution of employment. It may reasonably be concluded that the economy of the 1950's (and 1960's) had a larger percentage of the labor force employed in activities and occupations that are insensitive to mild cyclical fluctuations than has historically been so. This structural change, together with continued mildness of fluctuations, may underpin the proposal emanating from some labor quarters that employers adopt the salary basis of employee compensation for production workers. It will be seen from the record studied that the durable goods industries could be expected to hold out the longest against such a proposal.

The decrease in employment of wage and salary workers in nonagricultural establishments from peak to trough of 4.4 per cent was the most severe of the postwar recessions. The newly unemployed were added to the 2.8 million primarily frictional unemployed who had been out of work prior to the recession. In addition there was the usual annual increase in the civilian labor force, amounting to about 700,000 in 1958. From April to September of that year, total unemployment ran about 5 million, or 7.5 per cent of the labor force (Chart IV).

One of the fortunate aspects of the recession for the unemployed, as well as for the economy in general, was its relative brevity. There were eleven months of contraction in 1948–49, thirteen in 1953–54, and eight in 1957–58. However, the recovery failed to reduce the unemployment rate to the levels achieved in earlier recoveries (Chart IV). This pattern of ever higher unemployment rates as the economy proceeded through its recession and recovery sequences during the decade was one of the more disturbing aspects of the economic history of the times. Some blamed the automatic features of the Federal budget for this, as has been pointed out.

This dreary record was an important source of the new emphasis on the problem of slowing rates of economic growth, rather than instability, as the 1960's loomed ahead. As the economy entered the 1960's the employment configuration seemed to be one in which employment rose, but at a rate insufficient to prevent the concomitant increase of unemployment. As the economy moved upward from the mild slump of 1960–61, employment rose; but unemployment persisted at close to 7 per cent of the civilian labor force, i.e., close to the 1957–58 recession rates, in mid-1961. The problem was made increasingly large partly because the annual accretions to the labor force, assuming participation rates given, were destined to get bigger as time passed. The average annual increase was 800,000 between 1955 and 1960, but in the latter year the increase was 900,000.

The nation's experience with cyclical instability in the 1950's seems to add up to the forecast that such instability in the present era is likely to be of minor amplitudes. Should the secular trend become one of rising unemployment, however, the setting of cyclical fluctuations would thereby be altered. In such a context, recessions might well be more likely to become cyclical depressions by virtue of the persistently depressing effect of this trend on short- and long-run expectations. It *could* take the community so long to learn this that a severe depression or two might occur before action would be taken to forestall secular retardation.

5 | Contours of Change in in the 1950's: Prices, Money and Fiscal Policy to 1960

Inflation [1]

Demand-pull vs. Market Power

It has been shown that most of the rise in prices after World War II occurred in two waves. The first, which took place in the immediate postwar years, was caused largely by the unleashing of an explosive supply-demand disequilibrium through the removal of general price controls. The second was also generated by a supply-demand disparity, this time at the onset of the Korean War. But these two waves did not end postwar price rises; a new inflation got under way in 1955 and continued into the 1960's (see Charts I and VII).

The origins of the inflation in this later period of slow economic growth cannot be traced to immoderate increases in the money supply, even for short periods. The money supply (demand deposits and currency outside banks) rose much more slowly than GNP. The great bulk of the rise in GNP from 1955 to 1960 was accommodated by increases in the velocity of money, and a distinctly minor proportion by increases in its quantity. The whole period from 1945 to 1960 was marked by a strong upward trend in the ratio of GNP to the money supply, which was a reversal of the trend in the income velocity of money (GNP/M) that

1. This section relies heavily, though by no means exclusively, upon the *Eckstein Report*, especially Chapter 5, pp. 103–160.

had long taken place. Hence velocity increase was by far the most important monetary component of the inflationary process.

Three different explanations arose in accounting for the rising price trends after 1954. The first theory came to be called the "demand-pull" doctrine. Proponents of this doctrine often mistakenly claimed they based their analysis on the traditional theory of an excess of aggregate purchasing power superimposed on a competitive, price-flexible, full employment economy. In the equation of exchange, according to this traditional theory, the quantity of money, M, times its velocity, V, equals the price level, P, times total physical output, Q. Where $MV = PQ$, the Q cannot increase in the short run because of the full employment assumption, and V is stable; increase in M alone (or MV if the constant V assumption is relaxed) therefore *initiates* rises in P. (Note the mechanical cause-and-effect nature of the reasoning.) Increases in the public's holdings of M are assumed to go to the market promptly to buy goods and services.

The second explanation was the "cost-push" or administered price doctrine of inflation. This notion of "sellers' inflation" argued that the existence of some degree of discretionary power on the part of sellers—such as large firms, colluding or noncolluding oligopolists, associations or unions—made possible sustained price markups or nonreductions under cost-demand conditions that would produce opposite price adjustments if competition prevailed. For example, if capacity were excessive and prices were raised, the rise would be administered because under competition it could not be so raised. Or if demand fell, with cost conditions given, but price remained the same, the power to administer price was again imputed, since price would presumably fall under such conditions if competition were to prevail.

The third explanation was called structural inflation and was associated particularly with the name of Professor Charles L. Schultze.[2] According to this theory, inflation can be understood only through analysis of demand shifts in particular sectors or industries. Although the administered price analysis also resorted to disaggregation, the structural inflation theory typically was willing to start the inflationary process by a demand shift affecting some sector, rather than by an administered price increase. Following the price rises caused by the demand shift in a given

2. See Charles L. Schultze, *Recent Inflation in the United States*, Study Paper No. 1, Study of Employment, Growth and Price Levels, Joint Economic Committee, 86th Cong., 1st sess. (Washington, D.C., U.S. Government Printing Office, September, 1959.)

sector, these price rises, it was argued, were transmitted as higher costs to other industries and sectors, who then raised their prices in turn, even though their demand schedules had fallen. The lines which lost sales would at least not reduce their prices. This aspect of the structural inflation doctrine seems congenial to the administered price approach. It may be noted that the structural inflation theory did not employ the assumption of an excess of *aggregate* demand.

The demand-pull proponents actually based their notions most of the time on a disaggregated model of the economy rather than the crude aggregative theory of the traditionalists. They were inclined to define inflation not as a rise in general prices, but as a rise in some broad group of prices.[3] They differed from the structural inflation theorists, however, in that they minimized the role of sticky or rising costs, and particularly the alleged capacity of rising costs to induce an increase in the velocity of money.[4] They rejected at the same time, therefore, the administered price doctrine.

The greater attention to costs in the structural inflation doctrine was further reflected in the emphasis placed by Professor Schultze on the rising comparative importance through the 1950's of business overhead costs stemming from the increase in depreciation allowances and in salaried labor. The 125 per cent rise in capital consumption allowances, for example, far outstripped the percentage increases in other major business costs.

The treatment that follows leans toward a combination of the sellers' inflation and the structural inflation approaches,[5] while at the same time acknowledging, as will be seen below, some measure of validity at times and in certain sectors to the demand-pull interpretation.

Wholesale Prices

It has been shown that steady increases in consumer demand, implemented by sharp increases in consumer credit; equally continuous expansion in state and local government demand; the occasional booms in residential construction demand; and the plant

3. See, for example, Richard T. Selden, "Cost-Push Versus Demand-Pull Inflation, 1955–57," *Journal of Political Economy*, February, 1959, p. 2.

4. *Ibid.*, pp. 1–2.

5. For a critique of the *Eckstein Report* and Professor Schultze's Study Paper, see Romney Robinson, "Employment, Growth and Price Levels: The Joint Economic Committee Report," *American Economic Review*, December, 1960, pp. 996–1010.

and equipment investment wave of 1955–56—all these sectoral demand upsurges created strong demand-pull conditions in areas which for substantial periods, and especially during 1955, were experiencing tight supply conditions.

The investment wave of 1955–56, together with the rise in actual and expected military hard-goods demand in the latter year, go far to explain the concomitant price rises in the capital goods industries. And these industries, taken in conjunction with their chief suppliers, accounted for nearly two thirds of the rise in the industrial wholesale price index between 1955 and 1957. Within this total, a leading contribution to the wholesale price rise between 1954 and 1957 was made by iron and steel, which on a 1947–49 base increased from 133 in 1954 to 166 in 1957. In the first year of this price rise, the index jumped to 141, and associated with this rise was an increase in net profits after taxes for the industry from $182 million to $326 million. The explanation of the capital goods price rise and steel's role in it must invoke all three theories of inflation. After 1955 steel prices reflected chiefly a combination of administered price increases on the part of factor suppliers (labor, some materials) and of the steel producers themselves. Iron and steel prices continued to rise, and sharply until 1958; demand tapered off; production fell; capacity increased; and both aggregate profits and profit rates remained high through 1957. While these developments were taking place, the iron and steel wholesale price index, *however poorly it may have reflected, like other price indexes, quality changes or realized prices*, rose from 141 in 1955 to 169 in 1958. One of the rigidifying factors in the 1958 slump was the wage rate inflexibility stemming from a three-year contract settlement negotiated after the mid-1956 strike and under the comparatively favorable price, sales, and profit prospects obtaining in that settlement year.

Both auto and steel in 1955 and 1956 had set wage patterns for labor and management negotiators in a number of other important oligopolistic industries such as farm equipment, electrical equipment, aircraft, aluminum, copper, railroads, and meat packing— industries that contributed to the maintenance and even increase of wage rates during the 1957–58 slump. The general mildness of the slump in most of these industries no doubt helped to bolster the downward inflexibility of these wage patterns.

The record for the pervasive iron and steel industry is more or less representative of numerous other major manufacturing lines, especially finished producers' goods; the metals and all machinery components of the wholesale price index together accounted for approximately three fourths of the total rise in the index after 1955. Therein lies a significant key to understanding the inflation of the period.

The January, 1957, *Economic Report of the President* had this to say about the very important inflation year 1956:

Although the advance in industrial prices ceased for a while, rising costs became an increasingly pervasive factor. After the middle of the year, and especially after steel prices were raised following the strike settlement, industrial prices advanced again on a broad front. The combination of heavy demands from the investment goods sector of the economy, rising labor costs, and renewed advances in prices of many raw materials resulted in price increases for a broad range of semimanufactured materials, components, and supplies. And these price increases became cost increases to producers of finished goods, many of whom were also experiencing rising labor costs.[6]

The statement points up the mutually interacting, reinforcing effect of cost and price movements as a structural inflation process unfolds.

In the sphere of construction the price configuration was again developed out of a mixture of strong demand coupled with some moderate sellers' inflation influences. Price increases in residential nonfarm construction were slight between 1952 and 1955 and moderate after 1956 except for a modest upturn in 1959. The only year of significant increases was 1956. It may be that the rise in wages and labor costs in construction as in numerous other sectors during that year was an adjustment to their lag behind the price rises in 1955, although this would be less true in residential construction than in manufacturing. The cost of materials to the construction industry also increased substantially in 1956. For the construction industry as a whole, the 17 per cent price rise for residential nonfarm construction and the 23 per cent rise for other construction between 1954 and 1960 may probably best be explained as the result of both demand pressures and cost pressures, the latter emanating partly from wage factors within and wage-plus-materials prices from without. Prices in both sectors of the construction industry on an annual basis resisted the slump of 1957–58, a fact which must be related to the *rising* output during the latter year in the residential division and the *falling* output in the other division.

The post-1954 rise in the price indexes of wholesale commodities other than farm products may be ascribed largely to the influence of price administration in steel and to the pressure of

6. *Economic Report of the President*, January, 1957, p. 32.

demand on tight supply conditions in machinery. In most other manufacturing lines and in construction a combination of mutually interpenetrating cost pressures, sluggish productivity trends, market power to administer prices, and demand-pull was in operation. Rising costs and prices mutually reinforced one another as they permeated the whole structure of intermediate prices. In the case of administered price effects, rising overhead cost elements—centered in depreciation charges, salaried labor overhead, and interest costs—were a factor of unknown weight. It is also likely that indirect business taxes, which almost doubled over the decade, and social security taxes, which *more than doubled between 1954 and 1960,* were a notable inflationary force, albeit a force offset in part by their deflationary impact on demand.

The role of poor productivity achievement cannot be overlooked, particularly in manufacturing. Real value added per man-hour in that sector rose only 1.9 per cent per year from 1953 to 1957, which was a much lower rate than even the moderate output growth rate. Rising productivity exerts a downward pull on the trend of prices; and whenever productivity increases are sluggish the influence of this force is correspondingly vitiated.

The downward rigidity of wholesale industrial commodity prices in the 1957–58 recession, repeated in 1960–61, was ascribable largely to a combination of continued demand strength in many lines—associated with recession buoyancy—and market power to administer prices and wage rates despite particular demand decreases and excess capacity or unemployment. The downward inflexibility of wage rates during the slumps of the 1950's may be ascribed partly to strong unionism and partly to the brevity and comparative moderation of the recessionary forces. "Maximum employment" tended to remove the historic downward pressure on wages that had formerly emanated from large labor surpluses in cyclical downswings. In this connection, the comparative stickiness of most money wage rates during the recession phase of the great depression (i.e., during 1930 and even 1931), which were years of weak union organization, suggests that the amplitude and duration of the downswing may dominate the unionization factor in the recession behavior of such rates. It became evident that under contemporary conditions unemployment might have to reach intolerable rates before it would produce any significant reduction in money wages.

Consumer Prices

Turning now to consumer prices, the first important thing to recall is the great price increase in that heterogeneous category known as the service industries—housing, household operation, transportation, medical care, and miscellaneous. The entire rise in the consumer price index from 1951 to 1956 was accounted for by the rise in this service component. To understand the connections between the service component of the consumer price index and the remaining components, it is important to remember that during the course of the big jump in consumer prices following the removal of general price controls after World War II the service component rose only gradually while the other components rose very greatly. *On a prewar base* (1939) the service component in fact did not catch up with the others until 1961. This meant that at the beginning of the 1950's the components other than services, on a prewar base, were far above the prices of services. *Therefore, the rise in prices of services throughout the whole decade may be explained chiefly, though not entirely, in terms of the lagged infusion of rising prices elsewhere in the price system into the prices of services in their role as costs to the service lines.* These relationships are underscored by the fact that the rate of increase of the real output of services between 1951 and 1955 was not inordinate, but was approximately equal to the rate of growth of real GNP.

After 1955 all major components of the consumer index, except home furnishings, rose in varying degree. The rise in 1956 was the first notable increase since 1952.

Prices of services rose more rapidly than other components after mid-decade. The services were areas of strong demand-pull, and the demand influence exerted considerable pressure on the short supply in a number of cases. Medical care illustrates this relationship well. The short-supply condition here was no doubt aggravated by a complex configuration of market power leading back to the restrictive conditions surrounding the provision of medical training. In the case of a number of services afforded by the publicly regulated industries, such as gas, electricity, water, telephone, rail and air transport, and urban public transit, rising prices were of course based on the "fair return" principle. They therefore reflected past and expected cost increases emanating from elsewhere in the price system and incorporated into the full-cost prices set by these industries. In other service categories the upward movement of prices was attributable to diverse, interacting origins such as rapid growth of demand, low rates of productivity increase, market power, and cost infusion.

The retail price of food accompanied the slight rise in farm product prices and processed foods at wholesale from 1955 through 1958, but did not respond significantly to the drop in farm prices after early 1958 (Chart I). The fact that retail food prices rose less than all consumer prices may be attributed chiefly to the decline in farm prices.

The rise in the clothing price index of only about five percentage points between 1953 and 1961 was one of the more striking instances of price stability in the decade. The performance in both consumer durables and nondurables, according to the GNP implicit price deflators using 1954 as base, was one of moderate, steady rise to 106.5 and 107.6 respectively by the fourth quarter of 1960.

It needs only to be emphasized, beyond the summary points already made, that power to administer price, slow growth of productivity, and limitation of economic declines to mild recessions all combined to introduce an "inflationary bias" into the system, a bias that elicited much discussion toward the end of the 1950's.

As for the relation between sellers' inflation and demand-pull in the inflation process as a whole, it seems best to hypothesize that the phenomenon involved *reciprocal interaction between the parts of a disaggregated system.* In some parts and for some periods one influence dominated and spread its effects through the totality; in other parts during the same or different periods the other influence dominated. The older macrotheory of demand-pull inflation, employing a model which had general prices moving up while relative prices and the velocity of money remained fixed, could contribute little to an explanation of the inflation of the 1950's.

Aspects of Monetary Policy

Policy Goals of the Federal Reserve Board

The general policy of the Federal Reserve Board after the March, 1951, Accord with the Treasury was to rely overwhelmingly upon the general quantitative devices of credit control—the discount rate, open market operations, and changes in the reserve ratios. The Board and Congress abjured the use of selective controls, i.e., controls over the terms of installment loans and mortgages and over margin requirements for the purchase of common and preferred stocks. The latter have typically been included by the orthodox in the policy underworld of *direct* controls. As a policy alternative, direct controls were anathematized by almost all authorities throughout the decade.

From the end of the Korean War the Board was obsessed with the fear of inflation on the one hand and of direct controls over prices in the event of actual inflation on the other hand. The Committee for Economic Development sounded the alarm in a 1952 Policy Statement, when it announced that "the idea that we are living in an Age of Inflation is gaining currency." To this mixture of fears propelling the Board toward tight monetary policy was added after 1952 the urge to dissociate itself from the pre-Accord, pegged interest rate policy.

The Board inaugurated a moderately restrictive monetary policy soon after the recovery had gotten under way in early 1955 by raising the discount rate in April of that year from $1\frac{1}{2}$ to $1\frac{3}{4}$ per cent. There followed a series of small additional increases which carried the rate to $2\frac{1}{2}$ per cent in November. The rate reached 3 per cent in April, 1956, where it remained until August, 1957, at which time it was further increased to $3\frac{1}{2}$ per cent. Soon thereafter the rate was lowered to ease credit conditions in the 1957–58 recession. When recovery ensued, rates were raised again, to 2 per cent on August 15, 1958, and subsequently increased in steps to a peak of 4 per cent in September, 1959, on the threshold of the 1960 recession.

It can be seen that the Federal Reserve authorities attempted to lean against the wind. Their policy has been described as "vigorous" in this regard. Indeed, they did utilize the discount rate more actively than had traditionally been done. However, the absence of any change in the reserve ratios between August, 1954, and February, 1958, does not suggest excessive vigor, on the most liberal interpretation. Furthermore, open market operations were a minor control device until the 1958 recession. It is almost strictly true to say that the Board relied upon the discount rate exclusively to resist the controversial inflation following 1954. It has already been seen, however, that increases in the money supply were rather well curtailed. Also, net free reserves of the member banks (their excess reserves less their borrowings from the Federal Reserve) were negative from late 1955 to 1958. From the viewpoint of orthodox doctrine the Board generally followed the right policy during the latter half of the decade.

The chief aim of the Board's monetary policy was stable prices. Its failure in this regard was patent, but one can always safely argue that in the absence of its restrictive policy the price rises would have been greater. The continued uptrend of prices in the context of monetary tightness and the Board's apparent success in curtailing growth of the money supply served at the same time to spur the search for origins other than the quantity of money, such as the composition of the labor force, productivity trends, the degree of enterprise competition, the relation of money velocity to member-bank loan policy and to the activities of financial intermediaries, and the market power of unions. As Dr. Roy L. Reierson of the Bankers Trust Company (New York) put it, "The Federal Reserve has not been able to forestall a persistent upward trend in the general price level, but this inflationary bias appears attributable to forces in the economy over which the credit authorities have little or no control." [7]

The Board disavowed responsibility for qualitative, selective credit control (except during the Korean War and in the case of margin requirements). It was in consequence subjected to considerable criticism on the grounds that this was an ostrich policy. Criticism on similar grounds was leveled against it for ignoring the indirect influences exerted on the velocity of money by the operations of the growing financial intermediaries. To have responded positively to these criticisms would have involved a kind of integrated, planned public financial policy that the Board apparently abhorred. Its failure to exercise control in the spheres of housing and consumer credit was not criticized, however, in the 1961 report of the Commission on Money and Credit. (The Commission was a national committee of experts set up in 1957 by the Board of Trustees of the Committee for Economic Development to study public and private financial institutions.)

Housing and Consumer Durables

The Board's removal from direct policy participation in the residential construction field had some interesting results. It has already been pointed out that the availability and price of mortgage credit seems to have been the strategic cyclical factor in the housing market during the decade. More specifically, institutional investors compared rates of return on other types of investment, such as high-grade corporate bond yields, with interest rates on residential mortgages. The rates on conventional mortgages during the decade generally moved upward, sustaining the supply of funds and thus contributing to a rise (except for a plateau in 1955–57) in the volume of conventional mortgage recordings. The rates on FHA- and VA-insured mortgages, however, were subject to Federally regulated ceilings. In general during the

7. Updated version of paper delivered at annual meeting of American Statistical Association, Stanford University, Palo Alto, California, August 23, 1960, p. 2.

decade, as the excess of these rates over rates on alternative investments declined, government-underwritten mortgages became less attractive, and housing starts so financed would fall off. When the differential increased, government-supported mortgage commitments became more attractive, and residential construction was stimulated. These relations largely explain the counter-cyclical pattern of total residential construction during the decade. In this way the discount policy of the Federal Reserve, through its effect on other interest rates, more or less inadvertently influenced the volume of government-underwritten residential construction investment.

The Federal Reserve self-imposed segregation from the credit policies of other institutions led to some odd results in 1955. While it was engaged in tightening credit by raising the discount rate from 1½ to 2½ per cent, Fannie Mae was feeding a residential construction boom that added $3.1 billion or 23 per cent to the already high total of such expenditures in 1954. The rise in the total of outstanding Federally underwritten mortgages accounted for one half of the total rise in outstanding debt on one- to four-family dwellings in 1955. Toward the end of 1955, the lagged effect of the Federal Reserve's tighter monetary policy began to take effect, however, and housing starts began a precipitous decline (Chart V). The decline was hastened by Fannie Mae's co-operative move during the year to tighten up the terms on mortgage commitments. No sooner had this begun to take effect than the drastic fall in housing starts caused such alarm that measures were taken before the end of the year to stimulate the market again. By this time it was too late, however: the differential between other investment yields and mortgage paper, under the influence of the Federal Reserve's restrictive policy, was already too great to stem the drop in housing. If housing did not participate in the investment wave after mid-1955, i.e., if it acted as a drag on economic growth, the responsibility could reasonably be placed on the policy combination of monetary restriction by the Federal Reserve and Federal fiscal ineptness in the housing field.

It is true that the mechanism just described gave housing investment a counter-cyclical pattern in the 1950's, contributing to much lauded "stability." But concomitant monetary restriction meant that the long-run volume of housing investment was inadequate as a contributor to growth and also to the fulfillment of the nation's housing needs.

It seems doubtful that monetary policy influenced in a significant way the flow of consumer credit and the unstable pattern of consumer durable-spending associated with that flow. Extended consumer installment credit followed the course of recovery from 1954, climbing with great speed as interest rates rose during 1955 and tracing a more gradually rising path through 1956–57. There was a short but very brief drop in early 1958. Installment credit extension led in the recovery in 1958, rising rapidly again with interest rates in 1959. The demand for this type of credit appeared to be highly interest-inelastic and was chiefly a function of the demand for durables. Consumers were influenced on the financing side chiefly by the size of down payments and monthly installments, being scandalously indifferent to carrying charges. The moderate fluctuations in interest rates associated with changing monetary policy therefore were readily transferred by banks and sales finance companies to consumers without perceptible effect.

Consumer spending on durables as a percentage of disposable income reached a post-Korean peak in late 1955, at almost 15 per cent, and declined thereafter to peaks of slightly over 13 per cent of disposable income in early 1957 and late 1959. There can be no doubt that the upsurge of consumer spending on durables, aided by the growth of outstanding installment credit from $23.6 billion in 1954 to $34.2 billion in 1957, contributed greatly to the long expansion of 1955–57. At the same time, the enormous rise in the ratio of consumer debt to personal income in the 1950's endowed the 1960's with a great burden of debt service.

Monetary Policy and Business Fixed Investment

The most important activity relative to the impact of monetary policy was, of course, business investment in plant and equipment. This investment stream flowed in two waves, the first in 1955–57, already discussed, the second from the upturn in 1958 to a peak in the second quarter of 1960. These waves were roughly coincident with those for interest rates, including of course the Federal Reserve Bank's discount rate. This is not surprising, since monetary restraint is supposed to limit expansions when they threaten to become "excessive," and monetary ease to correct contractions. Here again, as always, nothing can be "proved" with the statistics. Nevertheless, there are good reasons for saying that monetary policy was at most a feeble limiting factor rather than an active and immediate determinant of the course of events. The proposition is designed to apply to the whole of the investment waves, including the upper turning points.

The impact of interest rate policy is supposed to be upon the *marginal* investment decision. The upward revisions of the discount rate, as in 1955–57, testify to the fact that as an investment wave proceeds and the economy expands along with it, the monetary authorities try to offset the concomitant rise in prospective yields on new investment. In technical terms, the schedule of the marginal efficiency of investment is shifting upward to the right. This schedule is not drawn from a series of points, but is a band or zone, and has a time horizon in the case of fixed investment decisions that extends considerably beyond the horizon of counter-cyclical interest rate policy, a fact recognized by both demanders and suppliers. The upward movement of the discount rate is designed to induce, allowing for a time lag, sufficient increases in long-term interest rates to overtake and arrest at the appropriate juncture in the expansion the rising prospective yields on additional plant and equipment investment.

It is implausible to assume, however, as does the conventional theory of monetary management, that the amplitude and the maximum of the rise in interest rates from 3.51 per cent to 5.09 per cent that occurred, for example, in the case of corporate Baa bonds (lower medium quality obligations having some speculative features, according to Moody's rating system) between 1954 and November, 1957, would be sufficient to arrest an investment boom that enjoyed favorable future prospects on other grounds. The Baa rate of 5.09 per cent was lower than its minimum level during the investment boom of the 1920's. During an actual investment wave, the *relevant range* of the investment demand schedule for durable capital goods is in all probability considerably above the equilibrium rate of investment where the marginal efficiency of an investment increment equals the expected rate of interest. The investment wave subsequently subsides not because business management confronts a problem of infinitesimal deviations from equilibrium values set by earlier schedules, but because the marginal efficiency schedule shifts sharply to the left—Keynes' "sudden collapse."

Furthermore, it is necessary in appraising the effective rate of interest relative to past history to consider the tax structure, just as that structure needs to be considered relative to prospective yields on new investment. For example, in the case of corporations on both sides of the market, if both were subject to the 52 per cent tax on corporate profits, the borrower's net cost and the lender's net return would be rather less than half the nominal rate of interest.[8]

8. See statement of William McChesney Martin, *Federal Reserve Bulletin*, June, 1959, p. 582.

Insofar as commercial bank loans to business were used directly or indirectly to finance fixed investment expansion, taking 1955–57 as a period for case study, one investigation concluded that

. . . tight money in 1955–57 apparently led those commercial banks which felt its impact to alter their asset portfolios significantly; they shifted to obtain funds to increase loans to profitable borrowers, especially business firms, even at the cost of liquidating government securities on a declining market. . . .
. . . the fact that increasingly tight banks continued to increase loans to good business customers, whose demand for money reflected partly heavy investment outlays and inventory carrying costs, means that tight money did not act to deter especially these prime movers in the investment boom. . . . tight money did permit funds to go extensively to the same borrowers who would have obtained them in the absence of tight money . . .[9]

The study also showed that business loans to large firms rose more than twice as rapidly as loans to smaller concerns, reflecting in all probability the differential increase in loan demand from the large firms.

Ineffectiveness of Traditional Credit Policies

It is the "other grounds" (other than interest rates) that economic theory came more and more to emphasize after World War II. Factors such as price-cost zones, current and prospective rates of utilization of capacity, and anticipated future sales volume were given increasing weight relative to interest as cost. Stress on these factors was based on an accumulating body of empirical investigation into actual business investment practices. It was recognized, for example, that many firms allocated investment funds on the basis of a payoff period, priority being given the projects which soonest returned the original amount committed. The discount rate applied in the payoff period—the "marginal efficiency of investment"—was typically far above current market interest rates. Where a firm's capital-budgeting policy employed a payoff period of five years, for example, the marginal efficiency of investment (rate of profit) would be 20 per cent; and interest rates between 4 and 6 per cent were therefore not likely to be an inhibiting consideration. (Critics attempted to whittle down the force of this hypothesis by arguing that the payoff period approach employed a gross profit concept,

9. G. L. Bach and C. J. Huizenga, "The Differential Effects of Tight Money," *American Economic Review*, March, 1961, p. 79.

and that a concept which first deducted depreciation, income taxes, and dividend costs would place interest cost in a more influential position.)

Where market power was substantial, investment commitments were typically made on the presumption that any increases in interest costs could be incorporated into price, all calculations being in terms of probability zones that left considerable tolerances for moderate, short-period interest fluctuations and a rising trend. As the apparent inflationary bias of the economy came to be built into business anticipations data, such calculations took on added validity. To the extent these became operative, tight money induced inflation instead of deflation. Also, it seemed most unlikely in the light of empirical evidence that a firm would turn over the employment of the large flow of internally generated corporate funds to outsiders for disposition, even in those improbable cases in which rising yields on the market appeared rather higher than on a project developed by the home management. Inside placement of internal funds would in general better serve management's long-run market strategy regarding product and geographical diversification, R & D programs, power posture vis-à-vis existing rivals or potential entrants, etc.

Another quite plausible hypothesis is analogous to the "permanent income" theorem regarding the consumption function. Perhaps a firm's investment outlays, to whatever extent they are sensitive to interest rates, are determined by its expectations regarding the *permanent* or *normal* or *average* interest rate over a number of years rather than to the short-run rate changes induced by monetary policy.

A more plausible case might be made for the effectiveness of tight money in regard to small and noncorporate enterprise. And the case could perhaps be strengthened by invoking the notion of credit *availability* in addition to interest cost. Studies of bankers' loan policy have indicated that when the Federal Reserve Board embarked on a restrictive program, member banks usually raised their sights and rationed credit more carefully. The major incidence of this more critical review fell upon the smaller borrower. For example, Mr. Theodore H. Silbert, president of the Standard Financial Corporation, asserted, in a talk before the Association of Commercial Finance Companies in September, 1959, that the "little fellow" stood to suffer most from the current credit tightening policy and warned that a great wave of small business failures would ensue unless the Federal Reserve Board insisted that lenders allocate a set proportion of their funds for small business loans.[10] This conclusion is consistent with the early spurt and later lag shown in Chapter 3 of nonlarge manufacturing corporations in the investment wave of 1950–52.

If monetary restraint were to be held efficacious in arresting the investment waves of 1955–57 and 1959–60, then the monetary authorities should be accused, as in fact they unjustifiably were, of being badly misguided in their policy of stabilizing prices by such restraint. Arresting the expansion of private investment at levels far too low and of too brief duration to meet the economy's minimal growth requirements was too high a price to pay for the attempt to achieve price stability, it was claimed. The charge cut the more deeply by virtue of the fact that the price stability goal had not even been achieved. Nevertheless, Board Chairman William McChesney Martin continued to reiterate the unilateral goal of price stability upon which the Board had fixed its eyes since the early 1950's when he declared in February, 1960, that ". . . the most constructive contribution monetary policy can make to the vigorous, healthy growth of the economy in the present circumstances is to maintain confidence in the value of money, and thus encourage people to save and invest. . . ." [11]

In perspective it may be hypothesized that the Board's defensiveness was an unnecessarily sensitive posture. If it slightly damaged the decade's growth achievement, the damage was largely confined to housing and fixed investment by smaller enterprise. On balance, these two factors aside, it is doubtful that monetary policy substantially affected the economy's rate of growth. If the Board failed to achieve price stability, this was primarily because of factors beyond its purview. Possibly it contributed somewhat to general economic stability by the counter-cyclical impact of its policies on residential construction, by the stabilizing effect of those policies on the economic atmosphere, and by curtailing the increase in the quantity of money during expansion.

So far as business fixed investment was concerned, the emergence of excess capacity in late 1956 was in all likelihood the major proximate factor in the cessation of the investment wave. *Given the high output capacity with which contemporary technology had endowed the typical investment dollar, the rate of increase of aggregate peacetime spending—including the investment spending itself—was insufficient to warrant a stronger, more lasting investment wave.* These relationships appear to be the real nexus of the slow growth problem during the late 1950's and early 1960's.

10. Reported in the *New York Times*, September 23, 1959.
11. *Federal Reserve Bulletin*, February, 1960, p. 132.

Fiscal Policy and Growth

Budget Policy

The Federal government complemented the tight monetary policy of the Reserve authorities with a commitment to classical public budget principles. As these principles were applied to the economy of the 1950's they meant the attempt to reduce the size of the Federal budget, keep it balanced or run a surplus to retire debt and inhibit inflation, lengthen the maturity composition of the publicly held debt, eliminate "nonessential" expenditures, improve the operating efficiency of departments, and prevent "waste."

Insofar as these objectives were related to implementing the goal of maximum employment, the implicit corollary was reliance upon the private market mechanism generally and private investment in particular. The same reliance on private investment underlay the presumed relation between the government's budget principles and the sustenance of satisfactory economic growth. Alternatively put, growth would take care of itself, provided the classical budgetary precepts were adhered to. Hence a balanced budget of falling magnitude was deemed compatible with maximum employment and growth.

This last proposition joins the issue regarding the growth role of the government's budget in the contemporary economic world. Aside from the questions of budget components and budget balance, the central question posed by contemporary economic history has been: Which policy assures economic growth, a rising or a falling (cash) budget? The hypothesis employed in the present historical review is that this question has *in fact*, though not in ideological controversy, been settled. (It was decided, in practice at least, after the publication of John Maynard Keynes' *The End of Laissez-Faire* in 1926; after the manner of the usual "American historical lag," the issue was explicitly decided in the United States with the coming of the New Deal.) It was resolved in favor of the secularly rising Federal budget. Without a large and rising budget, the actual rate of growth will in all probability fall well below the potential rate, i.e., the full employment rate. For reasons suggested at the end of the preceding section, to be elaborated in Chapter 10, private fixed investment apparently could not be relied upon to take primary responsibility for this growth objective as it did formerly. The performance of long-run private investment in the 1950's, as has been seen, was consistent with this hypothesis.

To the extent that the budgetary goals of the government in the last half of the decade were deliberately related to the maintenance of cyclical stability, major reliance was placed upon the built-in stabilizers and discretionary short-period increases in expenditures. Discretionary changes in the receipts structure were abjured. In the stabilization sphere heavy dependence was placed on monetary policy rather than fiscal policy—a traditional distinction in emphasis. It was believed the latter would help the monetary authorities prevent inflation, however, through balanced budgets or surpluses. Because the Federal government during the later 1950's was more interested in allaying the specter of severe inflation than in using public measures to stimulate growth, it followed a restrictive monetary policy and tried to follow a classical fiscal policy. Its emphasis on inflation and on monetary policy to deal with it may well have been misplaced. Besides, for the kind of inflation that actually occurred, the general quantitative monetary weapons applied were no doubt inappropriate and somewhat obsolete. More properly, the Administration should have attacked economic retardation and relied accordingly for the most part on fiscal measures, including rising, strategically placed expenditures and planned, short-period deficits to spur recoveries and a higher growth rate.

Where the classical budgetary principles impinged upon the welfare state, they were deliberately or inadvertently inimical to it. This has already been pointed out. Welfare-type expenditures of the Federal government other than social security (veterans, labor and welfare, agriculture, natural resources, commerce, and housing) were 5.3 per cent of national income in calendar 1952 and 4.3 per cent in fiscal 1960. Under the rapidly expanding Federal program of grants-in-aid to the state and local governments, the two chief components were labor and welfare, and the Federal-aid highway and airports programs. In 1954, grants for the former purpose, the chief component of which was public assistance, were almost four times as large as grants for the latter purposes. But by 1960 the highway and airports grants had become almost equal in magnitude to the labor and welfare subsidies. In absolute totals, the latter rose from $2,094 million in 1954 to $3,278 million in 1960, while highway and airport grants increased from $539 million to $3,105 million. It seems inescapable to infer that application of the budgetary precept to "restrain non-military spending" and minimize nonessentials had its major incidence in the welfare area. On the other hand, the monetary policy of raising interest rates frustrated the cost-minimizing budgetary principle, for it steadily raised budgeted interest charges until they equaled $9.3 billion in fiscal 1960, or 12 per cent of the total administrative budget. In the national product accounts, net interest paid in calendar 1960, amounting to $7.2 billion, was about 14 per cent of total Federal government purchases of goods and services.

The theoretical fiscal objectives which dominated the Federal government's declared policies during the decade may now fruitfully be compared with some relevant parts of the record. Table 5-1 shows both the administrative budget and the cash budget, together with the total and marketable debt and the average maturity of the latter, for *fiscal* years.

The Budgetary Record

The budgeted expenditures give an indication of the actual expenditure policy. The Korean War bulge is clearly seen, the total then dropping to a plateau through fiscal 1956 (ending June 30, 1956). Beginning in 1957 the goal of a reduced total budget was no longer attained. The trend was up, though mildly so, through fiscal 1959. Since the long-run purpose of the Administration, aside from its counter-cyclical policy in fiscal 1958 and 1959, was to reduce total expenditures, it must be noted that the uptrend in budgeted expenditures, due to the cold war, negated that purpose. At the same time, the Eisenhower administration did not *design* the budgets to stimulate growth; but that they had some such effect in the last years of the decade, partly because of the counter-cyclical rise in expenditures, is quite clear.

It will be observed that the growth of cash payments was greater than that for budgeted expenditures. The chief reason for the differential was the growth of transfer payments, which, like receipts into the trust fund accounts, are included in the cash budget but not in the administrative, or conventional, budget figures shown in the first two columns. The rising transfer payments represented an institutionally built-in expenditure requirement. The more rapid expansion of the cash payments series expressed a quasi-autonomous influence on the long-run budget philosophy of the government. (Objectives other than those related to budget philosophy prompted extensions of the Social Security Act in 1954, 1956, and 1958, which increased coverage, benefits, and tax receipts.) The secular rise in cash payments, which will of course be continued in the 1960's, was due to a

Table 5-1

Federal Budget Receipts, Expenditures, and Public Debt; Cash Receipts from and Payments to the Public; and Average Maturity of the Marketable Interest-bearing Public Debt; Fiscal Years 1950–60
(in billions of dollars)

Fiscal Year	Net budget receipts	Budget expenditures	Surplus or deficit (−)	Public debt, end of year	Cash receipts	Cash payments	Excess of receipts or payments (−)	Marketable debt	Average maturity Yrs.	Average maturity Mos.
1950	36.4	39.5	−3.1	257.4	40.9	43.1	−2.2	155.3	8	2
1951	47.5	44.0	3.5	255.2	53.4	45.8	7.6	137.9	6	7
1952	61.3	65.3	−4.0	259.1	68.0	68.0	0.0	140.4	5	8
1953	64.7	74.1	−9.4	266.1	71.5	76.8	−5.3	147.3	5	4
1954	64.4	67.5	−3.1	271.3	71.6	71.9	−0.2	150.4	5	6
1955	60.2	64.4	−4.2	274.4	67.8	70.5	−2.7	155.2	5	10
1956	67.9	66.2	1.6	272.8	77.1	72.6	4.5	155.0	5	4
1957	70.6	69.0	1.6	270.5	82.1	80.0	2.1	155.7	4	9
1958	68.6	71.4	−2.8	276.3	81.9	83.4	−1.5	166.7	5	3
1959	67.9	80.3	−12.4	284.7	81.7	94.8	−13.1	178.0	4	7
1960	77.8	76.5	1.2	286.3	95.1	94.3	0.8	183.8	4	4

Note.—Surpluses and deficits may not conform to differences between totals because of rounding.
SOURCE: Council of Economic Advisers.

combination of the rising transfer payments and the cold war. It may therefore be seen that the budget objective of reduced aggregate expenditures was a forlorn hope. If a rising volume of Federal expenditures contributed to economic growth, then this was the unplanned result of the record.

On the other hand, the explicit goal of balanced budgets and debt retirement was not nearly so severely trounced as the cut-the-budget goal. With the exception of fiscal 1959, Table 5-1 shows a fairly consistent record on this score for the budgeted receipts and expenditures.

The acid test is of course the cash budget. Here the record also appears rather consistent, although a somber year-by-year analysis reveals an uncomfortable number of fortuitous events. Fiscal 1954, which roughly coincides with the period of the 1953–54 recession, yielded an almost balanced cash budget. The no-change-in-receipts estimate turned out to be correct; and the drop in military expenditures coupled with the (from the standpoint of fiscal planning, fortuitous) mildness of the recession completed the achievement of approximate balance. (Note, however, that the Treasury had budgeted for a deficit of $3.1 billion.) The following year was one of both budgeted and cash deficits. The next two years—1956 and 1957—stand out as conforming to the goal of surplus with debt retirement. How did this come about? The planned rise in expenditures violated one of the Administration's budget principles; but the accurate estimate of rising receipts, because of prosperity, made it possible to fulfill another, and without any increase in tax rates. The public debt declined by about $4 billion. But this was the end of it. To the degree that the cash budget surpluses were the product of built-in features, they gave expression to the fact that *the built-in stabilizers work in two directions*. For those whose theories were opposite to the Washington administration's, the budget surpluses were considered fiscal depressants, just as the deficits in slumps were stimulants.

An important change occurring in calendar 1957 affected the trend of both the cash budget and the debt: the termination of the period of substantial surpluses in the trust fund accounts as broadening of OASI raised benefit payments to an annual rate of $7.2 billion compared with $5.5 billion in 1956. Thereafter the achievement of surpluses in the cash budget would have to be won without benefit of the former annual surpluses in the trust funds.

In both fiscal years 1958 and 1959 the balanced budget goal was forsworn. The last year of the decade witnessed a small surplus but an increase in the debt. Fiscal 1960 represented a real achievement for the fiscal philosophy of the Administration, however. Most important expenditure items were cut, including those for national security and for international affairs and finance. (The latter category had included in the previous year a nonrecurrent increase in the United States subscription to the International Monetary Fund.) Only the service charge on the debt rose, and that substantially. On the receipts side the budget was blessed with the fruits of economic expansion.

For the post-Korean period as a whole, then, the budget-balancing objective was not defeated too badly. The defeat on the debt-retirement front was more severe. The government tried to stay within the statutory debt ceiling of $275 billion and was forced to give up the ghost only under the blows of the 1957–58 recession-induced deficit, which finally brought the statutory limit up to $295 billion in the summer of 1959.

In spite of this defeat on the debt limit and the long record of defeats which had preceded it, the Kennedy administration, like the administrations of Franklin Delano Roosevelt a quarter century earlier, immediately professed its dedication to the principle of the secularly balanced budget. The economic historian is compelled to infer from the facts another "Parkinson's Law," premised on the postulate that appropriations exceed taxes: Congressional appropriations rise to burst Congressional debt ceilings.

In spite of the absolute rise in the size of the Federal debt, it should be observed that relative to GNP the portion of the debt held outside the Federal government (at the end of the fiscal year) fell from about 77 per cent in 1950 to 48 per cent in 1959. The gross debt per capita declined, in current dollars, from $1,697 to $1,607 over the same period.

A word is in order about 1959. Table 5-1 shows a huge deficit of $13.1 billion in the cash budget. This deficit was the joint outcome of the recession decrease in revenues (accounting for about 60 per cent of the deficit) and a substantial increase in expenditures (accounting for about 40 per cent). One of the more interesting aspects of the budget was the operation of the built-in tax stabilizer as it impinged upon revenues in the recession. For fiscal 1959 there was a *decrease* of almost $3 billion in corporate income tax receipts and an *increase* of $2 billion in individual income tax receipts. The former effect occurred mostly in the last half of calendar 1958 (first half of fiscal 1959); the latter effect occurred mostly in the first half of calendar 1959 (last half of fiscal 1959), as recovery from that typically mild recession raised personal incomes.

The rise in expenditures was partly recession-induced but mainly the result of planned expenditure increases all along the line: $2.3 billion more for national security; $2.1 billion for agricultural programs (the quantity of crops stored off farms under CCC loan increased by almost 150 per cent between January 1, 1958, and January 1, 1959); an additional subscription of $1.4 billion to the International Monetary Fund; and higher pay for both civilian and military personnel. Note that these increases possessed a quasi-compulsory character, since they were connected with larger commitments made independently of any concrete fiscal philosophy.

The pattern of Federal expenditures in the aggregate after Korea was generally not destabilizing in its short-run impact on the economy. The record was much better than in the period before. A computation by the Department of Commerce showed an average deviation from the trend of government purchases (all levels) of 12.0 per cent for the whole period 1948–60, but the deviation was only 1.4 per cent for the period 1955–60. Since the state and local expenditures were highly stable, the calculation for the total of all levels reflects the Federal influence overwhelmingly.

Debt and Tax Structure

It was pointed out above that the government was committed to lengthening the maturity of the public debt. The object of this policy was essentially anti-inflationary. The orthodox theory of debt management requires the flotation of long-term bonds when economic activity is high in order to compete with funds from the burgeoning capital markets. Hence the presumption that the normal state of the economy would be one of inflationary pressures led to the corollary plan of lengthening maturities. Furthermore, short-term securities are near-money and as such make for excessive liquidity, which is conducive to inflation. Finally, the frequent refunding required when the public debt is overwhelmingly short-term restricts the freedom of the monetary authorities to pursue appropriate open-market operations.

A glance at Table 5-1 shows the failure of the projected lengthening of the maturity structure of the marketable debt (gross debt minus Reserve System holdings minus government agency and trust-fund holdings); and the average maturity fell from 8 years 2 months in 1950 to 4 years 4 months in 1960. Hence the trend in maturity structure was inimical to the generally anti-inflationary objectives of the Federal Reserve and the Treasury. Perhaps the chief reason for this paradoxical outcome was the fact that the Treasury had to function within the limits set by law in 1918, that no more than 4½ per cent interest could be offered by the government on bonds having a maturity in excess of five years (because they would compete with funds sought by private corporations). Consequently, under the impact of the high interest policies of the Federal Reserve, particularly after the Korean War, together with increasing confidence in private long-term loans, the Treasury's 4¼ per cent long-term loans were unattractive to the market. The commercial banks also reduced their holdings of bonds in order to structure their portfolios more appropriately for the operations of such banks. Since there was no ceiling on the rates for Treasury notes, certificates, or bills, these were necessarily the chief types of government paper issued. In fact the Treasury more often than not had to sell bonds in recession and short-term paper during periods of high-level economic activity—just the reverse of the orthodox dictates. No bonds were issued by the Treasury during the period of high-level activity between mid-1955 and the fall of 1957. This result was, however, precisely that favored by the Joint Economic Committee of the Congress, since, as the Committee pointed out, borrowing through bond issues in times of high interest rates burdens the Treasury with high service charges for protracted periods. But from the standpoint of the Federal Reserve and the Treasury, the shortened maturity structure added to the inflationary potential of fiscal policy.

The Federal tax structure in the 1950's exhibited a remarkable degree of stability. It is doubtful that the slight changes which did occur during the decade had much effect on the distribution of the Federal tax burden by income level or on the distribution of spending streams or between consumption and investment.[12] After the Korean War there was evidence of some tendency for corporate tax accruals to decline as proportion of total Federal cash receipts and for receipts from the individual income tax to rise proportionately.[13] In particular, the provision for accelerated depreciation in the 1954 Revenue Act no doubt contributed to the dwindling significance of the corporate net income tax as compared with the personal income tax (and helped encourage the capacity expansion of 1955 and 1956). The evidence on this score shows at the very least that the Federal tax structure relaxed

12. *Eckstein Report*, pp. 260–61.
13. Committee for Economic Development, *Growth and Taxes*, Statement on National Policy, February, 1961, p. 5.

somewhat in its incidence on corporate profitability. Excises remained practically constant as a percentage of total cash receipts of the Federal government after Korea. The same may be said for estate and gift taxes.

The Last Recovery

It will be recalled that the trough of the 1957–58 recession was the second quarter of 1958. The recovery quarter, 1958 III, was not sparked by positive net inventory investment, but by the more usual sharp decrease in the rate of disinvestment. Moreover, the whole recovery movement had to function within the adverse impact of the sharp decline in net exports of goods and services.

The important leaders in the recovery were consumption, especially nondurables and services, the last-named having simply continued to rise throughout the recession; the intrepid state and local government purchases; expenditures for residential construction, which had already turned up in the third quarter of 1957; new orders for machinery and then for durable goods, as usual; and Federal government expenditures. Federal purchases for non-defense purposes rose at an annual rate of $3 billion between 1958 I and 1958 IV, primarily because of payments for agricultural price supports and higher government pay scales. New orders for defense goods, which in the latter half of 1957 were running at an annual rate of $12 billion, rose to an annual rate of $22 billion during the first half of 1958. These increased outlays slowed and finally stopped the liquidation of inventories by defense contractors.[14] Federal cash payments to the public rose $2 billion in the recovery quarter as compared with the trough quarter of 1958. Cash receipts from the public between the same two quarters were constant on a seasonally adjusted basis, but they fell $5 billion on an unadjusted basis (a typical seasonal factor).

Inventory investment performed its customary stimulative role in the recovery, not at the turning point but soon thereafter. The increase in this type of investment reached a dramatic $7.1 billion at seasonally adjusted annual rates in the first quarter of 1959 and an almost fabulous rate of $11.7 billion in the second quarter. An extremely significant factor underlying this inventory explosion was a wave of steel- and steel-products-buying in anticipation of an impending steel strike. The strike began on July 15 and lasted 116 days. The recovery movement was no doubt much

14. *Economic Report of the President*, January, 1959, p. 22.

accelerated by this event; but the price was paid in the third quarter. However, all three of the following quarters (1959 IV through 1960 II) enjoyed vigorous net investment in business inventories.

After contributing to the recovery so substantially, as can be seen on an annual basis in the series showing cash payments for fiscal 1959 in Table 5-1, Federal cash payments to the public leveled off. The defense category reached a plateau in the national product accounts after the last quarter of fiscal 1959, and this important spending stream no longer exerted an expansionary effect on the economy. Increases in interest and transfer payments offset the decline in purchases during fiscal 1960 to maintain the cash payments total.

Chart V shows that after spurring on the recovery, residential construction soon lost its potential efficacy as an expansion propellant, following the familiar counter-cyclical configuration. The reason, aside from minor real factors, was equally familiar: "exerting a dampening effect on demand for new residential construction was the condition of tight credit that prevailed in the latter part of 1959 and through most of 1960." [15]

Plant and Equipment Investment

Since business plant and equipment investment, in the absence of either expanding government balanced-budget outlays or government net-income-generating expenditures, has historically been so critical in the growth process, its performance at the decade's end is worthy of examination.

The fixed investment wave of 1958–60 was a weak recovery phenomenon that contained nothing of the virility required to spark a sustained expansion in the economy. In its annual review of economic activity for 1960 the *Federal Reserve Bulletin* surveyed the fixed investment patterns as follows:

At their high in the second quarter of 1960, business outlays for new plant and equipment were about one-fourth larger than they were at their low in the summer of 1958. This was a much smaller advance than in either of the two preceding periods of cyclical expansion. Furthermore, the high in 1960 did not attain the peak reached in the 1955–57 investment boom.

Manufacturers' outlays for fixed capital in the second quarter of 1960 were 10 per cent below their 1957 peak in current dollar terms. In real terms the decline was larger. Pressures on industrial capacity were generally less in the recent expansion than in earlier comparable

15. *Survey of Current Business,* February, 1961, p. 8.

periods. Estimates indicate that the average rate of capacity utilization for manufacturing industries as a whole was about 85 per cent at the peak of the 1958–60 expansion as compared with about 92 per cent in the preceding cyclical expansion. With unused capacity available and with strong incentives for more efficient operations, manufacturers devoted an increased proportion of their expenditures for fixed capital in 1958–60 to modernization and improvement of existing plant.[16]

Chart IX, from the same source, shows that non-manufacturing fixed investment, on the other hand, did reach the height attained in 1955–57. In fact, if fixed investment in mining, transportation, and public utilities were removed from the non-manufacturing curve in the chart, leaving chiefly the consumption-geared com-

Chart IX. Plant and Equipment Outlays

BILLIONS OF DOLLARS (annual rates)

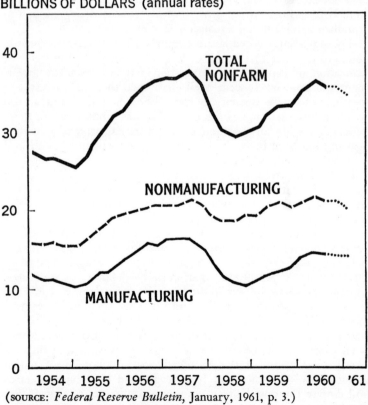

(SOURCE: *Federal Reserve Bulletin,* January, 1961, p. 3.)

16. *Federal Reserve Bulletin,* January, 1961, p. 3.

mercial investment, the line would rise above the height reached by the earlier wave. This can be inferred from the index of commercial equipment output shown in Table 4-3, wherein the output index for 1960 is 118.0, considerably above the previous peak of 104.5 in the first quarter of 1957. The record may be usefully compared with the index of 102 in 1960 for the crucial industrial equipment series. The outlays for commercial plant and equipment rose in part because "demand for shopping-center facilities reflected the continued shift of population to the new suburbs. . . ." [17]

Real gross investment in producers' durable equipment of all types was 5.4 per cent of real GNP in cyclical peak 1960, which compared unfavorably with the historically mediocre 6.2 per cent in cyclical peak 1956. There seems no question that capacity was still excessive relative to the slow rate of growth of consumption. Nor was the rate of growth of investment strong enough to stimulate a reinforcing expansion in consumption.

The statement quoted above from the *Federal Reserve Bulletin* refers to the fact that in the context of moderately low rates of utilization of capacity, modernization and improvement investment still proceed. It seems well established that such investment continues to raise capacity output although it does not absorb much, if any, net savings. Much of this was pointed out in theoretical discussions of economic growth over a quarter of a century ago and has been brought again to the forefront in a number of contemporary growth models.

Excess capacity, though it may permit continued cost-reducing investment that is at the same time capacity-increasing, does not breed capacity extensions as the primary object of investment. The sideshow is operating in the form of modernization and improvement; but the main event is bogged down. A good deal of whatever encouragement was given during the decade to the deliberate and extensive expansion of capacity may be traced to government expenditures, particularly defense expenditures. When these slowed down in the last half of the decade, so did the incentive to expand capacity. And no other spending stream of comparable magnitude appeared to fill the gap.

It does not seem that unsatisfactory rates of profit could have been a factor in the retardation of long-run investment during the post-Korean phase of the decade. Despite mountains of words about the adverse effect of high wages and high business taxes and despite the post-Korean corporate profits tax rate of 52 per

17. *Survey of Current Business*, February, 1961, p. 71.

cent as compared with 38 per cent previously, a striking fact remained: *the ex post rate of return after taxes on invested capital was as high in the 1950's as it was in the 1920's* [18]—and the 1920's was a decade of moderately high profits.

It has already been pointed out that a shortage of capital funds was probably not a barrier to the expansion of long-term investment, at least for the important group of large corporations. If fixed investment is mainly a function of (1) modernization to reduce costs and (2) the rate of increase of total income, then the growth rate of the latter becomes strategic for determination of the long-run performance of private investment.

Along with the failure of long-term private investment to top its previous peak went the failure of unemployment to decline to earlier minima. This has already been referred to and can be discerned from the curve of the unemployment rate in the three periods of relatively high level economic activity shown in Chart IV. Because of the human aspect, this matter is perhaps the most serious element in the legacy of retarded growth handed to the 1960's by the 1950's. As already noted, the problem is the more serious because of the large increases that are expected to occur in the annual additions to the labor force. The most important problem willed to the 1960's was how to overcome structural unemployment by achieving a full employment rate of growth.

18. Chase Manhattan Bank, *Business in Brief*, November–December, 1959.

6 | Developments in the Business Sector: Important Industries

The Business Population

The nonfarm business population failed to keep pace with the growth in real gross private product during the 1950's. This is another way of saying that production per firm rose, thus continuing an historical trend. However, the decennial rate of increase rose in the 1950's: dividing real gross private product (1954 prices) by the number of firms in operation (agriculture and the professional services excluded) yields a production per firm of $56,600 for 1929. The corresponding total for 1950 was about $72,200, and in 1960 it had risen to $87,000. Consequently, the absolute increase in output of $14,800 per firm during the 1950's was not too far short of the increase of $15,600 that it had taken two decades to achieve previously. The average firm was getting larger at an increasing rate. The affluence of the 1950's clearly found its expression in the business community.

Not only affluence, but a heightened degree of security also seems to have permeated the business sector taken as a whole. A fundamental security factor was implicit in the containment of cyclical instability. A notable further indication may be observed in the business failure rate. In the 1920's, which is often termed the heyday of prosperity, there were on the average about 100 industrial and commercial failures per 10,000 firms per month among the concerns listed in the Dun and Bradstreet Reference Book. In the 1950's, by way of contrast, the failure rate varied between about 40 and 65 per 10,000. During the first half of the decade the rate drifted upward, then leveled off to fluctuate between 50 and 60 from mid-1956 until the recession of 1960–61.

The number of nonfarm, nonprofessional firms in operation rose from 4,050,700 in 1950 to 4,658,700 in 1960, a moderate gain of 15 per cent. As might be expected, the largest gains were in the small-business industries, i.e., in order of growth rate: contract construction; finance, insurance, and real estate; service lines; and wholesale trade. It will be observed that these are all tertiary activities except contract construction. The high growth rate for the latter may be attributed chiefly to government (especially state and local), private institutional construction activity, and metropolitanization. The rate of increase in the number of such firms slowed after 1957.

Retailing was conspicuously absent from the high performers in terms of growth in numbers. With an increase of only 10 per cent in total firms over the decade, it lagged considerably behind the general average increase. The new entry rate in retailing was low, and after 1956 there was a steady absolute fall in the number of new retail businesses. High mortality in the important single-unit food stores group in particular dragged down the rate of increase of retail firms.

Manufacturing firms grew in number from 321,000 in 1950 to about 325,000 in 1960. The business population in this slowly growing sector remained virtually unchanged during the later years of the decade. Apparently manufacturing was almost as easy to enter, on a small scale at any rate, as many other activities; for the entry rate (ratio of new businesses to total in operation) was .087 in 1959—almost as high as the average for the economy. The entry rate was of course highest for the small concerns, decreasing as the size of firm increased. However, the turnover rate was also high in manufacturing. With 25,600 discontinuances and 28,200 new firms in 1959, the ratio of exits to entrants stood at 91 per cent. This was substantially higher than the 82 per cent for all business.

One of the more striking changes in the business population during the 1950's was the rapid gain in corporations as compared with other forms of business organization. Moreover the increase in number of corporations, stimulated by tax laws partial to the corporate form of business, accelerated during the latter half of the period, whereas the growth of numbers decelerated in the case of proprietorships and partnerships (agriculture included). The upward trend, which raised the number of active corporations from 552,000 in 1948 to rather over one million by the decade's end, affected even agriculture, forestry, and fisheries, wherein the number of corporations increased some 50 per cent despite the decrease in number of commercial farms.

A study of the size of business firms made by the Department of Commerce for 1956 and published in 1959, using number of employees as criterion, showed that the one per cent of all firms with 100 or more employees accounted for 50 per cent of all employment. Only one firm in 20 had in excess of 20 employees. Firms with fewer than 4 employees made up 75 per cent of all operating concerns but hired only 6 per cent of all employees. About 40 per cent of all firms had no employees at all. Manufacturing accounted for more than one half of all firms with 100 or more employees. *Fortune*'s list of the 500 largest industrial corporations in terms of sales contained the introductory statement that the group accounted for over half the sales of all United States manufacturing and mining companies *and over 70 per cent of the profits*.[1]

A list of the 300 largest manufacturing corporations (by size of assets in 1958) was published by *Business Record* in its February, 1960, issue. Among the industries represented in the list, the food, beverages, and tobacco category had the largest single number, with 41 firms, although the group accounted for but 8.0 per cent of all assets of the 300. The chemicals and allied equipment industry ranked second, with 37 concerns and 9.8 per cent of the total assets of the 300. The steel and petroleum groups ranked third and fourth in number of firms, with 12.1 and 26.7 per cent respectively of all assets.[2]

Size of Major Commodity-Producing Industries

It will be recalled that the five leading manufacturing industries toward the decade's end were chemicals (848,000 employees in 1959), aircraft (735,000 employees), motor vehicles (732,000 employees), steel (522,000 employees), and electronics ($11 billion of sales in 1960). It is at once apparent that the classification "leading" industry cuts across "rapidly growing" industry; for electronics, aircraft, and chemicals were included in both categories. However, there were some commodity-producing growth industries that fell outside manufacturing, notably certain public

1. *Fortune*, July, 1960, pp. 131 ff.
2. *Business Record*, February, 1960, cited in *Illinois Business Review*, March, 1960, p. 9.

utilities. It should also be noted that if assets or sales rather than number of employees were the criterion used for selection of leading industries, some substitution might be required. For example, the petroleum and coal products industry would be a likely candidate in terms of total assets, even though it had only 181,000 employees in 1958. This is understandable when it is seen that assets per employee among petroleum refining companies in *Fortune*'s 500 largest industrials in 1959 amounted to $63,838, whereas the figure for autos, aircraft, and shipbuilding was only $10,783.

Classification of industries is at best a risky venture. For some purposes the Census nomenclature in the case of manufacturing is satisfactory, for other purposes not. The Census' so-called 1-digit "chemicals and allied products" grouping is, for example, a much more heterogeneous collection than is desirable for present purposes. Furthermore, it is unfair in a strict sense to compare it in size with a Census subgroup such as the significant "mechanical measuring instruments" industry. It is not appropriate for the task at hand to adhere strictly to Census nomenclature, and the lines will be crossed wherever necessary to examine the inner workings of economic evolution in the 1950's.

The Slow Growers

Steel

At one time the oligopolistically structured steel industry was a growth industry; i.e., its growth rate was greater than the rate of growth of real GNP. It ceased to be such long before the 1950's. In that decade steel's growth rate lagged behind the rate of increase of GNP, and its own performance depended on the latter. Hence, the behavior of the steel industry may reveal the characteristics of a mature oligopoly.

In the discussion of inflation it was pointed out that the steel industry, whatever may be said about recession price-shading, etc., contributed to the price rise in the 1950's and did so to a considerable extent through the exercise of market power. The major steel buyers, despite much talk of substitute products, revealed that their "demand" schedules were relatively price-inelastic. This fact, in combination with rising incomes during the 1950's, made it possible for the industry to improve its profit position (in terms of rate of return on equity) relative to other manufacturing while at the same time absorbing greater than average wage rate increases; larger than average increases in employment costs per unit of output; very substantial increases in taxes and interest costs; and enormous increases in depreciation, depletion, and amortization.

The industry was able to approach the average rate of return on equity for all manufacturing despite a distinct late-decade trend toward lower rates of capacity utilization. Profitability had in general been positively associated with rates of capacity utilization in the past, a fact which made the maintenance of profitability in the face of falling operating rates all the more indicative of the possible exercise of market power. This may have been one factor in the decision of the industry in 1960 to cease publication of capacity and utilization rate figures.

One of the more remarkable features of the industry's performance, perhaps in small part under the lash of President Truman's criticism that it was laggard in building capacity, was the steady capacity expansion from about 100 million short tons in 1950 to nearly 150 million in 1960. Although the peak output of the decade was 117 million tons in 1955 (93 per cent of capacity), the industry's capacity continued to expand another 24 million tons by 1960. Some of the disparity between capacity and output can be attributed to fairly good production years in 1956 and 1957 and to the lag due to the long construction period for new facilities, but much of it was no doubt the result of modernization investment. Such investment was designed to overcome seriously obsolete fixed plant and equipment by replacing it with facilities that had greater output capacity because of their modernity. Such cost-reducing, inadvertently capacity-raising, or "modernization" investment was becoming increasingly characteristic of investment generally throughout the economy.

The industry evinced a strong partiality, like business in general, for internal financing of its investment programs. Such a program placed heavy emphasis on depreciation policy and substantial retained profits. Asked the American Iron and Steel Institute's *Steelways:*

What of the sources of funds for property, plant and equipment expenditures? With the first source, depreciation tax allowances, insufficient and the second source, profits, drained to meet that insufficiency, companies have been forced into the money markets. Evidence of this is ready to hand: the steel industry's long term debt from 1946 through 1959 increased 323 per cent.

It is a deceiving solution. In the long run it is no solution at all. For the interest and service payments on this extended debt could further compromise the future profit potential of American industries.[3]

Aside from the omission of any explicit reference to external equity financing in this statement, there are two references that call for comment: the first, to "depreciation tax allowances"; the second, to the diversion of profits to compensate for allegedly insufficient depreciation charges.

The inflation of capital goods prices, to which the steel industry contributed so liberally, exerted an upward pressure on new investment costs for all industry during the 1950's. One result, not applicable under a regime of constant prices, was that replacement investment was not fully offset by depreciation allowances, although the extent of the discrepancy was doubtless exaggerated. Traditional accounting theory typically endowed depreciation with the role of recording the economic wasting of a durable asset, not financing the replacement of that asset. With constant prices the distinction was of course not a substantive one, but with rising prices, with the contemporary stress on the desirability of internal financing of modernization investment, and with management's urge to maximize gross retained corporate income, the notion of financing replacement investment out of depreciation allowances was brought to the forefront. The notion was translated into a powerful and persistent demand that the Internal Revenue Code be revised to permit depreciation on a replacement cost basis. (There was no accompanying demand that the revaluation be treated as either income or capital gain and taxed as such; for such action, however correct, would of course offset the reduction in taxable income resulting from the inflated depreciation allowance.) By the decade's end the educated public was probably convinced, however incorrectly, that the purpose of a depreciation allowance was to finance replacement investment at current (though not yet expected future) prices.

A related piece of depreciation strategy was the companion demand for faster write-offs—accelerated depreciation. As mentioned earlier, a concession was made to this demand in the Internal Revenue Code amendment in 1954. The lay judgment was that with accelerated depreciation, total taxes would be the same over time by virtue of the presumption that the tax take with respect to any asset would merely be shifted from one period to another. However, in fact the government no doubt lost substantial sums

3. American Iron and Steel Institute, *Steelways*, May, 1961.

under the fast write-off rules, because for growing enterprises the tax reductions build up faster and stay permanently higher than would be the case under straight-line depreciation.[4]

The discussion of both methods of increasing depreciation allowances was notable for the failure to recognize that the investment decision to make a replacement is essentially the same as the decision to expand investment. That is to say, any investment decision is made in the context of expected future prices, costs, sales, etc.; *it stands or falls as a judicious decision in that context and no other*.

The most adequate interpretation of the steel industry's market strategy in the 1950's seems to involve a combination of price with investment policy. In the price area the industry followed what seemed to be the most commonly practiced policy among large corporations in oligopolistic markets: the so-called "target-return pricing," according to which the price leader in the industry attempts to administer a price that will yield a specified rate of profit on investment in the long run at some assumed rate of capacity utilization known as the standard volume. The demand schedule is implicitly viewed as what Joan Robinson has called a "smudge" surrounding the target price, allowing moderate upward or downward adjustments in price at given volume or moderate adjustments in volume at the target price, for any income level.

It can be inferred that under the conditions of rising capital and other costs, expectations of continuing cost increases, a desire to finance new investment internally, and the correct assumption of a price-inelastic "demand" schedule, the target-return price might well be raised from time to time. The pricing behavior and investment financing philosophy of United States Steel in the later 1950's was consistent with the notion of administered target-return price raising. Through such policy steel consumers rather than investors were induced to provide some of the "internal" funds to finance capital formation.[5] Professor John T. Dunlop has elaborated these propositions to hypothesize further that not only was the need to meet rising capacity costs the chief explanation of the inflation in steel prices, but also that the raising of target prices to yield greater returns stimulated extraordinary wage demands, the successful negotiation of which partially frustrated

4. *Illinois Business Review*, April, 1961, p. 2.
5. See the discussion by John M. Blair, "Administered Prices: A Phenomenon in Search of a Theory," *American Economic Review*, Papers and Proceedings, Vol. XLIX, No. 2 (May, 1959), pp. 441–444.

the attempts to raise returns.[6] It might be added that the slow growth in productivity in the industry rendered more difficult both the industry's adjustment to wage increases and its task of meeting the profit targets. (The productivity lag could have been aggravated by a low-level R & D effort.) Nevertheless each time wages were raised, the industry succeeded in raising prices more than per unit wage costs.

The central problem afflicting the industry was the slowed rate of growth in the economy after mid-decade. For a mature industry like steel, where product demand is linked so closely with capital goods and consumer durables, this consideration was overriding. Although demand was sufficiently strong and inelastic to accommodate the industry's administered price policy without too great a loss to substitutes (aluminum ingot prices rose substantially), it was not strong enough to overcome the increasing disparity between full capacity and actual output between 1955 and 1960.

Adverse developments, mostly in the form of slowed expansion, occurred during the latter half of the decade in the major markets for steel: auto, certain nonelectrical machinery lines, private construction, railroads, petroleum, wholesalers, and exports-imports. These adverse changes were accentuated somewhat by greater competition from aluminum, prestressed concrete, and plastics. On the other hand, the markets for light and stainless steels rose. Public construction was also a sustaining force. In the machinery lines, rising demand was recorded in radio, communication, and electronic equipment; office and store machinery; and electrical machinery. But these buoyant sources of demand could not compensate for the slowdown in orders for military hardware; business construction; producers' durable equipment (Table 4-3); automobiles (compact and otherwise); certain other consumer durables; and, after 1957, exports. The decade's terminal years also witnessed a nonrecurrent drop in the size of inventories of finished steel carried by middlemen who recognized that in the absence of impending strikes they could easily get steel from an industry so overloaded with excess capacity.[7] This was a dramatic case of smaller enterprise reducing its capacity (inventories) and

6. Cited in Otto Eckstein and Gary Fromm, "Steel and the Postwar Inflation," Study Paper No. 2, Materials Prepared in Connection with the Study of Employment, Growth and Price Levels, Joint Economic Committee, U.S. Congress, 86th Cong., 1st sess., November 6, 1959, p. 33.

7. Herman Roseman, "The State of Steel," *Challenge*, Institute of Economic Affairs, New York University, March, 1961, p. 17.

transferring the excess to the oligopolistic leviathan.

The steel industry in the late 1950's may serve as a possible dynamic model of a species of mature oligopoly in the context of slow general economic growth. Some of the components of such a model, as suggested by the steel case, would be continued modernization investment, low R & D outlays, growing output capacity, declining employment, slowly rising or declining production, formula or administered costing and pricing, rising costs and prices, and a strong preference for the internal financing of investment outlays.

Motor Vehicles

This industry was also mature long before World War II. The automobile market had become essentially a replacement market by the late 1920's, on the assumption of given income and population. After World War II there was a temporary period of rebuilding to the replacement market condition again (the period which permitted Kaiser-Frazer to be the first significant new entrant since Chrysler in the late 1920's); and this was probably accomplished by the year of peak sales for the decade, 1955. (Not only were the eight million passenger cars in that year a decade maximum, but so also were the million and a quarter trucks and buses.) Suburbanization gave a nonrecurrent boost to sales during the 1950's in the form of private vehicle commuting and two-car families. Rising disposable income and population, of course, would extend the number of new, first-car owners; and there will always be some of this. For example, at the end of the decade almost one half of the families with annual incomes under $5,000 did not own any car, new or used.[8] Since rapidly rising incomes are the most important single determinant, at given prices, of the growth of automobile demand, it can readily be inferred that the increase of excess capacity in this nongrowth industry toward the end of the 1950's was directly and chiefly attributable to the slowdown in general economic growth after mid-decade. During the years 1954–60 consumers adhered rather tenaciously to a pattern of spending about 4.7 per cent of their disposable income on automobiles.

Factory sales of trucks from United States plants to the domestic market showed a distinct downtrend from 1950 onwards. Export sales of trucks, on the other hand, exhibited a constant trend, averaging around 200,000 units.

After the advent of the small car in mid-decade, new registra-

8. *Ibid.,* p. 16.

tions of regular-sized passenger cars began a distinct downward movement, reaching about a 70 per cent position in total new car registrations at the end of 1960. The small-sized cars, led at first by imports, jumped dramatically to fill the gap. Factory sales of passenger cars in 1960 were 6,675,000, but the drop in unit prices due to compacts held total consumer expenditures down to the amount spent in 1959 for 5,591,000 units.

Foreign car sales, which during the 1950's for the first time in American automobile history seriously cut into the home market, zoomed after 1955 to a monthly peak of 57,211 units in June, 1959; and in September of that year foreign car sales in units approached the decade peak—12 per cent of total unit sales in the United States market. In 1960 foreign car sales of all major brands —including the English Ford, General Motors' Opel and Vauxhall, and Chrysler's Simca, but excepting the Volkswagen—fell off sharply. Meanwhile the export of United States passenger cars declined from 1955 to 1959 and turned up slightly in 1960. The excess of imports over exports, which had emerged during 1957, peaked in 1959. Imports (new foreign car registrations) totaled 499,000 units and exports 145,000 units in 1960.[9]

As the decade ended it was widely speculated that the new domestically produced compacts would cut deeply into the competition from imports, almost all of which were small cars. Over two thirds of all small cars sold during early 1960 were domestically produced.[10] But there was less speculation in the judgment that compacts and small cars had cut into the sales of regular-sized cars. Sales data in units had become less significant, while total expenditures on new and used cars had become more so, in tracing the career of the market. The rise of domestic compacts and foreign small cars also suggested that a growing portion of the market was more interested in price and operating expense than in the car as a prestige symbol. In fact, the 1950's brought about the subjugation of the automobile for most people to the rather pedestrian function of mere transportation.

The compact car was a product innovation of the 1950's for which foreign producers could take credit. American producers made compacts as a competitive retaliation move against the Volkswagen. The domestic industry could claim numerous product innovations as its own, however. Some of the more prominent among these were more powerful and faster engines, power

9. Estimated by Ford Motor Company, Marketing Research Office.

10. Robert M. Biggs, "The 1960 Automobile Market," *Illinois Business Review*, July, 1960, p. 9.

steering, power braking, jet-powered body design, longer and lower bodies, automatic transmission, and generally smoother performance. The great horsepower race was begun by General Motors' Chevrolet in 1956. (The petroleum industry was induced to develop more high powered—high octane—gasoline to accommodate the newer automobile engines.) Another product innovation, one of questionable merit from the standpoint of the industry's long-run advantage, was to make cars in all price ranges and from all producers very similar in appearance.

In the effort to boost sales, so it was alleged by many, the automobile industry also developed a type of product innovation which came to be termed "dynamic obsolescence," or "planned obsolescence." [11] The industry had long followed the apparel trade's established practice of designing new models to induce buyers to purchase more frequently than physical wear and tear would require. In the case of a consumer durable good, annual style changes seemed to many less justified than in the case of ladies' ready-to-wear. The auto industry seemed to make almost a fetish of this in the 1950's, contributing mightily to, and also reflecting, the fetish of a whole culture for "the new." In the production race with the Soviet behemoth many thought it somehow wasteful to undertake costly annual retooling and to add long, tapering, flamboyant "fins" onto the rear fenders.

More serious was the accusation that auto and auto accessory designers planned built-in engineering obsolescence that would bring on faster wearing out and quick repeat sales. (Household-appliance producers were similarly accused.) One result of this styling and engineering obsolescence was a boomerang effect. American Motors was proudly and pointedly advertising in the early 1960's that it changed models infrequently.

Nevertheless, the experience of the 1950's did not seem to lead the industry to the conclusion that simple, infrequent, limited-range styling was more acceptable to consumers than its emphasis on "product innovation." In 1961 the industry presented the market with 352 different models—more than ever before. No firm could afford to forego elaborate product differentiation.

The public interest in the product differentiation and innovation policy of America's most talked-of industry heightened the controversy which had emerged over the meaning and efficacy of consumer sovereignty. The need to look into the origins of consumer preference schedules became more and more insistent. Economists had traditionally taken the behaviorist approach

11. "Detroit's Next Decade," *Fortune*, October, 1959, pp. 114, 245.

that dollar votes in the market place were given data whose sources were of no concern to the economic scientist. However, the theory of monopolistic competition and Schumpeter's theory of innovation, with their recognition that sellers shape buyers' preferences, had since the 1930's begun to undermine this ostrich-like disclaimer. The undermining process was of course inhibited by a narrow view of the discipline of economics that assigned to psychology, philosophy, and sociology the unwanted task of probing into the sources of buyers' preferences. All these doctrinal limitations began to be passed over in the 1950's, however, as welfare propositions relating to the wastage associated with much product differentiation and pseudo-innovation came under scrutiny. Free choice was thus put under the microscope.

The rapid expansion of the West European economy in the 1950's stimulated a coordinate expansion in the auto industry there. Penetration of the United States market by Volkswagen and other foreign makes was a part of that expansion. The response to these developments by United States assemblers, a response including capital outflows which were a part of the vast volume of private capital export in the 1950's, created a "wheels within wheels" complex of competitive crosscurrents. American producers entered the European market in a big way, not to mention other areas from Australia to South America. Consequently, United States car-producers found themselves competing not only with foreign producers in foreign markets, but also with foreign producers in the United States market. This latter struggle for market shares was waged by United States auto-assemblers with their foreign-produced *and* with their domestically produced cars, particularly their compacts. At the same time, both their foreign-produced small cars and their domestically produced compacts competed with home-produced conventional sizes. It has been pointed out that this contributed to an absolute drop in the number of regular-sized cars sold after 1957, a monopolistic phenomenon aptly described by *Fortune* as "the cannibalization of the standard-sized car by its compact sibling." [12] However, the development of owned substitutes by diversified corporations has long been established practice: the cigarette industry is a prominent illustration.

The creation of an American-owned automobile industry abroad was a major development of the 1950's. General Motors and Ford alone owned or controlled facilities that produced ap-

12. "Detroit Is Flying by the Seat of Its Pants," *Fortune*, January, 1961, p. 84.

proximately one fourth of the vehicles sold outside the United States in 1960.[13] It was expected by many in the industry that the overseas market would overtake the United States market sometime in the 1960's, the European segment being of course the major one. This gave the auto industry an enormous stake in the movement for a unified free trading area such as the Common Market and the integration of it with some or all of the so-called Outer Seven countries under British leadership.

Concentration in the passenger car industry, reckoned in terms of numbers of firms, continued its rising long-term trend during the 1950's even as geographical decentralization proceeded apace. The decade began with nine firms producing cars: General Motors, Ford, Chrysler, Nash-Kelvinator, Hudson, Studebaker, Packard, Kaiser, and Willys-Overland. The remaining handful of "independents" was the end product of a long history of industry exits in a market where effective entry had been closed for many years. By 1953 the postwar Kaiser car was unable to compete in the automobile market, and the Kaiser-Frazer Corporation acquired the Willys car in a last-ditch effort to stay in the industry. The resultant Kaiser Motors Corporation exited as an effective competitor in 1955. Meanwhile in 1954 Nash-Kelvinator merged with the Hudson Motor Car Company to form American Motors, and Studebaker merged with Packard. From mid-decade there were therefore the Big Three and two "independents." The competitive connotations historically associated with the latter term had lost most of their substance, however, since there were more leading firms than there were independents for the first time in the industry's development. The little two began to experience a series of deficits running for several years after the mergers. *Fortune* headlined its discussion of their prospects in its December, 1954, issue, "Last Stand of the Auto Independents?" Prophetically perhaps, the Hudson and Packard cars were no longer in production in the late 1950's. Studebaker-Packard had only a 2.2 per cent position in the market in 1959. On the other hand, the compact Nash Rambler boosted its sales from 100,000 in 1956 to 500,000 in 1958 and 1959, a truly dramatic bit of market penetration.

The rise of the Rambler, however unusual and possibly transitory a phenomenon, was only one example of shifting market shares in the passenger car market. Even the General Motors share could shift noticeably, as evidenced by its drop from a 51 per cent position in 1955 to a 42 per cent position in 1959. It is

13. *Ibid.*, p. 196.

difficult to believe that this was a planned sideshow to counteract public criticism of possible auto monopoly, extortionate installment financing, the perennial exploitative policies toward dealers, corporate ties with du Pont, or conspiracy to monopolize the manufacture and sale of buses. On grounds of brute performance the shifting market positions among the Big Three testify to the existence of an important degree of non-price competition. Similar testimony is found in the fact that the independents were allowed to continue to exit, even though they probably represented only a moderate competitive threat, rather than be quietly supported by the leaders in order to retain a semblance of structural atomism in the industry. In other significant regards, however, the performance was no more in accord with competitive standards during the 1950's than it had been previously. Entry was closed; General Motors profits were far above the prevailing rate for manufacturing, as they had historically been; and prices were administered to rise, as in steel, in the face of growing excess capacity and falling sales after mid-decade. In a world of negotiated instead of secret-bid defense contracts, the industry, and General Motors in particular, fared noncompetitively well. For example, in perpetrating one of the most incredible statistical quips of all time, General Motors President Harlow Curtice declared before the Senate Committee on Banking and Currency, "During 1954 General Motors defense production totaled one billion, 233 million dollars, which was less than 7 per cent of the Defense Department's expenditures for the same period."

As the decade ended it was clear that the public attitude toward the industry, as focused on General Motors, was critical but permissive. Though the industry was "affected with a public interest" by virtue of large employment and provision of an increasingly essential commodity, and priced for a "fair return on a fair valuation" of its properties, there was no question of considering it for even public utility status. Nonetheless, its behavior was continually a matter for public concern. It was one of the pattern-setters in wage bargaining; and its wage and price policies, plant location decisions, investment program, and level of employment were of deep import to all persons and all levels of government.

The Growth Industries

The leading growth industries on the basis of the Federal Reserve Board's revised industrial production index, using 1947–49 as 100, together with their 1959 employment totals, are shown in Table 6–1. The criterion for inclusion in the table was that the index for the annual average production should equal at least 200 in 1960, thus exhibiting a doubling or better by 1960 of the industry's output rate on the threshold of the decade. The total

TABLE 6-1

Leading Growth Industries of the 1950's as Indicated by the Federal Reserve Board Industry Groupings Production Index (1947–49 = 100)

Industry grouping	Annual average of index for 1960	Employment 1959 (thousands)
Total index	164	—
Utilities	287	577
Electric	289	—
Gas	285	—
Electrical machinery	222	1,242
Aircraft and other equipment	368	735
Instruments and related products	221	339
Chemicals and products	255	848
Industrial chemicals	320	611
Rubber and plastics products *	200	93
Natural gas and gas liquids **	228	32
Item		
Stone and earth minerals (nonmetal)	194	
Equipment, including defense	195	

* Employment total is for fabricated plastics products only.
** Employment total is for 1958.

industrial production index is included for comparison. The five leading manufacturing industries, together with those shown in the table, will provide the focus for review of developments of the major commodity-producing activities, although it will not be possible to deal with all of them.

The table shows varying degrees of expansion, but those listed have in common growth rates far in excess of that for total industrial production including utilities and also of the 51 per cent rise in real GNP between 1949 and 1960. These industries spurred general economic growth.

Research and Development

The manufacturing industries listed in the table were by and large the R & D industries par excellence. If there is a functional connection between R & D and growth, the facts in the 1950's seem to bear it out. The bulk of all private R & D effort is centered in the aircraft, guided missiles, electronics, electrical equipment, machinery, chemical, and oil and gas industries. Over half of all industrial research in 1959 was performed in the first four industries just named.[14] The aircraft industry alone accounted for about one third of total R & D in the late 1950's.[15]

It is estimated that total R & D outlays rose from about $3.4 billion in 1950 to $12.0 billion in 1959. Part of this increase was of course attributable to inflation, and an additional portion to the inclusion of activities toward the decade's end that were not so included earlier when the subject had less renown.

There are three components to R & D: basic research, applied research, and development. The first, as the term denotes, is almost purely scientific in character; the second attempts to harness the results of pure science to products and processes; the third embodies the results of applied research in the more costly commercially operable equipment and techniques. Only about 8 per cent of total R & D outlays in 1959 were expended on basic research—a seriously low proportion; and in private industry only 3 per cent of the total of $9.1 billion passing through that sector for all R & D purposes was channeled to basic research activities.[16] An almost constant proportion varying between 19 and 20 per cent for the 1950's was channeled through the private industry sector for applied research.[17] This left about 78 per cent for development by industry in 1959. The important automobile industry has refused to make public its breakdown of expenditures between research and development.[18]

The Federal government was the major source of funds for R & D during the 1950's, although industry did between two thirds and three fourths of the work. The bulk of the Federal funds were for defense purposes.

14. Daniel Hamberg, "Does Big Research Get Big Results?" *Challenge*, Institute of Economic Affairs, New York University, June, 1960, p. 8.

15. Daniel Hamberg, "Less Noise, More Research," *Challenge*, Institute of Economic Affairs, New York University, May, 1961.

16. Leonard S. Silk, *The Research Revolution* (New York, McGraw-Hill, 1960), p. 236.

17. *Ibid*.

18. Daniel Hamberg, "Less Noise, More Research," *loc. cit.*, p. 7.

The trend of R & D effort has been noteworthy for an increase in the proportion devoted to development at the expense of research, particularly basic research, and a shift in sources of funds toward government. Also, an increasing proportion of the effort has been performed by industry as compared with government, nonprofit institutions, and independent inventors.

The overlap between R & D concentration, the most rapidly growing industries shown in Table 6-1, and the defense program will now be apparent. The defense program was extremely important even in the utilities industries. This takes much of the steam out of the arguments advanced by those followers of Joseph Schumpeter and others who rely heavily upon the continuous appearance of great new (private) industries to assure overall economic growth. As will be seen below, the growth industries of the 1950's by and large could attribute to government orders the margin between a mediocre growth performance and their striking actual record. The conclusions to be drawn point to the quasi-public character of the industries and to the importance of government expenditures for growth, however sluggish, during the 1950's. For the utilities, the steady expansion in consumption and the metropolitan "explosion" must be added onto the direct stimulus from expenditures by Federal and lower governmental levels.

Aircraft

Much could be said about the aircraft industry, but little need be said here. Toward the end of the decade the industry that received about 80 per cent of its business from military agencies, and that single-handedly contributed so much to the regional development of the Pacific Coast, began to decline. The production index, which stood at 368 for 1960, had seen its post-Korean peak of 415 in 1957. Employment naturally declined also as defense orders shifted from airframes to missiles. Profits as percentage of sales also dropped, from 4 per cent in the peak year 1954 to 1 per cent in 1959.[19] The airframe companies attempted with considerable success to break into space technology and to benefit from the switch to civilian jet propulsion, but they could not avoid substantial retrenchment. About 40 per cent of the 350,000 persons employed in the development and production of missiles in the second quarter of 1959 were employed in the aircraft industry. Meanwhile, apparently as a holding action for

19. Charles J. V. Murphy, "The Plane Makers under Stress," *Fortune*, June, 1960, p. 136.

the industry, the Congress in 1961 achieved considerable notoriety by continuing to insist upon making appropriations exceeding half a billion dollars for militarily questionable B52 and B58 bombers in the face of the Pentagon's and the Administration's persistent threat not to expend the funds if appropriated.

Electronics

Defining the electronics industry is next to impossible. The statement previously made that it was a big $11 billion market was at best an extremely loose guess. There is probably no more heterogeneous collection of products and firms. There is no official Census industrial classification by the title "electronics industry." Nevertheless, *some* collection of firms and products built around the term will persist in the literature; and because of its technological and economic importance, together with its linkage with automation, the electronics industry commands attention. In the table of leading growth industries, electronics is buried partly in the electrical machinery, aircraft and other equipment, instruments and related products, and the equipment-including-defense industries. These industries also produced outside the field of electronics even very broadly defined. Furthermore, much that would be included under a reasonable definition of electronics would fall in industries other than those listed in the table.

Broadly considered, the electronics industry comprises two chief product categories: component materials such as transistors, diodes, electron tubes, resistors, and capacitors; and end products such as computers, testing and measuring equipment, industrial control equipment, microwave communications systems, television sets, radios, phonographs, tape recorders, and high-fidelity components.

In order of sales importance, the electronics industry supplied the following markets: government military demand, industrial demand, households, and replacement parts. The government military demand accounted for about two thirds of the growth in aggregate electronics sales during the 1950's, the period of most rapid expansion in this category terminating with the end of the Korean War. A second and milder expansion phase for the decade began with the onset of the missile race in 1955 and was carried along by the accelerated electronification of military aircraft, warships, and weapons systems. While total defense spending rose about 15 per cent during the last part of the decade, the military sales of electronics firms rose about 100 per cent. It seemed doubtful that in the absence of enormous increases in the military budget such growth rates could continue in the 1960's.

As would be expected in a rapidly growing market, the member firms were in a state of great fluidity during the 1950's with respect to market shares, life span, corporate growth policy, product mix, price policy, type of ultimate market in which to concentrate, etc. It seemed clear by the end of the decade that business discontinuances through failure, merger, or acquisition would be high in the 1960's. New entry was becoming increasingly difficult, the degree varying with the particular product and other factors. In computers, *Fortune* estimated $100 million would be required for a frontal assault on International Business Machines' (IBM's) 75 per cent position in the computer market.[20] In the components division, the entry barriers were much lower. Here the reduction of numbers was discouraging to new entrants, however. For example, at one point in the 1950's the number of firms producing diodes and transistors approached 100, but by decade's end they were already down to 80.[21] There was little doubt that the process of concentration would eventuate in an industry with an oligopoly core and a small-firm fringe in the components division, with greater concentration in end products. The firms with annual revenue from electronic products in excess of approximately one-half billion dollars at the end of the decade were Radio Corporation of America, General Electric, Western Electric, Sperry Rand, Hughes Aircraft, IBM, and Raytheon.[22] The industry leaders in general fell into only two categories: large established firms whose entry into electronics represented commodity extensions as part of their product diversification program, or firms like Sperry Rand, Hughes Aircraft, and Raytheon that entered directly through the military contract route.

Industrial Chemicals

The heterogeneous chemicals and petrochemicals industry actually embraces many subgroups having divergent trends. Of primary interest from a growth standpoint is the field of industrial chemicals, the production index for which rose, with only slight recession hesitations, throughout the decade from 154 in 1951 to 320 in 1960. The growth was so rapid that employment in industrial organics (337,000 in 1960) and inorganics (104,000) rose

20. Charles E. Silberman, "The Coming Shakeout in Electronics," *Fortune,* August, 1960, p. 189.

21. *Business Week,* December 3, 1960, p. 58.

22. Charles E. Silberman, *op. cit.,* p. 130.

absolutely from 347,000 to 441,000 over the same period. Even production workers rose, though more moderately, from 258,000 to 278,000. It will be obvious from comparison of the output index with the employment totals that the link between rapid growth and substantial increases in man-hour productivity is clearly shown in the case of industrial chemicals manufacture.

In a diversified industry where every major producer is diversified, product innovation is a fundamental imperative for survival and growth of the firm. This is the chief reason why the chemical industry was a leader in R & D outlays. It also explains why the industry was outstanding for the number of mergers and acquisitions during a decade noted for such activity. The enormous variety of chemical products may also explain in part the fact that industry-wide collective bargaining was absent. Product heterogeneity is explained in part by the fact that firms in a number of formerly non-chemical and chemical-consuming industries entered the diverse market through the by-product route (e.g., petroleum, liquor, rubber, paper, and meat packing) and subsequently themselves diversified in order to exploit the industry's technological characteristics of joint products, common products, interrelated products, and common processes. These technological characteristics also explain why, during the 1950's when the industry was growing rapidly, the production of chemicals for the chemical industry itself (as raw materials and "intermediates") was an important component of the total output increase. Entry of firms formerly outside the chemical industry contributed strongly to the geographical dispersion of the industry into the Southwest and California and to the rapid growth of capacity. New entry and the pressure of more rapid growth in capacity than in output in many lines (this was an industry in which the capital-output ratio rose during the 1950's) no doubt held industrial chemical prices down to increases slightly less than those for all industrial commodities.

In the framework of rising demand, rising wage rates, and practically constant wholesale prices of chemicals during the last few years of the decade, the industry was still able to keep the rate of profit after taxes on stockholders' equity notably above the average rate for all nondurable manufactures. Productivity increase no doubt explains this in large part. As a result the industry was able to maintain payout ratios (proportion of dividends to profits after taxes) substantially higher than average and still finance the great bulk of its enormous new fixed investment outlays and capital exports from internal sources. The chemical industry is thus a good example of the proposition that rapid growth solves many problems by making it possible to increase productivity, raise wages, hold the line on prices, pay satisfying dividends, finance R & D, and provide internal funds for modernization and expansion.

The industrial chemicals market is outstanding among those reviewed here for the fact that it was a big and a growing industry during the decade yet apparently did not rely heavily upon defense orders or other public stimuli. This exceptional circumstance, aside from the ordinary interest attached to the industry, calls for some examination.

Bearing in mind the fact that the markets for industrial chemicals are extremely diverse, penetrating broad segments of the commodity-producing economy, the exceptional growth record may be explained, with necessary overlapping, in terms of the following:

(1) The displacement of older products, such as synthetic for natural fibers, e.g., acetates, textile glass, the noncellulosics; synthetic for imported natural rubber; synthetic detergents for soap; synthetic high-concentration fertilizers for standard fertilizers.

(2) The provision of chemicals to other industries that exhibited higher than average growth, such as paper and products, aerosols, plastics, fluorescent lighting.

(3) The creation of new and enlarged markets for new products, such as new drugs, additives, pesticides, plastics, liquid fertilizers.

(4) The production of intermediates for the industry's own use (growth stimulating and growth reinforcing—very important in an industry that uses so many of its own products).

(5) The increased chemicalization of industrial processes and products (this is an untested hypothesis to the effect that the contribution of the industrial chemicals industry to the average manufacturing process and the average manufactured commodity rose during the decade).

(6) The rise in export trade. The aggregate dollar value of industrial chemicals exports rose 73 per cent between 1951–55 and 1959, whereas imports rose only 42 per cent over the same period. In the case of some pesticides exports were frequently larger than domestic sales. Some important growth products, such as plastic and resin materials and ethylene glycol (used chiefly for antifreeze), experienced greater rises in foreign sales than in domestic. In the cases of ammonium sulfate and potash (fertilizer

materials) the United States changed from net importer to net exporter.

(7) The rise in military demand as compared with 1947–49. It may thus be seen that the growth of the industrial chemicals market at an annual rate of 10 per cent between 1947 and 1960 was a very broadly based development in which the industry improved its relative position sufficiently to overcome the general slowdown in investment and industrial expansion after mid-decade.

Long-Term Direct Foreign Investment

The chemical and allied products industry was a leading participant in the large export of long-term capital, especially by the growth industries, that characterized the 1950's. In the case of manufacturing alone, it appears that the investment expansion abroad during the decade was at a substantially greater rate than the rise in value of domestic fixed capital. The value of United States direct investments in manufacturing enterprises abroad jumped from $3.8 billion in 1950 to $9.7 billion in 1959. The coincident growth in direct investment by the chemicals and allied products industry was from $512 million to $1.7 billion, representing a slight rise in the relative position of chemicals to about 17 per cent of the total in the latter year and assuring its place as largest single-industry direct investor abroad. The industry's direct investments in plant, equipment, and inventories were concentrated in Canada ($742 million), Europe ($440 million), and Latin America ($361 million).

The outflow of private long-term funds during the decade reflected for the most part comparative long-term profit prospects in the United States and abroad. Even in the rapidly growing industrial chemicals industry, the internal generation of funds at home was so great that these funds called for larger offsets than domestic investment expansion warranted. *Business Week* pointed out in late 1960 that "as a measure of the scope of the trend to overseas business, one of the industry's top six companies figures that this year 70% of its expansion money has gone abroad. Next year it expects the rate will be between 75% and 80%." [23] Yet the industrial chemicals industry, with its favorable rates of return and rapidly growing markets, had far fewer domestic reasons than most industries to seek profitable foreign outlets for its funds. As *Business Week* stated it, "with so much excess capacity already existing in the U.S., and demand growing so slowly, there is little

23. *Business Week*, December 3, 1960, p. 51.

or no reason to believe that if the $1 billion (a year) were prevented from leaving the U.S., it would be invested in more domestic capacity. . . ." [24]

There were other reasons, largely in the nature of a "pull" rather than a "push," which induced a general outward migration of United States capital. The major pull factor was the rapid growth of foreign markets. The booming Canadian economy with its vital raw materials and favorable investment climate was the center of attraction during the first half of the 1950's. By 1957, when the Canadian boom had already slackened, United States direct investments in Canada were one third of its total direct foreign investments, and the Canadian total substantially exceeded that for all Latin America. Three fourths of Canada's oil and gas, one half of its mines, and over one half of all its manufacturing assets were in the possession of United States investors. At the end of 1956, United States firms accounted for 83 per cent of all Canadian business under foreign control. Over 80 per cent of Canadian exports consisted of raw materials or semiprocessed goods. So sensitive was the United States capital outflow to Canada, however, that with the slackening of economic activity there in the latter half of 1957 there was a sharp drop in the flow. The flows in 1958 and 1959 were both below 1957.

The favorable investment milieu in Canada included not only liberal tax concessions and the absence of nationalization or expropriation threats, but also involved very definite control considerations partial to American management and a source of irritation to Canadians. Such considerations included Canadians' inability to buy stock in many Canadian subsidiaries; the reservation of export markets for the parent United States company; the direction of Canadian subsidiaries by ambitious United States executives; the luring away of Canadian scientists and engineers by United States parent companies; the policy of keeping Canadian subsidiaries dependent, with respect to R & D work, upon the controlling United States parent; and the purchase of capital goods in United States markets.

A definite shift away from sluggishly growing Canada and toward Western Europe occurred in the late 1950's. The value of private United States direct investments in Canada increased about 18 per cent between 1957 and 1959; but it rose 28 per cent in Western Europe, 31 per cent in the Common Market countries as a group (Belgium, Luxembourg, France, Germany, Italy, the Netherlands), 37 per cent in West Germany, and 24 per cent in

24. *Ibid.*, December 31, 1960, p. 111.

Italy.

According to the Department of Commerce, during the whole decade United States private direct foreign investments of all types increased in the aggregate from $11.8 billion in 1950 to $29.7 billion in 1959. Some $10.4 billion of the latter total was in petroleum and $9.7 billion in manufacturing. Earnings (the sum of the United States share in net earnings of subsidiaries and of branch profits) on all direct investments totaled $3.3 billion in 1959. Private long-term portfolio (mostly foreign securities) investments totaled about $11.5 billion.

Rather over one half of the rise of $17.9 billion in the world total of United States direct foreign investments over the decade was associated with net capital outflow (of $9.8 billion). The remainder of the expansion in assets was financed largely from internal cash flow (chiefly depreciation in the case of manufacturing) of the foreign subsidiaries and affiliates, the dominant source of funds by the late 1950's.

Aside from the attraction of markets more rapidly expanding in Western Europe than in the United States, there were other inducements to the establishment of facilities abroad. These included circumvention of European tariff walls through foreign subsidiaries; liberal tax and depreciation policies of foreign governments; exemption from United States taxation of the unrepatriated profits of American firms with foreign branches; savings on transport costs; and, as some hypothesized but with questionable validity, possibly lower unit wage costs.

Long-term capital flows were of course not merely in one direction during the 1950's. Such investments by foreigners in the United States reached a postwar high of almost $17 billion in 1959. However, unlike the United States pattern abroad, foreign long-term investments in the United States were about 60 per cent portfolio items, of which by far the greater portion were corporate stocks.

The chemicals and allied products industry followed the pattern of all industry with respect to the shift from Canada to Western Europe in the late 1950's. While its direct investments abroad rose 20 per cent between 1957 and 1959, its Canadian assets increased 15 per cent and its European 38 per cent. This traditionally pro-tariff industry began to find itself in an ambivalent position as the 1960's began. It moved abroad in part to circumvent tariff walls against American chemical products, yet retention of United States tariffs on imported chemicals inhibited the sales prospects in the United States market of its foreign affiliates and partners and also created antipathy among influential foreign chemical interests that could eventuate in restrictive foreign government policies toward United States chemical investments abroad.

Other Growth Industries

The remaining industries in the table of leading growth industries were related to either the electrical or natural gas areas, except for instruments. The last named was in part associated with electronics, in part with the continued trend toward nonelectronic automatic control devices, mechanical measurement in industry, and increased use of instrumentation in scientific activity. The value of total shipments of electrical measuring instruments, for example, rose from $150 million in 1950 to $596 million in 1958.

The phenomenal expansion in the electric power utilities and the associated growth in electrical generating and transmission equipment and machinery were the result of a widely diffused increase in electricity use throughout the economy. Household consumption of electric power increased from 67.0 billion kwh in 1950 to 173.4 billion kwh in 1959, principally because of the vastly expanded stock of household electrical appliances, shown in Table 6-2. The table serves also to reveal indirectly the market growth rates for the appliances shown. The index of appliances production (excluding television and home radios, which were nongrowth lines) rose from 80.1 in 1951, on a 1957 base, to 117 in 1960.

Farm electrification also proceeded very rapidly during the decade, an important element in the phenomenal rise of agricultural productivity. While the total number of farms served by electricity rose slightly, from 4,424,000 in 1950 to 4,576,000 in 1959, sales of electricity increased from $12.3 billion kwh to $26.9 billion kwh over the same period. Scanning will show at once that the electricity consumption per farm served nearly doubled during the decade.

The accompanying indexes of electricity production for business and government (atomic energy being almost entirely for military purposes) reveal the growth rates in these markets:

	1950	1957	1959	1960
General industrial markets	60	100	110	115
Atomic energy	4	100	97	na
Commercial and other nonresidential	59	100	118	127

The broad base of the great expansion in the publicly regulated electrical utility industry during the decade is now abundantly

TABLE 6-2

Wired Homes with Selected Electrical Appliances Number (millions)
and Per Cent of All Wired Homes, 1950–59

End of year	Television sets		Refrigerators		Freezers		Vacuum cleaners (floor)		Electric washers		Dryers (electric and gas)		Air conditioners	
	No.	Per cent	No.	Per cent	No.	Per cent	No.	Per cent	No.	Per cent	No.	Per cent	No.	Per cent
1950	10.6	26.4	33.8	86.4	2.8	7.2	22.0	56.5	28.1	71.9	.6	1.4	.2	.6
1951	15.8	38.5	35.5	86.7	3.8	9.3	23.6	57.7	30.1	73.5	1.0	2.4	.3	.8
1952	21.2	50.2	37.8	89.2	4.9	11.5	25.1	59.4	32.2	76.2	1.6	3.7	.6	1.4
1953	27.7	63.5	39.4	90.4	5.8	13.4	26.4	60.5	34.2	78.5	2.2	5.1	1.2	2.6
1954	32.1	74.1	41.4	92.5	6.8	15.1	27.9	62.2	36.4	81.3	3.0	6.6	1.8	4.0
1955	35.0	76.1	43.3	94.1	7.7	16.8	29.6	64.3	38.7	84.1	4.2	9.2	2.6	5.6
1956	38.8	81.9	45.5	96.0	8.6	18.0	31.6	66.6	41.2	86.8	5.6	11.9	3.6	7.6
1957	41.9	86.3	46.8	96.3	9.4	19.2	33.2	68.3	43.0	88.5	6.6	13.7	4.6	9.6
1958	44.0	89.0	48.2	97.7	10.4	21.0	35.0	70.9	44.9	90.0	7.7	15.6	5.8	11.7
1959	45.5	89.9	49.6	98.0	11.2	22.1	36.7	72.5	47.1	93.1	9.0	17.8	6.5	12.8

SOURCE: McGraw-Hill Publishing Co. (*Electrical Merchandising Week*) and Council of Economic Advisers.

clear. The most spectacular element of market growth, it will be observed, was the expansion of electricity consumption for defense purposes. The almost 100 per cent rise in general industrial absorption of electric current may fruitfully be compared with the rise in the flow of manufacturing, mining, and utilities output during the decade. On the same 1957 base, the total joint production index for these sectors was:

1950	75
1959	105
1960	108

It may be inferred that, since electricity began the decade with a much lower index of 60, the absorption of electricity in the production of the average unit of industrial output rose substantially. The influence is of course supported by much other evidence, such as the increased use of electrolysis, electric steel furnace expansion, and the enormous output rise in the power-hungry aluminum industry, from 718.6 thousand tons of primary aluminum in 1950 to almost two billion tons in 1959.

Advertising

It is appropriate to be aware, in a survey of rapidly growing markets, of the very great expansion in advertising during the 1950's. The importance of this activity resided not in the volume of employment it afforded but in its significance as an emphasis in business policy and as a cultural influence. It may be that the growing gap between capacity and sales was the main reason for increased advertising effort. The seasonally adjusted *Printers' Ink* index of national advertising expenditures (1947–49 = 100) stood at 241 in March 1960, which definitely puts this activity in the rapid-growth category even if the index were to be adjusted for price changes. Total advertising expenditures increased from 2.36 per cent of national income in 1950 to 2.77 per cent in 1959. The breakdown of total advertising expenditures between national and local media reveals an interesting trend, steady through the decade, toward more national advertising:

	1950		1959	
	Amount ($ millions)	Per cent of total	Amount ($ millions)	Per cent of total
National	3,257	57.0	6,710	60.5
Local	2,453	43.0		

As perhaps the major device for product differentiation in the economy, advertising was concentrated in the consumer goods industries. This can be seen in Table 6-3, which shows all lines

TABLE 6-3

Advertising expenditures as per cent of 1957 sales

Industry group	Per cent
Tobacco manufactures	5.2
Beverages	4.9
Chemicals and allied products	3.6
Motion pictures	3.6
Furniture, housefurnishings	3.3
Amusements (excluding motion pictures)	2.8
Retail general merchandise	2.6
Apparel and accessories	2.5

that spent 2.5 per cent or more of their sales and receipts from operations on advertising in 1957. The "chemicals and allied products" ratio is heavily influenced by drugs. It is to be doubted that the 5.2 per cent for tobacco manufactures, where price competition was largely nonexistent, was justifiable on grounds of efficient allocation of resources. Much the same may be said of beverages.

Advertising was but one important component of the "miscellaneous business services" market, a fast-growing, heterogeneous collection of services whose total receipts exceeded $10 billion per year by the decade's end. This fact is a reminder that the growth in the service lines in the 1950's was by no means entirely for the consumer market.

The Laggard Industries

The tremendous growth of electricity and natural gas as energy sources was not without its cost to the output and employment record in substitute sources. Total energy consumption increased from 34.2 trillion British thermal units (B.t.u.) in 1950 to 42.9 trillion in 1959. This moderate rise, amounting to one fourth in a decade, did not permit the great growth of one source without stagnation elsewhere. The consumption of coal was most adversely affected, bituminous and lignite falling absolutely from 11.9 trillion B.t.u. at the beginning of the decade to 9.6 trillion in 1959. Exports and consumption by the competing electric power utilities themselves offset the decline to some extent, but not enough to compensate for the collapse of coal demand associated with the dieselization of railroads and the drop in industry and retail dealer deliveries. The number of bituminous-coal miners fell from 344,000 in 1950 to 149,000 in 1959, a serious blow to the labor union movement. This decrease was not entirely due to industrial decline; for mining, like agriculture, violated the usual link between rapid growth and rapid productivity increase. Output per man-hour in bituminous-coal mining, on a 1947 base, rose very rapidly from 114.5 in 1950 to 196.1 in 1959.

The petroleum industry also suffered, but by no means sufficiently to prevent noteworthy absolute growth based chiefly on expansion in petrochemicals, distillate fuel oils for household and railroad consumption, and refined motor fuels. The shifts in the comparative positions of the various mineral fuels and water power between the beginning and the end of the decade, in trillions of B.t.u. consumed, were as follows:

Year	Coal	Crude petroleum	Natural gas	Water power
1950	12,913	12,706	6,933	1,601
1959	10.047	18,340	12,826	1,691

Rather over one half of the energy consumed by electric utilities came from coal and about one fifth each from gas (natural and artificial) and hydro sources, with a minor shift during the decade in favor of gas.

A brief glance at the other important slow-growth or declining industries during the decade will increase appreciation of the aggregate growth trend as earlier discussed. Table 6-4 includes all industry groupings in the Federal Reserve Board index whose index in 1959 approximated 125 or less. The table also shows appropriate totals for purposes of comparison. The year 1959 rather than 1960 is shown because the effect of the 1960 recession in these activities, unlike the growth industries, would be misleading as to the decade trend.

It will be noted at once that all the stagnant industries shown in the table experienced absolute declines in employment over the decade, despite the fact that, in all cases except coal mining, production in 1959 exceeded that in the base period. In the case of iron and steel the 1950 index stood at 112. Productivity increases, therefore, explain most of the absolute employment declines.

Further perusal of the table will suggest, in the case of activities not already mentioned, that the poor performance shown may frequently be traced to the expanded demand of substitute products marketed by the rapidly growing industries discussed earlier in this chapter. This was particularly true of textile mill products, which suffered from the increased use of artificial fibers, and leather, which suffered especially from the growth of plastics.

TABLE 6-4

Major Slowly Growing or Declining Industries of the 1950's as Indicated by Federal Reserve Board Industry Groupings Production Index for 1959, and Their Total Employment in 1950 and 1959

Industry grouping	Production index (1947–49 = 100)	Employment (thousands) 1950	1959
Mining	125	889	676
Coal	68	443	184
Metal mining	107	97	80
Iron and steel *	107	611	522
Lumber products	125	805	658
Textile mill products	126	1,292	966
Leather and products	119	392	372
Beverages	117	214	209
Total		4,743	3,667
Total employment (thousands)			
All manufacturing		14,967	16,168
All mining		889	676
Total production index			
All manufacturing	158		
All mining	125		

* Production index for 1960 was 110 (steel strike in 1959 lasted from July 15 to November 7; both 1958 and 1960 were marked by recessions).

Public transportation should also be added to this group of slow-growing or declining activities. Although employment in trucking and warehousing rose from 619,000 in 1950 to 853,000 in 1959, this rise of over one-quarter million was more than offset by the 513,000 drop in employment in interstate railroads and local railways and bus lines. A great part of the decrease in employment in Class I railroads from 1,221,000 to 815,000 may be attributed to very substantial productivity increases—another violation of the principle of association between rapid industrial growth and rapid productivity rise. Discontinuances of and deterioration in the quality of railroad passenger service also contributed to the decrease of railroad income and employment. The slowdown in the growth of commodity output during the later years of the decade likewise helped depress rail and other forms of transport. (Chart X)

Chart X. Intercity Freight Traffic

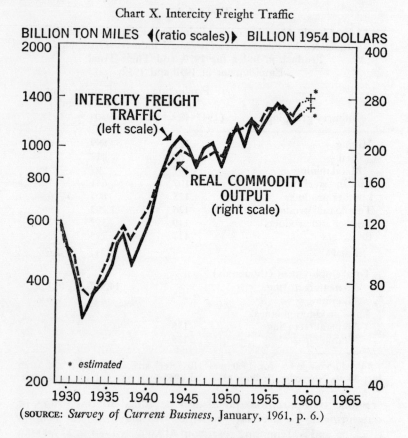

BILLION TON MILES ◀(ratio scales)▶ BILLION 1954 DOLLARS

(SOURCE: *Survey of Current Business*, January, 1961, p. 6.)

Regional Pattern of Economic Change [25]

Regional shifts in rates of growth and in welfare indexes are the product of many secondary influences outside the sphere of direct decisions by business firms. For example, householders may pour into a state such as Florida, attracted as they continued to

25. This section relies heavily upon H. S. Perloff, E. S. Dunn, Jr., E. E. Lampard, and R. F. Muth, *Regions, Resources, and Economic Growth*,

be in the 1950's by favorable climatic features. Again, the influence of a Congressional delegation, responding to both its own and its constituents' impulses, may contribute to a very high concentration of government contracts in one area, such as has been the case in California during the decade of the cold war. On the whole, however, the proposition that "the critical elements in the changing patterns of regional economic development are the locational and production decisions of business firms flowing from the input and market requirements of the major industries" [26] seems to place the emphasis where it belongs. For this reason it is appropriate to review briefly some of the more striking regional changes of the decade.

Perloff *et al.* distinguish the regional employment impact of locational shifts in the volume of activity within various industries, which they term the differential employment shift, from the regional impact of geographical specialization in rapidly growing or slowly growing industries, which they term the proportionality employment shift.[27] In any particular region these two effects may neutralize, reinforce, or overcompensate each other.

The preceding discussion of the growth rates of certain important industries together with changes in the agricultural sector offers the key to the contours of regional economic growth in the 1950's. The varying growth rates and spatial shifts of these important industries produced, and were further stimulated by, secondary effects in the form of population migration and economic activities.

A glance at Table 6-5 showing the regional pattern of personal income at the beginning and the end of the period under scrutiny, and of average annual growth rates, reveals great disparities between regions and certain selected states. On a regional basis the rates of increase of total personal income for the entire period range from a low of 68 per cent in the Plains to a high of 118 in the Far West. Yet population changes wrought remarkable compensating effects, so that per capita incomes remained surprisingly stable for the period in any one region. The per capita relations also show a tendency toward convergence upon the national figure in the cases of the Mideast, Great Lakes, and Southeast.

The large effect of population out-migration is strikingly shown

Resources for the Future, Inc. (Baltimore, Johns Hopkins Press, 1960); and U.S. Census of Population: 1960, *General Social and Economic Characteristics, United States Summary*, Final Report PC(1)—1C (Washington, D.C., U.S. Government Printing Office, 1962).

26. Perloff *et al.*, *op. cit.*, p. vi.
27. *Ibid.*, pp. 70–71.

TABLE 6-5

Per cent Rise in Total Personal Income, 1950 to 1961, Per cent of U.S. Per Capita Personal Income, 1950 and 1961, Annual Growth of Real Gross Product Per Capita, 1950–57, and Average Annual Growth of Retail Sales, 1948 to 1958, Regions and Selected States

Region and state	Total personal income: per cent rise, 1950–61	Per capita personal income, per cent of U.S. 1950	Per capita personal income, per cent of U.S. 1961	Average annual growth rate of real gross product per capita, 1950–57	Average annual growth rate of retail sales, 1948–58
United States	84	100	100	1.9	4.5
New England	80	109	112	2.0	4.1
Massachusetts	75	112	115		4.1
Mideast, or Middle Atlantic	73	118	116	1.7	3.9
New York	72	126	125		3.8
Great Lakes, or East North Central	73	111	105	1.8	4.0
Illinois	71	122	118		3.9
Plains, or West North Central	68	95	94	1.8	3.3
Southeast, or South Atlantic and East South Central	91	68	73	2.7	5.1
North Carolina	84	68	72		5.5
Georgia	87	68	73		5.3
Florida	187	86	88		9.6
Southwest, or West South Central	93	86	86	2.2	5.0
Texas	86	90	87		5.2
Mountain, or Rocky Mountain	92	96	96	1.5	5.4
Far West, or Pacific	118	120	119	1.4	5.6
California	133	123	123		6.2
Alaska	99	150	120		7.6
Hawaii	120	94	102		3.4

SOURCES: *Survey of Current Business*, May, 1961, p. 28, Table 1, and April, 1962, p. 7, Table 1; E. F. Denison, *The Sources of Economic Growth in the United States*, Committee for Economic Development, Supp. Pap. # 13, 1962, p. 10.

by the fact that the Southeast had the highest growth rate of per capita product in the nation, although the percentage rise in its personal income was below that for three other regions. In significant contrast, the Far West—a region of high in-migration—had the lowest growth rate of per capita product in the country, despite the fact that its personal income rose proportionately faster than any other region. One half of the native population in the Far West in 1960 was in a state other than the state of birth, but in the Southeast ratios approximating as low as one seventh were widespread (Florida—a state of in-migrants, climatic amenities, retired people, and tertiary industries—was an obvious exception).[28]

Diversification in New England

The New England region fought a rear-guard action in the 1950's to prevent a serious lag in economic growth as compared with the rest of the nation. Total employment increased from some 3.6 million persons to about 4 million. The region's textile industry continued to contract, leaving many depressed, labor-surplus cities, such as Lowell, New Bedford, and Providence. Employment in shoes, leather, and other traditional products stagnated (see Table 6-4 on slowly growing industries), so that total employment in nondurable goods manufacture declined from 726,411 in 1950 to 658,545 in 1960. But there were compensating forces. For one thing, durable goods manufacture in the region as a whole not only came to supersede nondurables in importance, but kept pace with the nation's 27 per cent rise. New England's manufacturing product mix became more diversified during the post-World War II era, while total manufacturing employment, at 36.6 per cent of total employment in 1960, represented only a slight drop from the 38.5 per cent of 1950.

The decline in farm employment that beset the nation and all regions in the 1950's had little power to drag down the growth rate of employment in New England because of the small proportion of that section's employment devoted to farming. Whereas agricultural employment in the East South Central region fell by over one half, from 27.4 per cent of total employment to 13.2 per cent, calling for substantial alternative opportunities and out-migration, New England's almost equivalent proportionate drop from a mere 4.0 per cent to 2.3 per cent of total regional employment exerted but a negligible influence on the employment pattern.

28. U.S. Census of Population: 1960, *op. cit.*, pp. xiii–xiv and Figure 2.

A glance at Table 6-1 on leading growth industries provides an important clue to New England's industrial performance. Aircraft in Connecticut and electronics, electrical machinery, and defense equipment in Massachusetts lent a noteworthy proportionality shift to New England's regional employment pattern. With $1,353 million of prime defense contract awards in fiscal 1960, Massachusetts was one of the leaders in the nation in such business; and Connecticut led big manufacturing states like Michigan and Illinois in the same spending category. Other expanding activities were non-electrical machinery (mainly in Connecticut), apparel, R & D, metalworking, the broad category of "professional and related services" (which includes engineering, scientific, and kindred services), financial services, and the inevitable state and local government category. Employment in the Boston metropolitan area expanded from 915,000 in 1950 to 1,024,000 in 1960— an unimpressive gain compared to Phoenix, Los Angeles, or Atlanta, but notable for an old manufacturing-belt region. Boston's Route 128, an outer-belt highway, became famous for its new industrial complex signifying the union of higher education, R & D, engineering services, electronics, and the defense budget. Employment in professional and related services in the Boston metropolitan area grew dramatically from 105,000 to 155,000 during the intercensal years. In all New England this category of employment rose from 9.4 per cent to 12.8 per cent of total employment, moving the region up from third to second place in the nation, surpassed only by the Mountain region.

The Central Manufacturing Belt

Like New England, the western side of the nation's long-established manufacturing belt (Great Lakes region) basically held its position in relative share of manufacturing activity. This area employed in manufacturing approximately 35 per cent of its total workers in both 1950 and 1960, while its share of the country's manufacturing employment slipped only from 28.6 per cent to 26.7 per cent, a remarkable stability in view of the far-reaching westward economic shifts within the nation as a whole. In contrast to New England, the Great Lakes region experienced a slight increase in the ratio of slow-growing nondurables to durables employment (Table 2-2). For one thing, Michigan and Indiana were adversely affected by the decentralization of automobile assembly operations; Detroit, for example, was beset by consequent serious chronic unemployment in the later years of the decade. Nevertheless, some of the slow-growing industries of the region, like iron and steel and leather, found an offset in fast growers such as chemicals, metal hard goods, and rubber.[29]

Outside manufacturing, the region's employment changes were not particularly significant. Total employment rose somewhat less than the national average. However, a combination of moderate birth rates, out-migration, and a low ratio of population to employment kept per capita personal income above average despite the distinctly below-average rise in total personal income.

At the eastern edge of the old manufacturing belt the great industrial state of Pennsylvania faced very serious stagnation. Its growth rate of total personal income of only 50 per cent between 1950 and 1961, its declining per capita personal income as a percentage of the average for the nation, and its 3.4 per cent average annual growth of retail sales showed that Pennsylvania was bearing the brunt of the westward movement of industry and the decline of coal mining. Much of the state was becoming a depressed area by the end of the decade. In early 1962 Pennsylvania had 426,000 unemployed—over 9 per cent of its labor force.[30]

Industrialization in the Southeast

The performance of the Southeast, while leaving per capita personal money income the lowest in the nation, nevertheless exhibited a number of gratifying trends over the decade. High birth rates and insufficient out-migration failed to prevent a rise in the area's standing with respect to per capita personal income, as shown in Table 6-5. Also, the average annual growth rate of real gross product per capita was notably above the national average, as was the growth rate of retail sales.

The Southeast went against the national trend by raising the proportion of its employment devoted to construction. Both the South Atlantic and East South Central sub-regions also increased the proportion of their employed engaged in manufacturing, the latter from 18.4 to 23.8 per cent. This placed the two sub-regions on a par with each other and with the Far West in this important respect, and indeed left the Southeast only about three percentage points below the national average. Manufacturing employment in the Southeast rose almost 30 per cent as compared to the national expansion of about 20 per cent.

It is true that in manufacturing the more slowly growing non-durables employment in the region continued to dominate the durables, and early processing of products of the extractive industries, such as textiles and lumber, continued to be very important. The Carolinas' textile industry endowment, so important in

29. Perloff *et al.*, *op. cit.*, p. 480.
30. *Business Week*, April 21, 1962, p. 85.

former decades, exerted an adverse shift in employment and acted as a drag on growth in the 1950's. However, the net differential shifts in the area as a whole were generally upward and typically dominated the net behavior of manufacturing employment.[31] In this category of shifts are to be found automobile and truck assembly; manufacture of household furniture, paper and allied products, food and kindred products, apparel; and printing and publishing. Major growth industries in the area included machinery and transportation equipment, especially ships and boats.

The Atlanta metropolitan area paced expansions in personal incomes and retail sales for Georgia that exceeded the nation's. The employed population of the standard metropolitan area (SMA) grew 45 per cent and, perhaps more significant, manufacturing employment a remarkable 64 per cent between 1950 and 1960. Within the latter, employment in durables more than doubled, to approach total nondurables employment. The number of persons engaged in personal and related activities in the Atlanta SMA almost doubled.

Major Shifts in Texas

As is well known, the fast-growing regions were and remain the Southwest, Mountain, and Far West. Texas and California may be taken as representative of the more dramatic changes operating in these regions. Moreover, they are by far the most important states in the three areas, accounting for two thirds of all personal incomes in the three regions combined.

The Texas performance was not remarkable for its overall expansion, which only modestly outdistanced that for the country as a whole. Rather, its striking characteristics are found in the very substantial growth offsets to Texas' stagnating or declining sectors.

Accompanying a great shift from crops to livestock, the number of persons employed in agriculture, forestry, and fisheries in Texas fell from 446,000 in 1950 to 292,000 in 1960, reducing thereby the proportion of the state's total so engaged from 16 to 9 per cent. Among the slowly growing industries, textiles and leather products, though stagnant, were not important enough to pull down the state's record significantly. Lumber and wood products, however, did occupy a position of some importance and did decline from 31,000 employed in 1947 to 17,000 in 1960.

On the other hand, our table of leading growth industries of

31. Perloff *et al.*, *op. cit.*, p. 484.

the 1950's (Table 6-1) could almost have been constructed from Texas' experience. For example, employment in certain Texas growth industries rose as follows between 1947 and 1960:

Industry	1947	1960
Machinery	25,000	47,000
Transportation equipment (including aircraft)	21,000	65,000
Instruments and related products	1,000	5,000
Chemicals and allied products	24,000	39,000

Furthermore, Texas became the nation's leading producer of natural gas, increasing the total dollar value of this product three and one-half times over the decade to reach well over one-half billion dollars at the end.[32] Natural gas, crude petroleum, sulphur, and salt became the resource base of Texas' great new petrochemical industry centered in the Houston-Beaumont-Port Arthur industrial complex. Exploitation of this resource base explains in major part the fact that Texas went against the nation's trend in mining to *increase* its employment in that activity from 90,000 to 100,000 during the decade—despite great man-hour productivity advances.

Related in substantial part to the expanding mineral and natural gas power base in the state and the general market expansion associated therewith, numerous other lines of manufacturing exhibited substantial differential upward shifts. Notable among these were the primary metal industries (including aluminum reduction and basic steel) and fabricated metals products. Total manufacturing employment in the state rose from 370,000 in 1950 to 540,000 in 1960, the leading component of the rise being in durables. The entire expansion process was given a fillip by very large defense procurement allocations. With $2,143,000,000 prime contract awards in fiscal 1960, Texas ranked third in the nation, exceeded only by California and New York. At the end of the decade approximately one fourth of Texas' annual income was derived from the Federal government.[33]

California's Dramatic Growth

California's prime defense contracts totaled $6,409 million in fiscal 1960. This substantially exceeded New York and Texas combined, making California the epitome of the state defense

32. Janus Howard, "Out Where the Southwest Begins: A Prospectus," *Current History*, May, 1961, pp. 286–287.

33. *The New Yorker*, April 22, 1961, p. 49.

economy. Military procurement wielded a crucial influence over the state's economy throughout most of the decade. The main chains of causation from World War II through the 1950's ran from directly defense-related growth industries to both indirectly defense-related industries and expanding market-oriented activities. In addition, California agriculture, while dropping some 30,000 persons engaged, maintained that state's leading position in value of all farm products sold.

It would be hard to overstress the importance of manufacturing in the growth of the state during the decade. Total employment in that sector rose from 764,000 to 1,391,000, or 82 per cent. Total employment rose about 47 per cent, so the vital role of manufacturing is eminently clear. As percentage of total employment in the state, manufacturing rose from 20 per cent to 24 per cent. California increased its proportion of the nation's manufacturing employment from 5.2 to 8.4 per cent. The greatest expansion was in the fast-growing durables.

A glance at the growth-strategic Los Angeles-Long Beach SMA shows a rise in the proportion of persons employed in manufacturing from 25 to over 30 per cent during the decade. What were the important and the rapidly growing industries in the area? Ignoring the slowdown in aircraft during the waning years as that industry fought first for its obsolete planes and then for its conversion to missiles, the major lines for the whole decade were aircraft, electronics, machinery, and primary and fabricated metal products. The first two, high on our list of leading growth industries, were directly defense-related, the latter two to a considerable degree either directly or indirectly defense-related. Almost 40 per cent of all factory workers in the Los Angeles area in 1960 were employed in the aircraft, missile, and electronics industries.[34] The chemical industry was a negligible factor.

The smog-ridden seven or eight southernmost counties embracing the Los Angeles-Long Beach SMA, with a population of some 9,000,000 in 1960, came to be the country's leading example of urban sprawl, with all its attendant problems. The kind of unplanned metropolitanization represented by this megalopolis, and to a lesser degree San Francisco-Oakland to the North, was extremely important to California's growth. The contrast with Chicago, greatest city of the old manufacturing belt, is enlightening. Total employment at the beginning and end of the decade was:

34. C. Page Smith, "The Pacific Coast: A Study of Southern California," *Current History*, May, 1961, p. 293.

	1950	1960
Los Angeles	1,690,000	2,616,000
Chicago	2,363,000	2,512,000

The heart of the change which saw Los Angeles overtake Chicago may be discovered in the fact that the latter lost 66,000 "operatives, craftsmen, and foremen" while Los Angeles gained 250,000 such workers. It should also be borne in mind that economic expansion in Los Angeles and all of Southern California was greatly facilitated by the in-migration of some 2,000,000 persons during the decade, about one fourth of these being relatively low-paid Negroes with primarily urban backgrounds.

Another aspect of California's growth derived from enormous and primarily manufacturing-connected increases in the number of government, private professional, service, and trade-connected workers. California came to share with Massachusetts the leading position in scientific and engineering R & D employment. Furthermore, nowhere else in the nation was higher education favored with such solicitude by the people of a state.

A final major influence on the state's expansion was the fact that it had exceptionally easy access not only to its rapidly growing home market, but also to a market area encompassing in many products the entire region west of the Rockies, insulated as this region is by transport costs from much eastern competition.[35] As the entire Pacific Coast developed, California could sell to it and to the whole Mountain West. With respect to farm products the same held true, in addition to the continuing national markets for California produce.

This cursory review of certain regional changes during the 1950's bears out the thesis that the magnitude, and as may now be appreciated, the spatial dispersion, of economic activity were heavily dependent upon government budgets, particularly the Federal defense budget. This thesis has been pinpointed by continual cross-referencing in the above discussion of regional changes to the analysis of leading and lagging industries earlier in the chapter. To be sure, there were many related factors at work, such as interregional migration of people and capital, climatic amenities, political influences, access to inputs, metropolitanization, and the distribution of consumption activities. The allocation of appropriate weights to all these must await the further endeavors of the location theorists.

35. Perloff *et al.*, *op. cit.*, p. 475.

7 | Other Developments in the Business Sector

The Capital Markets

Corporate Financing

Emphasis on long-run growth performance involves analysis of the sources and uses of long-term funds by the corporate sector. It will be possible here to deal only with the corporate sector as a whole and to treat it in a highly selective way. The present concern is with the capital markets, as distinguished from the money markets. In the latter the chief new money instruments usually traded are checks drawn on balances held in Federal Reserve banks ("Federal funds") and short-term Federal obligations such as Treasury bills, tax anticipation bills, certificates, and other paper of up to one year maturity. The heterogeneous capital market deals largely in mortgages, corporate and noncorporate bonds, stocks, long-term Federal obligations, and customers' loans. Contemporary capital markets are notable for the existence of oligopsony. Indeed, in the important direct placement market, where securities are usually sold to some financial intermediary, bilateral monopoly for any given issue is widespread.

Since corporate financing of long-term requirements draws upon both external and internal sources, it is necessary to examine the historical record of both sources in order to appreciate fully the changes in financial policy through the 1950's.

It has already been remarked that the chief source of funds for long-term investment in plant and equipment (P & E) for the corporate sector was internal cash flow. The extent to which this was the case may now be seen clearly by perusal of the data in Table 7-1, which show that retained profits plus depreciation and amortization allowances averaged about 100 per cent of total P & E outlays between 1955 and 1960, a higher average than that for the first half of the decade. It should not be inferred that all such cash flow went into fixed capital: some went into working capital, but the great bulk typically did find its real investment offset in fixed assets.

It will be observed that the major proximate reason for the rising importance of internal funds was the growth of depreciation and amortization allowances from less than half of total P & E investment during the early years of the decade to about three fourths toward the end. This result was of course due to a combination of the plateau in P & E investment and the growth of such allowances. It is therefore apparent that the relaxation of the Treasury's depreciation policy in 1954 must have gratified to a considerable degree the preference of business for internal financing of long-term investment. Even had that type of investment been substantially higher toward the close of the decade, it seems evident that depreciation and amortization would have amounted to at least as much as two thirds of P & E outlays. Since a portion of retained profits was also allocated to fixed capital outlays, corporate enterprise had to submit to the explicit judgment of the market for only a minor percentage of such long-term needs.

There seems to have been a mild tendency for retained profits as a percentage of P & E investment to drift downward from 1955 through 1960. Higher payout ratios (ratio of dividends to profits after taxes), together with the post-Korean 52 per cent tax rate as compared with the previous 38 per cent rate, could sufficiently account for the weakening of the retained earnings series.

The payout ratios in turn may be explained as the attempt by corporate executives either to maintain stable dividend-sales ratios or to maintain some reasonably satisfactory dividend-price ratios on common shares in the face of the great upsurge of stock prices. This latter ratio, which began the decade at an annual average of 6.27 per cent, descended to 3.46 per cent in 1960. The downward plunge carried common stock yields below the averages for all classes of bonds in 1958. The average yield on all types of bonds rose from 2.86 per cent in 1950 to 4.73 in 1960, largely

TABLE 7-1

Selected Sources and Uses of Corporate * Funds, 1950–60
(Billions of dollars)

	INTERNAL SOURCES			EXTERNAL LONG-TERM SOURCES									
Year	Retained profits °°	Depreciation & amortization	Total	Bonds, debentures and notes	Preferred and common stock	Total new securities offered	Debt instruments as % of total	Internal plus external long-term	Total plant & equipment investment (P&E)	Internal + external − P&E invest.	Ratio intern. sources to P&E invest.	Ratio depr. & amort. to P&E invest.	Cash dividends †
1950	13.0	7.8	20.8	4.9	1.4	6.3	77.7	27.1	16.9	10.2	1.23	.46	9.2
1951	10.0	9.0	19.0	5.7	2.1	7.8	73.2	26.8	21.6	5.2	.88	.42	9.0
1952	7.4	10.4	17.8	7.6	1.9	9.5	80.0	27.3	22.4	4.9	.80	.46	9.0
1953	7.9	11.8	19.7	7.1	1.8	8.9	80.0	28.6	23.9	4.7	.82	.50	9.2
1954	6.3	13.5	19.8	7.5	2.0	9.5	79.0	29.3	22.4	6.9	.88	.60	9.8
1955	10.9	15.7	26.6	7.4	2.8	10.2	72.5	36.8	24.2	12.6	1.10	.65	11.2
1956	10.5	17.3	27.8	8.0	2.9	10.9	73.4	38.7	29.9	8.8	1.21	.57	12.1
1957	8.9	19.1	28.0	10.0	2.9	12.9	77.5	40.9	32.7	8.2	.86	.58	12.6
1958	5.7	20.3	26.0	9.7	1.9	11.6	83.6	37.6	26.4	11.2	.99	.77	12.4
1959	9.1	21.5	30.6	7.2	2.6	9.8	73.5	40.4	27.7	12.7	1.10	.78	13.4
1960	7.4	22.9	30.3	8.1	2.1	10.2	79.4	40.5	31.0	9.5	.98	.74	14.0

Notes.—* Excludes banks and insurance companies unless otherwise specified as all corporations. ** Includes depletion allowances. † New securities offered for cash sale (gross proceeds.) A small portion of the debt paper was no doubt for short-term uses, as was a minor portion of the equity issues. The universe for the securities series is all corporations; hence the columns relating internal to external financing overstate the lattersomewhat. (See first note.) ‡ All private corporations.

SOURCES: Securities and Exchange Commission, Council of Economic Advisers, Federal Reserve Board, Department of Commerce. Totals rounded.

under the influence of the high-interest-rate policy of the Federal government. While high-grade bond prices slipped from $121.9 per $100 bond in 1950 to $94.7 in 1960, Standard and Poor's common stock price index (1941–43 = 100) rose from 18.40 in 1950 to 55.85 in 1960. Despite the emphasis by most investors on price appreciation and the notion of stocks as a hedge against inflation, corporate policymakers were hard put to it to increase the flow of dividends sufficiently to prevent equity investors' possible disquietude over their current rate of return. In view of this kind of pressure, the mounting clamor directed at the Treasury by business for even more liberal depreciation and corporate income tax policies as a hedge against further declines in retained profits becomes more understandable.

The long expansion from 1954 through 1957, seen clearly in Table 7-1 and previous tables and charts, brought with it typical increases in corporate requirements for fixed and working capital funds that could not be met sufficiently from internal cash flows. These fixed capital fund requirements were augmented by the disproportionate rise in capital goods prices during that period. Also the corporate nonfinancial business sector had to finance a net increase of $5 billion in trade credit extended to other sectors between 1954 and 1957. Total new securities annually offered rose in consequence from $9.5 billion to almost $13 billion over the same period. Net new money, after allowing for retirement of securities (which was substantial in 1954 and 1955), increased from $6.8 billion to $11.8 billion. Between two thirds and three fourths of these funds were designed for P & E acquisitions, the remainder for working capital purposes. Bank loans to the corporate nonfinancial sector also rose, from −$1.2 billion (net repayment) in 1954 to +$3.6 billion in 1956. External financing through new security issues leveled off, however, during the last three years shown in Table 7-1. During the middle years of the decade a given volume of such issues was associated with much lower rates of P & E investment than was the case later. For example, total new offerings of $10.2 billion were associated with P & E investment of $24.2 billion in 1955 and with $31 billion in 1960. The new offerings total and P & E investment for 1959 may be similarly compared with the appropriate figures for 1952 and 1954. It seems reasonable to relate these contrasts to the higher total internal cash flow available in the later years of the decade. Some might argue that the rising interest costs on debt instruments discouraged resort to external financing as the decade waned, but this interpretation has already been dismissed.[1]

1. See Ch. 5, "Monetary Policy and Business Fixed Investment."

A general preference for debt instruments in external financing is clearly shown in Table 7-1. There was no apparent trend, for the corporate sector as a whole, however, in favor of either debt or equity instruments (the latter overwhelmingly common shares) through the decade, despite much talk of the desirability of equities as low dividend-yield rates gave stocks an advantage in the late 1950's. (In this connection it should be realized that the use of internally generated funds is a kind of equity financing— one which skirts the judgment of the market, however.) The general preference for debt financing stemmed largely from reluctance to dilute stockholder interests and from the tax deductibility of interest paid as contrasted with dividends. Corporate bonded indebtedness of the nonfinancials rose more than 100 per cent, from $35.7 billion in 1950 to $74.9 billion in 1960. Nonfinancial corporations therefore just about kept pace with the rise in total long-term debt of the whole private corporate community from $72 billion in 1950 to about $156 billion in 1960. (Compare with the increase in Federal debt in Table 5-1.)

A very small proportion of equity issues, but an average of 47 per cent of all debt issues, was directly (privately) placed, mostly with life insurance companies and trust institutions, rather than offered publicly on the capital markets. Commercial banks took some of the shorter maturities. Direct placement bypasses to a great degree the wider influences of the public capital markets. If the $3.8 billion of privately placed corporate securities in 1959 is added to the $30.6 billion of internal funds for that year, one may say that 85 per cent of the total of internal plus external long-term funds for the corporate sector circumvented the public capital markets. The latter were of course not competitively structured.

The Financial Intermediaries

The most important changes in the relation of the private financial intermediaries to the capital markets for long-term funds during the decade involved, aside from the Federal Reserve and commercial banking system, the private life insurance companies, mutual savings banks, private and government pension funds, savings and loan associations, and investment companies.

LIFE INSURANCE COMPANIES

The life insurance companies held only 2 per cent of their assets in industrial and miscellaneous bonds in 1930; but 24 per cent was in railroad and public utility bonds, mostly railroads. A long-run shift in favor of the former category and against railroads was already evident in 1950, with 14.9 per cent in industrials and only 5 per cent in bonds of the economically declining railroads. Meanwhile, public utility bonds had grown to 16.5 per cent of life insurance assets. During the 1950's these intermediaries absorbed savings in enormous amounts, largely in the form of premium payments on policies, which crept upward from 3.46 per cent of disposable personal income in 1950 to 3.77 per cent in 1960. The absorption is represented in the fact that life insurance policy reserves expanded from $54.9 billion at the beginning of the decade to $98.5 billion in 1960. The allocation of the bulk of this increase in individual savings, as decided by life insurance management, favored three types of credit market instruments: mortgages (primarily home), industrial bonds, and public utility bonds. The following tabulation, taken from the Institute of Life Insurance *Fact Book*, shows the amounts involved and the percentage of total life insurance assets that they represented:

| | Mortgages | | Industrials | | Public utilities | |
| | amount | | amount | | amount | |
Year	($ billions)	per cent	($ billions)	per cent	($ billions)	per cent
1950	16.1	25.1	9.5	14.9	10.6	16.5
1960	41.8	34.9	26.7	22.4	16.7	14.0

Holdings of state and local government bonds, not shown in the table, almost tripled. It is evident that these intermediaries generally favored active and growing sectors of the economy and disfavored declining sectors and lower-yield paper. The life insurance companies were the largest single factor on the lending side of the corporate bond "market."

These intermediaries reduced their proportionate holdings of railroads (to 3.1. per cent), foreign government bonds, and United States government securities (from 21.0 per cent in 1950 to 5.4 per cent in 1960). The decrease in government securities, largely long-terms, reflecting for the most part a reticent attitude toward the statutory 4.5 per cent interest rate ceiling, was from $13.5 billion to $6.4 billion over the decade.

The life insurance companies moved directly into the real estate field by developing large urban apartment projects (Stuyvesant Town and Peter Cooper Village in New York City, for example). Beginning in mid-decade, life insurance firms also began to exhibit a new interest in stocks, apparently responding to some extent to the permanent inflation psychology which led to the acquisition of common stocks as an inflation hedge. Urban real estate, of course, was also an inflation hedge.

The growth of life insurance companies slowed down between 1955 and 1960, as did their net purchases of industrial and public utility bonds—a serious matter, in view of their dominant importance in the corporate debt field. At a time when the securities markets were moving toward equities as an inflation hedge, the slower growth of the chief single source of demand for bonds no doubt contributed to the decline in bond prices and the coordinate rise in bond yields (rates of interest).

SAVINGS AND LOAN ASSOCIATIONS

Although life insurance companies were one of the fastest growing intermediary channels for the absorption of personal savings during the decade and remained at the end the largest single factor, they were outdone in growth rate by the savings and loan associations. These institutions, which the states usually prohibit from investing in equities and most corporate bonds, confine their conversion of other people's money very largely to real estate mortgages for the promotion of home ownership and, to a lesser extent, to government securities. Savings and loan associations were among the few intermediaries that remained active in the government obligations market.

In view of the moderately high rate of home construction, the great increase in home ownership, the rise in price of the average mortgaged house, and the increase in the ratio of mortgage loan to average price, it is not surprising that total mortgage debt on one- to four-family nonfarm houses jumped during the same period from $45 billion to about $142 billion. Financial institutions held 84 per cent of this total in 1960, with savings and loan associations by far the largest single holder. The spectacular expansion of these associations was one of the more dramatic features of the postwar capital markets, their total outstanding mortgage loans rising from $13.6 billion to $60.1 billion over the decade ending in 1960.

MUTUAL SAVINGS BANKS AND COMMERCIAL BANKS

Other major holders of residential nonfarm mortgages in 1960 after the life insurance companies, which held second position, were the mutual savings banks ($24.2 billion) and commercial banks ($20.4 billion). These last two institutions were both slow though substantial growers in the residential mortgage field. The important role of Federal lending institutions in this sphere has already been discussed. As of 1960, 40 per cent of the total mortgage debt outstanding on nonfarm one- to four-family properties was either FHA-insured or VA-guaranteed.

INVESTMENT COMPANIES (MUTUAL FUNDS)

Investment companies constituted another spectacularly growing type of financial intermediary. These institutions (the "open-end" variety of which is referred to as mutual funds) sold their own shares to individual and institutional investors and used the savings thus garnered to buy other securities, chiefly equities, for investment. They constituted an increasingly important factor in the equity capital market during the decade, and their rapid growth attested to a general rise in the investment community's preference for equities. The investment companies that were registered with the Securities and Exchange Commission under the Investment Company Act of 1940, comprising almost all such institutions, increased in number from 366 in 1950 to 570 in 1960 and in aggregate market value of assets from $4.7 billion to $23.5 billion over the same period.

CREDIT UNIONS

Credit unions, though remaining a relatively small factor in the aggregation of personal savings, expanded their savings accounts from less than a billion dollars to almost 4½ billion in 1959. The savings deposits of commercial banks, while growing at a slower rate than the credit unions, maintained their position through the whole period as largest single holder of savings accounts, although the savings and loan associations had almost overtaken them as the decade ended.

One criticism leveled against the intermediaries by those beset with inflationary fears was that intermediaries were under continuous constraint to invest the steady flow of savings at their disposal and that they therefore often circumvented the restrictive aims of the monetary authorities with the easy conditions upon which they extended funds to borrowers. It was also claimed that intermediaries were partial toward large corporate borrowers and that, with such a large proportion of the community's capital disposal under their command, the small firm, however worthy, was deprived of a free market. Again, it was argued that the management of most financial intermediaries was unduly safety-conscious and that the intermediaries had the power, through their command over savings, to transmit this security-consciousness to the directing boards of nonfinancial firms that habitually came to them for funds. It was also noted that many intermediaries in fact acquired bonds or mortgages only on condition that the borrower subordinate his dividend policy to certain strictures regarding minimum income retention. As might be expected, none of the problems raised by these allegations were resolved, but rather passed on to the next decade.

Growth of Pension Funds

One of the most dramatic developments impinging upon the capital markets during the 1950's was the enormous growth in private pension funds from about $11 billion in 1950 to about $44 billion in 1959. State and local government retirement funds also burgeoned. The expansion in pension funds paralleled that for private health and medical care insurance. The pension funds were an outgrowth of increasing public sentiment for the socialization of personal risks as the main focus of the search for material security. The spread of private pensions accompanied the successful movement for extension of social security coverage (old-age benefit coverage rose from 1.9 million persons in 1950 to 9.6 million in 1959, for example) and the escalation of social security benefits to compensate for inflation. Furthermore, as emphasized by Father Paul P. Harbrecht in a study in 1959,[2] the expansion of private corporate pensions was stimulated by the fact that they were tax deductible and by their frequent inclusion in union demands as a fringe benefit, especially after a 1948 National Labor Relations Board ruling that made such pensions a proper subject of collective bargaining by classifying them as deferred wages. Private pension and disability retirement plans were generally viewed as supplements to the Federal old age and disability programs. Indeed, an additional stimulus came from the lag in social security benefits behind rising living costs.

One of the striking changes associated with the growth of pension funds was the very great expansion in their equity portfolios during the 1950's. Before 1950 it was unusual for a pension fund to invest in common stocks. Less than 15 per cent of corporate pension fund assets consisted of common shares in 1952; but this had risen to 27 per cent in 1958, and by 1960 about 50 per cent of the annual increase in such funds was going into the acquisition of equities. Purchases out of total pension funds were the most rapidly growing single category of stock purchases during the

2. Father Paul P. Harbrecht, *Pension Funds and Economic Power* (New York: Twentieth Century Fund, 1959).

decade, although they constituted a small proportion of the total market. Despite this latter fact, the concentration of pension fund purchases of equities in a small group of blue chip issues made pension fund placement a significant factor with respect to those particular shares. This is not to imply that the funds were unimportant in the debt paper category, for in 1958 corporate pension funds alone held about 11 per cent of the aggregate market price of all bonds listed on the New York Stock Exchange. Corporate debt held was about twice the amount in equities, but the trend was toward the latter. In any case, it was certain that the swing to equities by the pension fund investor was an inflation hedge that bolstered the market for common shares and thus contributed to the upward pressure on stock prices. As one writer put it, "Buying a hedge against inflation has been so popular for the past decade that we may well have an inflation in hedges against inflation." [3]

Many new problems were raised by the growth of pension funds. The flimsy structure of pensioner's rights suffered under a system of regulation that lagged behind the rapid expansion of the funds. The employee's rights were generally limited to his claim against a fund upon retirement. For most workers, pensions were partially vested or not vested at all; i.e., their benefits did not go with them if they changed jobs. Also, there was a high concentration of pension funds in the hands of a small number of big banks acting as trustees of the funds. This fact, together with the purchasing emphasis on a relatively narrow range of issues, raised the possibility of corporate control by bank trustees.

A mincing forward step was taken by the passage by Congress in 1958 of the Welfare and Pension Plans Disclosure Act to protect participants in private employee welfare and pension plans by requiring plan administrators to disclose significant information regarding financial operations and other related matters to plan beneficiaries. But much still remained to be done. The Act of 1958 required pension plan administrators to file very general financial reports with the United States Department of Labor, but the Department lacked authority to check upon their accuracy. Further improvement in reporting and greater power of enforcement was provided for in March, 1962, legislation, however.

One of the central questions regarding the capital markets in the 1950's was whether savings were allocated optimally for economic growth, under the prevailing highly institutionalized ar-

3. Robert Tilove, "Social and Economic Implications of Private Pensions," *Industrial and Labor Relations Review*, October, 1960, p. 33.

rangements. No doubt weakness on the demand side for plant and equipment procurement was the major difficulty. This demand has traditionally been considered the strategic one from the standpoint of growth and, possibly, for the increase of productivity in the economy. Yet the question was still legitimately raised whether those institutions which dispensed other people's savings employed proper criteria in channeling about 55 per cent of the new funds in the capital "markets" after World War II into mortgages and only 30 per cent into corporate securities. As Dr. Roy L. Reierson of the Bankers Trust Company of New York declared, "It thus seems pertinent to ask whether a disproportionately large share of available investment capital is moving into residential and other private building and into types of public projects which do not contribute to rapid economic growth, and whether too little is being directed into channels which lead to greater expansion of our truly productive resources." [4]

The Stock Market

A glance at Chart XI shows that the decade's inflation in stock market prices got under way at the *end of the Korean War*. Stock prices, on the basis of Standard and Poor's index, *led* the upturns from the 1953–54, the 1957–58, and the 1960–61 recessions. This was a striking feature of the 1950's. The delay in the emergence of the great bull market of the decade, together with the recession buoyancy of the market, points to the most likely hypothesis regarding the behavior of stock prices during the 1950's. The hypothesis is that the stock market boom expressed chiefly two things: the conviction that government spending would prevent severe depression, and the conviction that commodity prices would secularly rise. In addition to these two probably correct insights, the market no doubt increasingly responded to the built-in tax condition whereby capital gains (if realized) were taxed at only 25 per cent, while dividend income was taxed at much higher rates. Hence, tax considerations introduced a bias in favor of price appreciation and against current dividend income.

There is no money-making activity anywhere that can compare with the stock market when it comes to making speculative expectations justify themselves by events. In the stock market, expectations are far removed from the pedestrian profit-making activity of producing enterprises. This quasi-autonomy of stock-price expectations gains strength as an upward (or downward)

4. "The Changing Capital Markets," February 9, 1960, p. 10.

movement gains momentum. At the beginning of the decade, stock market traders and investors were reluctant to pay more than seven times annual earnings for common shares and to accept less than 7½ per cent yield; by 1959 they were eager to pay eighteen times earnings for conservative stocks and would accept dividend yields (dividend-price ratios) of 3.23 per cent.[5]

Chart XI. Stock Prices and Volume of Trading, 1952–60

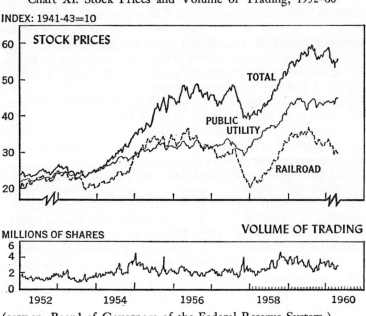

INDEX: 1941-43=10

(SOURCE: Board of Governors of the Federal Reserve System.)

The two convictions just mentioned reinforced each other in the minds of stock market traders. Because the economy was expected to be depressionless, commodity prices could only go up, never down. (Everyone knew stock prices and commodity prices moved in the same direction.) When they actually did go up, even in the slump of 1957–58, the convictions became fetishes. Chart XI shows the result: the second great upward wave of the decade in stock prices following the brief, halting drop in the early phase of the 1957–58 recession.

Yet the quasi-autonomy of the stock market was, as the term

5. Sam Shulsky, "The Year That Glamour Faded," *Challenge,* Institute of Economic Affairs, New York University, February, 1961, p. 10.

implies, by no means complete autonomy. Stock prices did not lose complete contact with underlying business conditions, as shown by the temporary setbacks in late 1957 and early 1960 and by the fact that the components of the total index moved differently and at differential rates of change. For example, industrial stock prices rose about 45 per cent between 1955 and early 1961; but utilities—on the whole the more rapidly expanding sector, as has been shown—rose 88 per cent; and by contrast, railroads barely held their ground. The utility and railroad trends, shown in Chart XI, are consistent with the notion that the market correctly sensed the growth and associated stock-price appreciation potentials of these sectors under the existing general economic conditions. Of course, the market reflected what Thorstein Veblen called the "acquisitive instinct" of traders in that it exaggerated underlying trends, particularly the expansionist ones. The exaggeration was especially acute in the case of the so-called growth stocks, such as IBM, which doubled its assets every four years beginning in the late 1940's and which was being traded at 75 times earnings in early 1961.

The glamour stocks also included many new firms whose names contained "electronics" or "tronics" or just plain "onics." These stocks, along with those of numerous long-established concerns, brought "every physician and college professor" into the market, just as in the fabulous 1920's. Reports of popular participation have historically been much exaggerated, of course. Nevertheless, among middle and upper income groups, share ownership was no doubt widespread. It was estimated on the basis of a sample study that 29 per cent of all professional and semiprofessional heads of spending units in 1957 owned some stocks. The total number of individual shareholders was estimated to be 12,490,000 in 1959 (and 15,000,000 in 1961).

The Large Corporation and Corporate Policy

New Features of the Corporate Environment

Most of the changes that occurred in the large corporation and in corporate policy during the 1950's were extensions of well-established structural and behavioral patterns. A number of these have already been touched upon. Certain further aspects of corporate policy will be sketched in this section. First, however, it is important to note four comparatively new features of the corporate environment.

The most far-reaching new aspect of the corporate and general business environment in the 1950's was the practical absence of depressions and the governmental assurance that severe and protracted depression would never again be permitted. The profound significance of an underwritten economy for business has been mentioned in connection with the discussion of the psychology of the stock market. But underlying that psychology was the more basic fact that a depressionless capitalism was a kind of capitalism that afforded general enterprise security with respect to a major source of risk in the historical past. The implications of this for applied profit theory, among other things, were hardly noticed by the economics profession.

It is true that severe depression under twentieth-century conditions rarely spelled bankruptcy or even temporary insolvency for the overwhelming majority of large corporate enterprise. But a contraction like that of 1930–33, followed by anemic recovery, did cut drastically into profitability and the intermediate prospect of stable growth, even for many large concerns. The remarkable stability of aggregate consumption and real GNP in the 1950's had thus eliminated one of the great sources of business insecurity that had plagued the system of industrial enterprise for generations. This fact must be thrown into the balance in appraising the impact on private business of the new role of government.

The fruits of the new general economic stability of the 1950's may be seen in the fact that business gross retained earnings rose *steadily* from $26.6 billion in 1948 to $51.2 billion in 1960, dropping only *once* during that entire period—by $1.0 billion in 1958. The range in fluctuation of corporate profits after taxes between 1950 and 1960 was from a low of $16.8 billion (1954) to a high of $23.8 billion (1959). In no recession year did corporate profits after taxes drop more than 17 per cent. This was a truly remarkable record for an eleven-year period.

A second new feature of the corporate environment was the existence of a substantial and continuing flow of military spending. Defense business enjoyed the close security of bilateral negotiation on a cost-plus basis rather than through competitive secret bidding. The great bulk of the prime contracts in value terms were drawn with a relatively small number of large corporations. These latter in turn subcontracted much of the business to a considerable number of defense-business satellites. Twenty firms received over half of and one hundred firms accounted for 74 per cent of the total value of prime military contracts awarded during 1959.[6] This last represented a steady increase from 63 per cent in 1953.

A third somewhat novel element in the corporate business environment of the 1950's was the development of foreign competition to historically new and threatening heights. This competition was centered where it could in the long run seriously hurt American business—finished manufactures. A major reason for the deterioration in the United States position both at home and abroad was the lag in American industrial productivity that has been pointed out earlier. Industrial output per man-hour rose 33 per cent in Germany, 35 per cent in Italy and 40 per cent in France,[7] compared with about 11 per cent in the United States between 1953 and 1958. Productivity in Japan, where the rate of growth of output also exceeded the United States rate, was likewise rising more rapidly. A second reason for the deterioration in the United States position, closely tied up with the first and with the greater excess capacity and slowed growth in the American economy, was the more rapid rise in the United States in employment costs per unit of output in manufacturing. This rise was due primarily to an increase in the salary component, since unit wage costs, despite higher money wage rates, drifted downward in the later years of the decade.

On the export side, total merchandise exports stood at $20.7 billion in 1957 and $20.3 billion four years later. An absolute decline in five commodities (petroleum and products, coal and related products, iron and steel scrap, iron and steel mill products, and raw cotton) offset increases in other components to achieve this stability.

A fourth new characteristic of the corporate environment was the long-term labor contract. Although the decade was marked by numerous big strikes in industry, the spread of the two- or three-year contract and of pattern wage determination introduced a new element of stability into the factor markets which considerably enhanced the degree of calculability in market administration enjoyed by corporate management.

Prominent Features of Corporate Policy

The major objective of management with respect to the corporate realm under its purview is typically the long-run security

6. Murray L. Weidenbaum, "Some Economic Aspects of Military Procurement," *Current Economic Comment,* November, 1960, p. 8.

7. Emile Benoit, "European Competition," *Challenge,* Institute of Economic Affairs, New York University, February, 1960, p. 31.

of operations, achieved by the minimization of the uninsurable risks undertaken. Under conditions of competitive pressures and substantial internally generated funds, this requires expansion and market diversification of the total assets of the firm. Internal fund (gross business savings) generation is maximized. Since asset growth is highly and positively correlated with sales growth, such a proposition can readily be reconciled with Professor Baumol's presumption that corporate management's "ultimate objective" is to increase sales. It can also be reconciled with his corollary proposition that executive compensation is closely correlated with size of firm.[8] The difference in emphasis between the first proposition and those of Professor Baumol resides chiefly in the inclusion of the notion of enterprise security in the former. The reason for the difference in emphasis is the writer's conviction that gross business savings maximization explains a wider range of business policy phenomena. In the long run the difference is certainly not a substantive one.

The 1950's produced little that was new in the sphere of business policy. Traditional methods, such as product diversification through either product innovation or merger and acquisition, were vigorously applied. Merger and acquisition proved generally more enticing from the standpoint of the firm, as devices for expanding assets rapidly through product diversification, than commodity extensions (internal diversification). One prime consideration here was the fact that through merger and acquisition a corporation gained a fresh bundle of managerial and technical talent trained in the problems of producing and marketing the additional products. Some authorities claimed, and many corporate executives asserted, that acquisitions were accelerated by the tax deductions that the losses of many acquired firms afforded to profitable acquiring firms, but this was of course no significant long-run motivation to an acquiring firm. Motivation aside, however, the important fact from the economy's standpoint was that mergers and acquisitions were a widely chosen alternative to the creation of new capacity and additional output, with possibly attendant price reductions. In the late 1950's particularly, mergers and acquisitions indirectly retarded the rate of P & E investment and contributed to the maintenance of prices. Avoidance of such results undoubtedly prompted Joseph Schumpeter's insistence that an enterprise system have sufficient free entry to assure a flow of new firms with fresh entrepreneurial leadership. Mergers and acqui-

8. See W. J. Baumol, *Business Behavior, Value and Growth* (New York, Macmillan, 1959), esp. pp. 46–47.

sitions of manufacturing and mining concerns as reported by Moody's Investors Service and Standard and Poor's Corporation totaled 4,089 from 1950 through 1959 (substantially less than the 6,818 for the 1920's, however).

One interesting study of mergers showed that of the 1,001 largest manufacturing companies in existence on January 1, 1951, 854 survived as of September 15, 1959. Of the 147 disappearances, almost all—138 firms—resulted from mergers.[9] *If mergers are excluded from the business mortality category, this gives a 99 per cent survival rate for large manufacturing concerns for the decade* —strong evidence for the degree of security enjoyed by large manufacturing enterprise and against Schumpeter's theory of the "perennial gale of creative destruction." The large and the very large manufacturing and mining corporation was by far the most active size-group among acquiring concerns in the 1950's.

Diversification of expanding assets by all traditional techniques continued to represent the corporation's chief strategy for achieving security through growth during the decade. Associated therewith was the spread of decentralization in managerial responsibility. Operating units in particular were given substantial autonomy, with major policy decisions and coordination retained in central offices. (It was these central offices that contributed to the maintenance of the economic life, and to the commercial building boom, in several stagnating "core cities" of large metropolitan areas.)

It was not at all certain that high R & D outlays were in general positively correlated with high rates of productivity increase, despite the fact that important cases of such correlation could be found. Neither was it clearly established that industries dominated by large firms, wherein such administered R & D outlays were important as elements of price policy, revealed a productivity performance any better than small-firm industries. Some studies showed, in fact, that innovation activity tended to be centered either in small firms or in areas external to the particular industry affected. Finally, the strategic *basic* research for industrial innovations was conducted overwhelmingly outside the business sector of society.

The pressures of the cold war in the context of slowed productivity gains during the decade called into question with a new urgency the legitimacy of the time-honored seventeen-year patent monopoly privilege, and also even the exclusive possession of technological knowledge by corporate managers. Said Pro-

9. Frank J. Kottke, "Mergers of Large Manufacturing Companies, 1951 to 1959," *Review of Economics and Statistics,* Vol. XLI (1959), pp. 431–432.

fessor Wassily Leontief in a memorable introduction to Leonard Silk's *Research Revolution*, "the costs of the technical advance resulting from . . . privately financed research are covered by license fees or an equivalent markup included in the price of the new or improved goods. This means that the practical application of many of the path-breaking discoveries of recent years is necessarily restricted. In an era in which economic progress depends so much on scientific research, such chronic underemployment of technical knowledge might have, in the long run, an even more deleterious effect on the rate of economic growth than idle capital or unemployed labor." [10] All this bordered not only on the matter of the locus of responsibility for optimal decision-making but also on the ever more insistent question of the 1950's: the public responsibilities of private corporate directors. The historic patentee rights of restricted use or nonuse increasingly seemed to conflict with the national growth goal and its requisite rapid productivity gain. The conflict was frequently reflected by the courts in antitrust decisions opening patents to more liberal licensing arrangements, prohibiting tying contracts, requiring the sale as well as lease of equipment, and in general assuring greater access to technological knowledge.

During the 1950's the subjugation of the shareholder by corporate management to the position of quasi-creditor, as long ago noted by Joseph Schumpeter, seemed to have reached an extreme. The dominant managerial objective for the firm, referred to above, dictated that stockholder payments, like interest payments, be subject only to the restriction that external equity funds be available to the degree that internal equity and external debt money were insufficient.

Other evidence is equally consistent with the stockholder-subjugation hypothesis, as well as with the general view that managerial objectives are controlled by the impulse to expand managerially controlled enterprise assets. In the study earlier referred to by Professor Irving Kravis on relative income shares, the following percentages for corporate profits components in the national income are given:

Year	Dividends	Undistributed profits	Total after-tax profits
1919–28	5.3	1.4	6.7
1949–57	3.3	3.0	6.3

10. Leonard S. Silk, *The Research Revolution* (New York, McGraw-Hill, 1960), pp. 7–8.

The contrast with our base decade, the "new era" of corporate prosperity in the 1920's, is very striking. Kravis' data show that dividends as proportion of national income conceded to shareholders fell drastically. On the other side of the coin, the percentage of profits withheld by corporate managers more than doubled.[11] Computations for 1958 and 1959 yield similar results.

Professor Edith Penrose has pointed out that in the typical large management-controlled corporation, wherein the ownership equity is widely diffused, "salaried managers have little or nothing to gain by paying out more than is necessary to keep existing shareholders from complaining in force, to attract any additional capital that may be needed, and in general to build up or to maintain the reputation of the firm as a good investment. On the contrary, the managers of a firm have much more to gain if funds can be retained and reinvested in the firm. . . . dividends would be looked on as a cost to be kept to a level no higher than necessary to keep investors happy." [12] (This is the same view as that taken toward creditors.) The inflation in share prices during the decade, although generating some pressure on corporate directors to raise aggregate dividends, also helped keep them down by virtue of the market's growing emphasis on appreciation with its attendant promise of capital gains.

Meanwhile, corporate executives apparently proceeded to administer dividends as a cost, as they did other costs that entailed a considerable degree of discretion. Theorists have searched, under great informational handicaps, for the dividend-payout criteria employed by management. It seems clear that payouts were not related directly either to profits before taxes or profits after taxes. It may be that traditional rates of return in the given industry were applied to stockholders' equity (net worth) to yield a total payout for a particular year. Another likely possibility, as suggested in Table 7-2, seems to be total sales. The stability of the ratio of dividends to sales for the sample of 180–200 large manufacturing corporations during the 1950's is certainly remarkable. Although the matter justifies a great deal more research, the proposition that corporate managers use sales as a guide for dividend payouts seems consistent with the record of the 1950's. The proposition is also congenial to the absorption of corporate administrators and public relations departments with the ratio of profits to the "sales dollar." Great interest in the ratio

11. *Ibid.*, p. 931, Table 7.
12. Edith Penrose, *The Theory of the Growth of the Firm* (New York, Wiley, 1959), pp. 27–28.

TABLE 7-2

Sales, Dividends, and Ratio of Dividends to Sales, Large
Manufacturing Corporations, 1950–60
(Billions of dollars)

Year	Sales	Dividends	Per cent dividends to sales
1950	45.8	2.3	5.1
1951	52.9	2.1	3.9
1952	54.5	2.1	3.6
1953	63.3	2.2	3.4
1954	88.3	3.2	3.7
1955	105.0	3.8	3.7
1956	107.7	4.1	3.8
1957	114.2	4.2	3.7
1958	105.1	4.1	3.9
1959	115.9	4.4	3.8
1960	120.7	4.5	3.6

Note.—The data include little or no representation of some important nondurable goods groups such as meat-packing and rubber.

SOURCE: Board of Governors, Federal Reserve System, *Federal Reserve Bulletin*. The sample covers 200 corporations for the years 1950–53 (see *Federal Reserve Bulletin*, June, 1956), and 180 corporations beginning in 1954.

of profits to sales is a phenomenon of the last two or three decades, and has never been a matter of basic concern to the sophisticated investor.

Oligopoly and Antitrust

Public Monopoly Policy

The economist's pure monopolist or monopsonist is rarely found in unregulated industry. The problem of "monopoly" in a practical sense therefore resides generally in markets wherein business structure, policy, and policy results evince characteristics that resemble those of monopoly. Aside from situations where the government has intervened, such characteristics are typical of the concentrated, oligopolistic industries in the private relations of very large firms to one another and to suppliers or customers.

The yardstick for testing the presence or absence of inimical monopoly power in the United States has traditionally been a set of either structural or performance criteria generally associated with perfect or workable competition, such as numerous producers, free entry and exit, absence of interfirm agreements, absence of price discrimination, non-uniform prices through time, "average" profits through time, temporariness of patent monopoly, and technological progressiveness. Monopoly is a phenomenon of market power, and the traditional indictment by economists has run in terms of the potential or actual exercise of such power to do one or more of the following: reduce the rate of growth; inhibit the rate of technical progress and investment; depress the level of employment; distort the distribution of income; frustrate new entry; harbor excessive idle capacity; maintain inflexible prices; induce inflation from the side of supply rather than demand; depredate smaller rivals; weaken the nation's capacity to compete in foreign markets; and unduly influence government to get tariff protection, public contracts, tax concessions, and other discriminatory measures. All elements of the indictment have derived their meaning largely by comparison with appropriate competitive yardsticks.

In its defense of large numbers of enterprises against widespread oligopoly, public policy has been motivated not only by its objective of improving the economy's efficiency, but also by its desire to protect small enterprise as a disadvantaged and politically salutary group. Unfortunately, these two objectives have often conflicted in varying degree, for small enterprise is itself not necessarily efficient or competitive enterprise. But government has preferred, perhaps wisely, to rely on a larger number of firms in the apparent belief that numbers are on balance more salutary than any possible offsetting inefficiences or noncompetitive concomitants.

Such conflict explains in large part the furtherance of monopolistic policies in some areas by the government itself. One prominent case is that of the misnamed state fair-trade laws, which in an effort to protect small retailers make it illegal to resell a branded item below a minimum price stipulated by the manufacturer of such item. These laws, by eliminating price competition at the retail level and thus also reducing the pressure on manufacturers to compete on a price basis, violate competitive pricing principles. The Justice Department, the Federal Trade Commission (FTC), and the economics profession have for decades opposed fair-trade laws despite their legalization in the Federal Miller-Tydings Act of 1937 (an "amendment" to the Sherman Antitrust law). Both houses of Congress overwhelmingly joined in strengthening the monopolistic principle of resale price maintenance in the McGuire Act of 1952 (an amendment to the Federal Trade Commission Act), which provided not only for the continued exemption from antitrust prosecution of resale price maintenance, but also for the right of the individual firms to (1) enforce fair trade contracts against non-signers and (2) fix stipulated as well as minimum resale prices. Despite these developments there was considerable weakening of fair trade during the decade because of opposition by some businesses, consumers, and the courts.

Another effort to protect small business, in this case against price discrimination, is represented in the 1936 Robinson-Patman Act, outlawing such discrimination where it would substantially lessen competition. Even if it were acknowledged that the law was designed to sustain larger numbers of firms than would otherwise obtain in most markets and thus possibly keep competition more virile, the application of the law and its judicial interpretation probably contributed more to shoring up inefficiency than to eliminating monopoly. The 1950's saw no significant changes in the methods of applying this act.

An additional major governmental violation of its own professed antimonopoly principles, in this case again in the name of small enterprise, is of course the price-support, production-restrictive cartel program in the agricultural sphere.

It is apparent that the government has legislated exemptions and exclusions from antitrust in important areas of the economy. The Webb-Pomerene Act (1918) exempted collusion in the export trade. The Reed-Bulwinkle Act (1952) exempted railroads from public approval of agreements relating to "rates, fares, classifications, divisions, allowances or charges." Other regulated monopolies and activities affected with a public interest were subject not to the antitrust laws, but to the Federal Communications Commission, Federal Power Commission, Civil Aeronautics Board, Interstate Commerce Commission, Securities and Exchange Commission (public utility holding companies), and the United States Maritime Commission. Agricultural cooperatives were exempt. Prices of crude petroleum were subject to formulas set by Congressional action, and production to prorationing rules. Congressional legislation exempted rate-making in insurance. Investment and commercial banks could not be proceeded against under the antitrust laws without the initiative of the Federal Reserve Board. The inroads of protectionism against antitrust prosecution even extended to defense contracts, inasmuch as 86 per cent of such procurement contracts were subject to bilateral negotiation between seller and government.

The two chief pieces of Federal legislation in the monopoly field during the 1950's, other than the increase in 1955 of the penalty for violating the Sherman Act from $5,000 to $50,000, were the McGuire Act, noted above, and the Celler-Kefauver Antimerger Act of 1950. The Antimerger Act was designed to plug up the legal gaps in Section 7 of the Clayton Antitrust Act (1914). Its expressed purpose was to prevent the consummation of mergers and acquisitions, through purchase of all or part of the stock or assets of other corporations, if the effect would be to lessen competition substantially or tend to create a monopoly in any line of commerce in any section of the country.

Application of this law appears to have carried on an antitrust tradition of protecting competitors but not necessarily protecting competition. As pointed out by Professor M. A. Adelman,[13] of 76 complaints by the FTC and Justice Department up to November, 1960, the overwhelming majority called for dissolution of a merger because it would be a "detriment" to competitors. Although in many cases the weakening of the competitive position of certain firms in a market might contribute to monopoly, in many others it might be associated with cost savings transferred to buyers. Certainly the doctrine of forbidding mergers simply because they might make life harder for other firms *could be* merely a form of protectionism for the high-cost producer. The doctrine was a blunt instrument indeed, for it failed to provide a clear alternative to the choice between monopolistic resource misallocation and misallocation due to the public sustenance of enterprise inefficiencies. Indeed, as the Court pointed out in the Bethlehem-Youngstown case (1958), the Congress did not intend enforcement to proceed upon distinctions between good and bad mergers.

Significant Court Decisions

The historical record of antitrust prosecution in consummated mergers under Section 7 was as feeble as that for any other aspect of enforcement. Virtually none of the 6,818 mergers of the 1920's were prosecuted. The FTC won no more than a handful of merger cases between the passage of the Clayton Act and the Celler-Kefauver Act. A major reason was, as usual, the emasculation of antitrust by the courts; the milestone in this case was the Thatcher decision (1926), which ruled that the FTC's powers under Section 7 were limited to *stock* acquisitions, thus opening

13. M. A. Adelman, "The Antimerger Act, 1950–60," *American Economic Review*, Papers and Proceedings, Vol. LI, No. 2 (May, 1961), pp. 236–244.

the door to *asset* acquisitions and mergers.

Subsequent to the passage of the 1950 Antimerger Act, and as part of the somewhat accelerated rate of antitrust prosecution during the 1950's, a number of merger and acquisition cases were instituted, some under the original Section 7. These cases included *Hamilton Watch Company v. Benrus Watch Company, Inc.* (1953); the *Pillsbury Case* (FTC Complaint, 1952); the *Crown Zellerbach Case* (1954); and *United States v. Brown Shoe Co.* (1959). Perhaps the two outstanding cases were *United States v. E. I. du Pont de Nemours and Company et al.* (1957) and *United States v. Bethlehem Steel Corporation and The Youngstown Sheet and Tube Company* (1958). The decision in the former was rendered under the original Section 7 as narrowly construed to apply only to stock acquisitions and dealt with a *vertical* acquisition (du Pont's acquisition of a 23 per cent stock interest in General Motors). It was held that du Pont's interest resulted in the foreclosure of du Pont's competitors from an important share of the market, and the firm was ordered to divest itself of its General Motors stock, a move which was still under way as the decade ended. It was in this case that the court defined the market for a commodity as, in part, one class of purchasers of the commodity.

This decision, like that in *United States v. United Fruit Company* (1954), broke through the historic reluctance of the courts to disrupt the corporate *status quo* by divestiture. In the United Fruit case, one of the more significant cases of the 1950's, the company agreed, under a consent judgment in February, 1958, to use its assets to create a new firm, capable of importing nine million stems of bananas (about 35 per cent of United Fruit's 1957 imports) into the United States annually.[14] Presumption: duopoly is better than monopoly; duopoly is the best that can be accomplished in the given situation.

In the proposed Bethlehem-Youngstown merger, the Celler-Kefauver amendment was invoked to forbid the merger on the grounds that it would substantially reduce the degree of competition, primarily by increasing the degree of concentration, in the purchase and sale of certain steel products in "substantial relevant markets." The Court's decision was premised in large part on its definitions of "relevant markets," an exercise in which it was hardly more successful than were the industry defendants in submitting their own definitions.

The Supreme Court rendered in 1951 a significant decision in-

14. Donald Dewey, *Monopoly in Economics and Law* (Chicago, Rand McNally, 1959), p. 247, n. 6.

terpreting the Robinson-Patman Act. In *Standard Oil Company (Indiana) v. Federal Trade Commission*, the court held that the "good faith" defense advanced by Standard Oil was complete. It rejected the FTC argument that the impairment of competition had removed the necessity to consider whether or not the seller had met competition in good faith.

In *United States v. United Shoe Machinery Corporation* (1953, 1954), initiated under Section 2 (involving the "attempt to monopolize") of the Sherman Act, the courts added to what many interpreters believed was a new and more adequate judicial trend toward recognition of the link between oligopoly, via large size, and monopolization. Until the 1940's the courts had insisted that size alone was no offense (*United States v. United States Steel Corporation*, 1920), applying only the 1911 Standard Oil case "rule of reason" decision to determine whether monopolization had occurred through the use of aggressive, predatory, or repressive practices exhibiting *intent* to monopolize. This current of judicial subversion of antitrust in the context of an oligopolistic economy seemed to have suffered a setback in the 1945 Alcoa and 1946 American Tobacco cases, wherein large shares of the market were related by the court to a broadened concept of monopolization that involved growth through restrictive rather than predatory behavior. In the *United Shoe Machinery* case the judge again applied this modified rule-of-reason concept (restriction of competition by practices not directed at any particular rival but merely intended to enhance market power through various defensive, protective, and security measures) to another example of large size. Intent to monopolize was inferred from United's nonpredatory policies of achieving and maintaining market domination, such as refusal to sell shoe machinery; restrictive, long-term leases; sale of machinery and repair service in a single package; and purchase for scrap of all second-hand machines in order to prevent the emergence of a second-hand market. This decision detected unlawful results where large size was associated with combative corporate growth policies and expressed what some authorities believed to be a judicial trend toward concern with market power as a monopoly criterion. However, these authorities could not deny that the criteria of behavior, intent, and rule of reason were still very much alive under their so-called "new Sherman Act."

It was thus obvious that the courts were, and for a long time had been, wrestling rather clumsily with economic matters that were much too sophisticated for legislators and judges, who had enjoyed a conventional monopoly of the antitrust field for decades. The problem was highlighted in the (to economists) somewhat amusing Cellophane case (*United States v. E. I. du Pont de Nemours and Company*, 1956), where the court, in dealing with this differentiated oligopoly situation, had to define a "market" and make decisions on the cross-elasticity of demand for cellophane (plain and moistureproof!) and other flexible packaging substitutes such as glassine, paper, pliofilm, foil, polyethylene, and saran. Some economists hailed the court's rejection of the Justice Department's allegation that cellophane represented a gap in the chain of substitutes, invoking in support the impressive authority of J. M. Clark's doctrine of workable competition. Other economists disagreed, thus pointing up the confusion that prevailed even in the house of economics.

Judicial insistence that particular business practices, other than price-fixing and output-limitation arrangements, were not illegal per se, but only when they foreclosed competitors from a substantial portion of the market, was reiterated in two important decisions in the early years of the decade. The first (*United States v. J. I. Case Company*, 1951) involved an exclusive dealing arrangement, the second (*Times-Picayune Publishing Company v. United States*, 1953) a tying agreement under which buyers of advertising space were required to insert their ads in both the morning and evening New Orleans papers owned by the Times-Picayune Publishing Company, the *Times-Picayune* and the *States*.

Antitrust enforcement, both public and private, awoke somewhat in the 1950's from a long period of comparative somnolence, particularly with respect to monopolization among the few. Nevertheless, bipartisan public antimonopoly enforcement still had to cope with annual appropriations (between $3.5 million and $4 million each for Justice and FTC in the late 1950's) that little more than kept pace with inflation, pressures on the Appropriations Committees of Congress to reduce antitrust appropriations,[15] inadequate staff, noncompetitive attorneys' salaries, paucity of economists, restrictions on the subpoena powers of the Attorney General, bottlenecks of court dockets, absence of injunctive relief, ineffectiveness of final dispensations under court decisions and consent decrees, and poor coordination of effort between the two agencies with enforcement power. More im-

15. "The Effects of Monopolistic and Quasi-monopolistic Practices," *Hearings before the Joint Economic Committee*, 86th Cong., 1st sess., September 22, 1959, pp. 2, 103.

portant were the ever-growing areas of *exclusion from the purview of antitrust* and the misguided enforcement policy, referred to above, involving *pure protection of existing enterprises* regardless of the contribution to either competition or long-run industrial efficiency represented by such enterprises. The latter policy reflected the same economic philosophy as that underlying the various small-business agencies of the Federal government and, indeed, the "family farm" program. In the last-named instance, at least, the policy redounded mainly to the benefit of the large firm.

Beyond these difficulties was the more basic one of distinguishing the legitimate, superior competitive power of the large and growing corporation from what was supposed to constitute monopolization. The failure of public policy to discover this distinction is largely traceable, on the legal and doctrinal level, to the almost insurmountable difficulty of determining the comparative roles of market structure, business behavior, and market performance in the generation of monopoly conditions. On the level of political power relationships, the control of monopoly may have been much vitiated by an underlying tendency to protect both monopoly and monopolistically competitive enterprise. Both represent influential political forces in a world of "countervailing power," the former by virtue of its wealth and economic importance, the latter because of its numerical preponderance. The prospect for successful solutions to the task of monopoly control was still rather bleak at the end of the decade, as major sections of the business system continued to exhibit a lack of effective, built-in limitations on the undue growth of private market power.

Small Enterprise

Small business has been one of the sectors long afforded special treatment by public policy. In the 1950's small business continued to be viewed as a disadvantaged group subject to unique competitive obstacles in the performance of its presumed role as a mainstay of free enterprise.

The definition of "small" in any quantitative way is unfortunately quite arbitrary. However, industrial organization theorists agree that small enterprise in the economy, outside agriculture and the professional services, is located chiefly in the sectors where the number of firms is large, such as retailing; the service trades; contract construction; and finance, insurance, and real estate. In the case of manufacturing the distinction between large and small firms has been the object of a great deal of theoretical study for many years.

The basic problems of the small firm stem either from lower efficiency or from its lack of market power vis-à-vis the large competitor, supplier, or customer. The latter deficiencies are amply illustrated in the discussion of small-enterprise difficulties in the various markets treated in the *Final Report* of the Select Committee on Small Business of the House of Representatives (1960), which provides a review of the Committee's activities during the decade.[16] The difficulties typically relate to such matters as price and quantity discrimination, weaknesses in antitrust enforcement by the appropriate Federal agencies and the courts, the nondiversified character of the small firm, the disadvantages of private food brands compared with nationally advertised brands, the unequal contest for shelf space in retail food stores and for shopping-center locations, loss-leader selling, discriminatory advertising allowances, deprivation of the power of independent decision-making at the retail marketing level in petroleum products and automobile accessories, and incapacity to participate in export markets.

Other important problem areas of major interest to the Select Committee during the decade were the perennial shortage of inexpensive short-term bank credit, intermediate credit, and long-term external capital disposal; the small business share of the military procurement, foreign aid and the Federal research-grant dollar; and the relation of taxes to small-firm growth.

Such a complex of interfirm market relationships between the large and the small concern, only a few of which are discussed in the *Final Report*, affords the best approach to a functional as distinguished from a merely quantitative definition of small enterprise. It also provides a proper focus for consideration of the small-business problem in the economy.

However, there had long been a tendency on the part of government agencies to exaggerate the "credit and capital problem" of small business and, indeed, to lend credence to the notion that this was the heart of the difficulties experienced by that group. Beginning with the studies by the New Deal's Temporary National Economic Committee, the credit and capital problem tended to become a political football. In the 1950's concern with this aspect continued unabated, although there did emerge a greater

16. 86th Cong., 2nd sess., House Report No. 2235 (Washington, D.C., U.S. Government Printing Office, December 27, 1960). Hereafter referred to as *Select Committee Report*.

appreciation of the more relevant matters relating to market power. The other new feature of the approach to this problem during the decade was the attempt to assure to the smaller enterprise a fair share of expenditures under the new regime of large peacetime Federal military budgets.

Federal government responsiveness to the small-business pressure group was registered not only in the bipartisan House Small Business Committee, created on a temporary basis in 1941 and reconstituted during each succeeding Congress. It was also represented in the creation of the United States Senate Select Committee on Small Business in 1950; the Cabinet Committee on Small Business in May, 1956; and the Small Business Administration (SBA), to absorb the remaining functions of the Reconstruction Finance Corporation and the Small Defense Plants Administration as a temporary organization in 1953 and as a permanent Federal agency in 1958. The last-named was, of course, a direct slap at the Department of Commerce, which was supposed to represent the interests of *all* business. The SBA was established "for the prime purpose of rendering aid and assistance to small business concerns, including financial, procurement and technical assistance." Note the emphasis. It was to be the "advocate for and spokesman of the small business community in its relations with the various departments of the Federal government; and should assist it in its attempts to secure adequate financing in order that it might attain and maintain an effective competitive position in our American economic system of private enterprise." [17] The last part of this statement of SBA purpose expresses the unashamed continuation, despite a quarter-century of experience with ineffective efforts to deal with the subordinately important credit and capital aspect, of a policy premised upon the misleading proposition that "adequate financing" could bear the brunt of the task of assuring to the small competitor an "effective competitive position."

As if to underscore the perpetuation of the historic emphasis on financing problems, Congress passed the Small Business Investment Act (SBIA) in August, 1958. The act provided for the licensing by the SBA of small-business investment companies to provide equity funds and long-term credit—the chief types of funds ordinarily not readily available—to small enterprises. The passage of this act was hailed by the subcommittee on SBA of the House Select Committee on Small Business as "one of the greatest opportunities to help small business in the history of our

17. *Ibid.*, p. 62.

country." [18] The subcommittee noted immediately thereafter, however, that the results had been most disappointing up to the beginning of 1960. The *Final Report* of the Select Committee as a whole, published in late 1960, was able to give the results of two years' experience under the SBIA. Although this was an admittedly short time in which to judge the effectiveness of a new agency, the gloomy and critical appraisal by the Select Committee [19] cannot be brushed aside, particularly in view of the long and dismal experience of other Federal government and Federal Reserve System attempts to open the channels of intermediate- and long-term funds to small business. The basic, nominal difficulty was always that small firms were, in the view of loan administrators, poor credit risks. Behind this essentially correct judgment was the unfortunate and abiding fact that small firms were often inefficient and typically lacked market power; they were therefore subject to high mortality rates ("really big firms never fail"), short life spans, low and unstable profit records, low current ratios, and weak liquidity.

In the sphere of military procurement, foreign aid, Federal grants for R & D, and the movement of household goods of military personnel, the Select Committee and the SBA were rather active in securing orders and funds for their (undefined) small-business charges. Despite this activity, however, the percentage of total Department of Defense procurement awarded to small business, on the Committee's own definition of "small," declined steadily from 25.3 in fiscal 1954 to 16.1 in 1960.[20] The Committee argued that the dominant system of procurement through negotiated contracts militated against the small firm, which it believed could do better under a system of secret, competitive bidding.[21] It was also pointed out that small firms under subcontract to a prime contractor, or even under direct procurement, were required to submit, either to the prime contractor or the Defense Department, complete proprietary data on products or techniques as well as trade secrets which they had designed,

18. "Organization and Operation of the Small Business Administration," *Report* of Sub-committee No. 1 on Organization and Operation of the Small Business Administration to the Select Committee on Small Business, House of Representatives, 86th Cong., 2nd sess., House Report No. 1252 (Washington, D.C., U.S. Government Printing Office, 1960), pp. 2–3.

19. *Select Committee Report,* pp. 86–91 *passim.*

20. *Ibid.,* p. 129.

21. *Ibid.,* pp. 130–131.

developed, or otherwise acquired.[22] In the matter of allocating Federal R & D funds, some 85 per cent of which was dispensed by the Defense Department in the late 1950's, "small business" received on the average about 4 per cent. On a monthly basis, the highest percentage received between October, 1957, and June, 1960, was 8.5, in April, 1958. The Committee further pointed out that, of approximately $37.6 billion spent for foreign aid under the mutual security program over a ten-year period, about $28.7 billion was spent directly within the United States, and that the small business potential in this area was not being fully utilized.[23]

In regard to taxation and the growth of small enterprises, the House Ways and Means Committee pointed out that the peculiar difficulties of small and medium firms in securing external funds, particularly on long-term, necessitated greater reliance on internal sources than was the case with large corporations.[24] From this fact the chief conclusion regarding taxation was that the tax laws should provide for depreciation on a replacement-cost basis and for greater earnings-retention in the case of smaller firms in order to leave them more internal funds, to be provided, on the "plow-back principle," by a tax deduction allowed small firms for re-invested profits.

As the decade drew to a close it was apparent that the historically subordinate market status of small enterprise had been but little changed during the 1950's. Traditional forces making for survival and short life spans continued to obtain.[25]

22. *Ibid.*, pp. 131–132.

23. *Ibid.*, p. 143.

24. House Report No. 2198, 85th Cong., July 16, 1958. Cited in *Select Committee Report*, p. 151.

25. For a summary statement of these, see Joseph D. Phillips, *Little Business in the American Economy*, Illinois Studies in the Social Sciences, Vol. 42 (Urbana, University of Illinois Press, 1958), pp. 60–66.

8 | Labor and Agriculture in the Mixed Economy

Economic Change and the Worker

The Underwritten Economy

The publicly underwritten economy afforded business a new measure of market security through the elimination of major depressions. Similarly for labor, the absence of mass unemployment, together with the national commitment embodied in the Employment Act and backed up by labor itself, created for all but a small percentage of the labor force a kind of security such as had never before been experienced in the history of industrial capitalism. Security from cyclical mass unemployment must be counted as one of the great human achievements of the American economy in the 1950's, however much grumbling took place about the alleged costs in terms of inflation, government planning, etc.

It is true that military spending connected with the cold war was a major prop of the underwritten economy and involved a waste of resources unknown before in peacetime. Nevertheless, the experience did reveal that the scourge of cyclical mass unemployment could be dispelled by sufficient public spending of almost any kind.

Labor Force Shifts

Aside from the public-budget basis of the cyclically moderated economy, there was a direct public employment aspect. Table

2-2 shows an increase in state and local government employment of over 2 million from 1950 to 1960. This 52 per cent rise in cyclically insulated employment carried state and local government employment to the point in 1960 at which it accounted for 12 per cent of the total number of wage and salary workers in nonagricultural establishments. Civilian government employment at all levels was 16 per cent of the 1960 total of civilian employees in nonagricultural establishments—a substantial proportion of the labor force to be cyclically immune (to mild recessions at least).

The shift to government employment, associated with the underwritten economy, calls to mind the corollary relative employment decline in the cyclically sensitive lines. There are two temporal aspects to this decline: the trend for the whole decade and the slackening during the years of slowed growth after 1956. For the whole decade, production employment in manufacturing plus total employment in mining, contract construction, and interstate railroads (not shown in Table 2-2) together rose slightly in absolute terms but fell relative to total nonagricultural employment. For the period of slowed growth, these lines taken together fell both absolutely and relatively. The absolute decline was almost 1.5 million—a reduction in cyclically unstable types of employment at the cost of declining growth.

At some point during the mid-1950's, the number of persons engaged in goods-producing activities fell below 50 per cent of the civilian labor force. Although this historic change was also hastened by the growth difficulties in the goods sectors as well as by the big expansion in state and local government employment, there can be little doubt that the secular trend had moved in that direction.

The implications of this complex of trends within the labor force went beyond the matter of added security for labor against the vicissitudes of severe cyclical unemployment. Another development was the increasing difficulty of organizing labor into unions. Historically, workers in the goods-producing industries (except agriculture) and in transport had been much easier to organize than those in the service lines. Toward the end of the decade, well over three fourths of all union members were in manufacturing, mining, construction, and transportation industries. The difficulty of organizing other lines may have been due partly to the smaller scale of enterprise, partly to the high concentration of women in service occupations, partly to a middle-class, white-collar aversion to unionization, as well as other factors. Certainly the white-collar group had traditionally been more difficult to organize; and white-collar employment rose about 27 per cent during 1950–60, while total nonagricultural employment increased some 17 per cent.[1]

The Wage Earner in the Abundant Economy

One benchmark of the economy in the 1950's that has been repeatedly stressed was the elimination of poverty for the great bulk of Americans. Although available data unfortunately are not always segregated to isolate the wage earner from the salary- or property-income receiver, leaving much to inference, it seems clear that the income and the material consumption of wage earners rose moderately during the 1950's. Average real weekly earnings (1960 prices) in the highly unionized manufacturing industries, for example, rose in the case of a worker with three dependents from $70.37 in 1950 to $77.76 in 1955 and increased again to $81.50 in 1959, after making deductions for social security and income taxes.[2] This represented a 16 per cent increase in spendable weekly earnings for the decade, most of it being concentrated in the first half. Increases in other industries varied, of course. On the basis of gross undeflated weekly-earnings data, the rise in manufacturing wages may be compared with the relatively unorganized wholesale trade, where the increase was roughly equivalent, and with the similarly unorganized retail trades, in which the rise was rather less. The increase in building construction was notably greater than in all manufacturing.

The decade also witnessed a noteworthy reduction in the proportion of the population occupying a low income status (a "low income" person, according to one study by Robert Lampman for the Joint Economic Committee, being one with an income equivalent to that of a member of a four-person family with total money income of not more than $2,500 in 1957 dollars), from 26 per cent in 1947 to 19 per cent in 1957.[3]

The contribution of social welfare programs to the community's income, the bulk of the benefits from which programs accrued to wage earners, was increased during the 1950's. This has been emphasized in part in connection with the earlier discus-

1. *Illinois Business Review*, March, 1961, p. 91.
2. *Economic Report of the President*, January, 1961, p. 158, Table C-27.
3. Robert J. Lampman, *The Low Income Population and Economic Growth*, Study Paper No. 12, Materials Prepared in Connection with the Study of Employment, Growth and Price Levels, Joint Economic Committee, 86th Cong., 1st sess. (Washington, D.C., U.S. Government Printing Office, December 16, 1959), p. 4.

sion of the growth of transfer payments. Public social welfare expenditures of all types, but excluding educational outlays, rose from $16.6 billion in 1950 to $32.9 billion in 1959. Rather over half the latter figure was under social insurance programs that expanded to an important extent because of labor's pressure.

The improvement in material consumption of wage-earner families must generally be discovered by inference. It has already been shown that the proportion of all families possessing electrical appliances in the home increased so sharply that families in the labor stratum without doubt participated importantly in this index of material well-being. Automobile ownership among wage earners was apparently not as widespread as ownership of most appliances, however. Of some 57 million spending units in the country in 1959, about 71 per cent owned at least one car. A study referring to the year 1956, when 70 per cent of all spending units owned (or were buying) a car, showed that 85 per cent of the heads of spending units among the skilled and semiskilled owned at least one car. However, 67 per cent of the heads of spending units in clerical and sales occupations, and only 47 per cent in unskilled and service occupations, owned one car or more.[4] In addition, wage earners more often bought used rather than new cars.

The construction of over a million dwelling units each year was in excess of the number of new households and therefore substantially reduced the backlog of need inherited from the years of depression and war. However, for the 39-year period between 1920 and 1959 there was a net shortage of approximately 1.5 million new nonfarm dwelling units relative to the number of new nonfarm households formed.[5] The economy's housing stock at the end of the decade was about 57 million units, or rather more than 50 times the annual new additions during the 1950's. It may be deduced that approximately one fourth of the nation's stock had been built during the decade. The Census' *1956 National Housing Inventory* reported that 54 per cent of the dwelling units in the country had been built in 1929 or earlier. Because of the very low levels of construction in the 1930's and 1940's, the age distribution of the nation's housing plant was bimodal, with substantial proportions in each of the very old and the very new categories.

4. U.S. Department of Labor, Bureau of Labor Statistics, *Economic Forces in the U.S.A. in Facts and Figures*, 6th edn. (Washington, D.C., U.S. Government Printing Office, May, 1960), p. 95.

5. *Ibid.*, p. 93.

The metropolitan configuration of housing ages was significant of levels of living inside and outside the central portions of large cities. The *Housing Inventory* revealed that only 37.4 per cent of the dwelling units had been built in 1929 or before in places within standard metropolitan areas that were outside the central cities, but that 68.8 per cent had been built in 1929 or before in places that were inside the central cities. Correspondingly, the newer units were concentrated outside the core city of the typical metropolis.

Home ownership increased quite dramatically during the decade, as shown in Chart XII. In early 1959, 58 per cent of all nonfarm families owned outright or were buying the house they occupied (excluding 400,000 owner-occupied trailers), 56 per cent of those owner-occupied dwellings being under mortgage. This meant that there were 12.8 million nonmortgaged, owner-occupied houses out of the approximately 57 million dwelling units. As would be expected, the incidence of home ownership was distinctly smaller among wage earners, only about 40 per cent of families with pretax annual incomes of less than $4,000 owning their homes.

On a per capita basis, the apparent civilian consumption of major foods changed but little during the decade. A number of nutritional indexes, calculated on a per capita basis, suggest some slight deterioration when 1950 is compared with figures for 1959. Cases in point are the drop in dairy products from 29.4 to 25.6 pounds per year, the drop in fresh fruits from 107.4 to 101.5 pounds, and the drop in fresh vegetables from 139.5 pounds to 125.2 pounds. However, there were offsetting increases in meats, processed fruits and fresh frozen vegetables, so that on balance the per capita figures lead to no clear conclusion one way or the other.

The physical health of the total population appears to have improved moderately. Life expectancy at birth rose for both sexes from 68.2 years to 69.7 years between 1950 and 1959. For whites of both sexes it climbed from 69.1 to 70.5; and for nonwhites slightly more—from 60.8 years to 63.5 years for both sexes. The death rate declined from 9.6 in 1950 to 9.4 per 1,000 in 1959. Infant deaths per 1,000 live births fell slightly, from 29.2 in 1950 to 26.3 in 1959. In some areas of disease, such as heart disease and cancer, little progress was made; in others, such as acute poliomyelitis, diphtheria, tuberculosis, typhoid fever, pertussis, and the venereal diseases, substantial advances were recorded during the decade. The number of physicians per 100,000 of population

Chart XII. Housing Status: Number of Nonfarm Spending Units, Selected Years

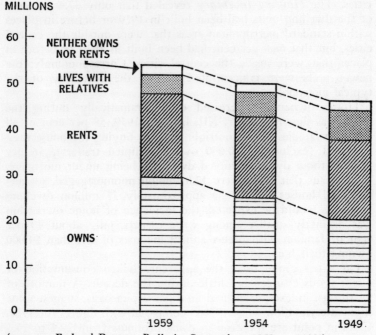

(SOURCE: *Federal Reserve Bulletin*, September, 1959, p. 1103.)

was practically constant at 133.

Yet one of the striking aspects of the diffusion of well-being was the fact that substantial poverty continued to exist. General affluence had by no means solved the distributive problem. The Joint Economic Committee's study of the low income population, for example, revealed that 32.2 million persons, or almost one in five among all persons, suffered low income status in the generally prosperous year 1957. Who were these people? About 8 million of them were 65 years of age or older, 6.4 million were nonwhite, 8 million were in consumer units headed by women, and about 21 million were in households headed by persons with an eighth-grade education or less. Other characteristics were farm residence and nonemployment. About one fourth of all low income persons were farm residents. Regionally, the group was unduly concentrated in the South, which, while accounting for one third of the nation's population, held 39 per cent of the low income population.

The reduction in the numbers of low income people between 1947 and 1957 was attributed in the aforementioned study for the Joint Economic Committee to the declining incidence of low income in most occupations, the greater-than-proportional growth of employment in higher-paying occupations, the out-migration from farming, and the increase in number of workers per family. It was concluded that the poverty of this low income group would not yield to general economic growth in the future to the degree it has in the past and that special measures would have to be taken to erase modern poverty. Economic growth in the 1950's expanded the proportion of persons in the upper income groups more rapidly than it reduced the proportion in the lowest income bracket.

The low income population was not the only group significantly deprived of the fruits of an abundant economy. Between those at the poverty level and those living in comparative comfort were the millions located in the minimum comfort range. An appreciation of the distribution within the lower rungs of the income ladder for selected wage-earner occupations in 1958 is shown in Table 8-1. For comparative purposes it may be noted

TABLE 8-1

Percentage of Total Spending Units Within Selected
Wage Earner Groups (Pretax Money Income, 1958)

Occupation of head of spending unit	Under $1,000	$1,000– $1,999	$2,000– $2,999	$3,000– $3,999	$4,000– $4,999	$5,000 and over
Clerical and sales	2	6	9	15	16	52
Skilled	1	2	6	10	11	70
Semiskilled	2	6	14	16	22	40
Unskilled and service	10	23	20	16	14	17
Item						
Farm operator	10	23	19	12	11	25
Retired	25	34	16	9	5	11

SOURCE: *Federal Reserve Bulletin*, July, 1959, p. 713, Supplementary Table 2.

that the median income for all spending units was $4,400 and the mean income $5,150. It has been said that "labor has no reservation price." The extent to which this may or may not have continued to be true in the 1950's is intimated by the fact that in early 1959 one fourth of all spending units had no liquid assets, 73 per cent had no United States savings bonds, 50 per cent had no savings accounts, and 45 per cent had no checking accounts.

The level of living involves effort expended as well as satisfaction received. For example, it is important to know that the average hours worked per week in industry, aside from cyclical fluctuations (notably in manufacturing), showed no trend during the decade. The quality of an hour's work with respect to such a thing as the intensity of labor probably changed little, but this is almost impossible to estimate. Injury-frequency rates in all manufacturing and in contract construction, taking 1950 as a base, seem to have declined slightly until mid-decade.[6] Multiple job-holding, which may be taken in general as a rough measure of undue labor effort to maintain a target plane of living, affected only a modest per cent of the labor force; and Labor Department statistics on this phenomenon were for the first time being collected toward the end of the decade. The increase in women workers indicated more clearly a high proportion of cases of the extension of input effort by the family in order to achieve a minimum comfort level of living: the lower the husband's income, the more probable that the wife would be working. One of the great disutilities suffered by wage earners along with others was the enormous amount of commuting to and from work—not a new phenomenon, but one which was aggravated by the spreading urban sprawl with its attendant separation of worker residence from place of work.

It must be remembered that many millions of workers, for reasons of layoff, sickness, or other disability, did not work the year round. In the year 1956, which was among the least affected by recession and only moderately affected by industrial stoppages, about 10,000,000 men, or one out of four in the 25- to 64-year age group, were either part-time or part-year workers or were unemployed.[7] In the same year of high employment a New York survey revealed that, in the $2,000 to $3,000 income bracket, one in ten received unemployment compensation benefits at one time or another.[8] In the relatively prosperous year 1957, slightly over one fourth of all employee spending units were employed less than a full year. Thus part-time employment and temporary

6. *Statistical Abstract*, 1960, pp. 232, 233.

7. Eleanor M. Snyder, "Low Income in Urban Areas," *American Economic Review*, May, 1960, p. 245.

8. *Ibid.*, p. 248.

layoffs seriously qualified the generally favorable condition of employment security obtaining during the decade.

Labor's Response to Inflation

Organized labor had pursued its economic goals within the framework of a more or less constant or falling consumer price level for almost two decades, from the recovery of the early 1920's to the onset of World War II. With the new and dramatic price rises thereafter, labor was faced with a powerful and potentially destructive attack upon its plane of living. The response to this attack explains much of the history of industrial disputes and their resolution from 1940 to 1960.

In referring to Table 8-2 on average weekly spendable earnings, it is assumed that worker experience in manufacturing was generally decisive with respect to labor's behavior, and that real take-home weekly earnings were for labor the most important guide to action. It will be observed from the table that in both current and real terms the average worker was able during World War II to improve his position substantially by virtue of a 70 per cent increase in this current weekly earnings (1940–44), an important though minor portion of which was due to an extension of the workweek by about five hours.

With the war's termination in 1945, the worker was faced with a drastic rise in the cost of living, as the table shows, coupled with a sharp reduction in average hours worked per week from over 45 in 1944 to slightly over 40 two years later. Consideration of the reduction in hours leads to the conclusion that the rise in average hourly earnings from $1.02 to $1.24 between 1944 and 1947 afforded insubstantial protection against the overwhelmingly demand-induced inflation of the period.

During the years of great industrial strife, when the postwar patterns of collective bargaining settlements were being hammered out, the real spendable take-home pay was almost stagnant at levels substantially below the wartime peak of 1944. Indeed, the manufacturing worker, who had to confront the immediate postwar and Korean inflations, together with a continually larger bite for Federal income and social security taxes (and with hours steady after 1946), made little headway in the years at the threshold of the decade. Nor did he overtake his wartime real take-home earnings—input effort aside—until 1955. Thereafter, in the years of the famed seller's inflation and slow economic growth, he edged gradually upward from his 1944 real-earnings position. If 1946, the year when hours became stabilized, is taken as a

TABLE 8-2

Consumer Prices and Average Weekly Earnings of
Production Workers in Manufacturing Industries,
Selected Years, 1939–59

| Year | Consumer price index (1947–49 = 100) | Net spendable weekly earnings,* worker with three dependents | |
		Current dollars	1947–49 dollars
1939	59.4	$23.62	$39.76
1940	59.9	24.95	41.65
1942	69.7	36.28	52.05
1944	75.2	44.06	58.59
1945	76.9	42.74	55.58
1946	83.4	43.20	51.80
1947	95.5	48.24	50.51
1948	102.8	53.17	51.72
1949	101.8	53.83	52.88
1950	102.8	57.21	55.65
1951	111.0	61.28	55.21
1952	113.5	63.62	56.05
1953	114.4	66.58	58.20
1954	114.8	66.78	58.17
1955	114.5	70.45	61.53
1956	116.2	73.22	63.01
1957	120.2	74.97	62.37
1958	123.5	76.05	61.58
1959	124.6	80.36	64.49
Per cent rise,			
1939–59	110	240	62
1950–59	21	41	16

* Gross earnings minus social security and Federal income taxes.
SOURCE: U.S. Department of Labor, *Economic Forces in the U.S.A.*, 6th
edn., pp. 73, 80; and *Statistical Abstract*, 1960, p. 336.

base, real full-time spendable weekly earnings, ignoring fringe
benefits, had risen about 25 per cent in the thirteen years ending
in 1959. Most of this had already been achieved when these earnings stood at $63.01 in 1956, on the eve of the seller's inflation
period.

The achievement was no doubt moderately satisfying to labor,
but was certainly not breathtaking for an economy as potentially
productive as the American. Furthermore, it was surely a neces-

sary achievement if aggregate consumption was to rise at a rate sufficient to assure a satisfactory overall growth—a frequently overlooked requisite.

The immediate postwar years of inflation and comparative stagnation in real take-home earnings were notable for their great industrial strife, for several "rounds" of wage boosts designed to keep up with inflation, and for the formation of the chief elements in labor's collective bargaining policies during the whole postwar era.

1946 was a memorable year: the year of passage of the Employment Act (which committed the government to promote maximum *purchasing power* as well as employment and production), of the termination of all wartime wage and salary controls, of the first big breakthrough in the wartime price dike, and of 116,000,000 man-days of strike idleness—the peak for the postwar era in terms of strike idleness relative to total working time (1.43 per cent). Strike actions in that year (and in late 1945) ushered in several years of vigorous action designed in the main to deal with inflation. Of the ten leading idleness-producing disputes during the whole period 1947–59, no less than six occurred in the first four years of the period. These were comparatively widespread among industries: coal, steel, telephone, auto, and meatpacking. It is noteworthy that of the other four disputes, occurring over the nine remaining years of the period, three were in the steel industry. (There were big strikes in the auto industry throughout the 1950's, but since disputes were usually with particular companies, rather than industrywide, their magnitude was less than those in steel.)

During the period of greatest labor action, 1946–50, the negotiated agreements initiated the major new and significant features found in labor-management contracts during the ensuing decade. In this period also there was established, beginning about the time of the widespread acceptance of the steel industry's "first-round" wage settlement, the practice of *pattern settlements*, whereby wage agreements in certain big industries, such as auto and electrical manufactures, were copied in other industries.

The link between wage adjustments and the cost-of-living index, to which labor had historically been opposed, had been established at least as early as 1942, when the National War Labor Board handed down the "Little Steel Formula" for wartime wage adjustments, based at that time on a 15 per cent rise in living costs from January 1, 1941, to May 1, 1942. The formula was later flexibly extended to other industries.

Wage escalation in terms of the consumer price index was provided for in most of the leading contracts beginning in the immediate postwar years. Long-term contracts were often "reopened" (periodically, automatically, or optionally) before termination in order to allow wage renegotiation to keep pace with rising prices. Many contracts provided for semiannual escalation. Suspicion that inflation was a permanent mode of life was evinced when the historic five-year United Auto Workers (UAW)-General Motors contract of 1950 was reopened in 1953, and 19 cents of the 26-cent cost-of-living adjustment was transferred to the base straight-time wage rate.

The United Steelworkers union clung longer than other leading unions to the notion inherited from the era of the old-fashioned business cycle that it was against labor's interest to tie wages to price changes, including possible declines. It was not until the 1956 contract in steel that the union was willing to bow to the presumption of permanent inflation and incorporate escalation into its three-year agreement. The presumption and the decision in this case also turned out to be correct: escalation added 17 cents to steel hourly wages during the life of that agreement (the union's first long-term contract of the decade).

The rise in the long-term contract, it was variously hypothesized, reflected the maturation of bargaining procedures, the growth of a sense of mutual interest between management and labor, and a new-found confidence in economic stability.

During World War II the War Labor Board had also fostered a private version of the more advanced European institution of "social charges"—pensions, paid vacations and holidays, sickness and hospitalization benefits, supplementary unemployment insurance—mostly paid by employees in this country. These "fringe benefits" were a response to inflation in two ways: first, they were initially a means of circumventing the wartime wage freeze to allow some compensation for inflation without seeming to contribute to it; second, the average OASI benefits and unemployment compensation payments were seriously lagging, and in the 1950's continued to lag, behind the cost-of-living increase. Hence pensions, health insurance, and supplementary unemployment income came about, not as in Europe in the form of public expenditures to implement the welfare programs of Social Democratic parties, but mainly as a typically pragmatic response to the immediate pressures of current and anticipated inflation. The proportion of average hourly labor costs represented by social charges in the 1950's was much higher in a number of leading

European countries (e.g., Germany, Belgium, France, Italy) than in the United States.

An additional component of collective bargaining contracts, by no means entirely new but becoming widespread in the 1950's, was the so-called annual improvement factor, which attempted to transfer to the wage earner each year a portion of the gains from improved productivity. A milestone in the development of this practice was reached in the two-year agreement negotiated in 1948 between the UAW and General Motors. This was the first agreement of significance to establish a definite formula relating wage increases to general productivity increases.[9] The settlement waived all wage-determining factors other than productivity and the cost of living. The annual improvement factor was again incorporated in the 1950 agreement, and the rate raised from 3 cents to 4 cents an hour.

It is not so easy to assert that incorporation of the productivity increment into labor-management contracts was overwhelmingly a response to inflation. Certainly this practice represented in part the substitution of a collective approach for the traditional employer policy of linking wages to the performance of the individual worker or shop unit. However, inflation did enter into the matter. Insofar as productivity gains were not transferred to the suppliers of a particular industry in the form of higher prices (an unlikely case), or to buyers in the form of lower prices, the annual-improvement productivity formula, through its capacity to shift relative prices in a partly administered price economy, could both generate inflation and redistribute its incidence. This effect would depend, *ceteris paribus*, on the actual productivity increase, the wage formula, and the property income share as incorporated into price.

The notion of a "package settlement" that combined a cost-of-living adjustment with so many cents per hour for fringe benefits, to which there was ever more frequently added a separate productivity increment, also gained a secure foothold during the immediate postwar years. All three features, plus linkage of pensions with OASI, were contained in the famous 1950 UAW-General Motors settlement previously mentioned. Another such prominent post-strike settlement was that of the steel industry with the United Steelworkers (CIO) in 1949, which provided for noncontributory $100-monthly pensions at age 65, plus certain death,

9. U.S. Department of Labor, *A Guide to Labor-Management Relations in the United States*, Bulletin No. 1225 (Washington, D.C., U.S. Government Printing Office, March, 1958), Chap. 2:06, pp. 4–5.

sickness, and accident benefits.[10]

It may be concluded that the outstanding new and widely used features of collective bargaining in the 1950's—escalation, fringe benefits, package settlements, contract reopening arrangements, pattern settlements, the annual improvement adjustment, and the long-term contract—were already firmly established at the beginning of the decade. All but the last can be seen as direct or indirect responses to the threat posed by inflation.

This is not to say that other causes were inoperative. It cannot be doubted, for example, that the fringe-benefit movement reflected a steadily expanding drive, characterizing all social strata, for greater income security. Indeed, this motivation was unquestionably primary in the emergence in the early 1950's of the demand by the CIO and many AFL unions for a guaranteed annual wage and subsequently for its sibling, salary status rather than hourly rates for production workers.

The concern with inflation meant not only that labor had a stake in public anti-inflation policies, but also that labor had a responsibility, in whatever bargaining posture it assumed, not to contribute to cost-push by inordinate wage demands in the pattern-setting negotiation centers. A further implication that engaged public attention during the decade was that joint wage-price administration in such negotiation centers (e.g., steel) needed to consider the impact of settlements upon the general price level. The public-interest aspect of this matter was pinpointed when, in connection with the 1959 steel strike, the companies built their public case against wage increases around the proposition that such increases would be inflationary (which the union denied). In the end, of course, both management and labor were advertising the fact that their dispute was affected with a public interest. But management had the most to "lose" because it was the companies that kept the books. In the historic battle of the books the business position had always been that books of account were a private affair (although with the establishment of the income tax, considerable ground had been yielded to the Internal Revenue Service).

Labor's concern with inflation extended beyond the confines of direct labor-management relations. Labor was active in bringing the lagging levels of social security payments and Federal and state minimum wages into line with the rising price index.

10. U.S. Department of Labor, *Brief History of the American Labor Movement*, Bulletin No. 1,000, 1957 revision (Washington, D.C., U.S. Government Printing Office, 1957), p. 78.

Noteworthy progress in these realms was made in the course of the decade. Along with the steady extensions of OASI coverage through the decade, which began in 1951 as a result of the 1950 amendments to the Social Security Act, the average monthly benefit was raised (taxes, too) from $26.00 in 1949 to $72.78 in 1959. The rise in average monthly benefits was of course partly due to higher income received by workers. Under the unemployment insurance program the average weekly payment increased much more modestly, from $20.48 to $30.41 over the same period, leaving the ratio of such payments to the average weekly wage about constant at approximately 35 per cent. It is interesting to note that long-term unemployment in 1957–58 became such a drain on state reserves that the Federal government had to extend loans to the states to lengthen the duration of payments made to workers.

The Federal minimum hourly wage was also "escalated" to 75 cents in 1949 and $1.00 in 1955, where it remained until 1961, at which time it was again raised, to $1.15. The poor showing of the minimum wage rise was matched by a secular decline in the proportion of all workers in interstate commerce who were covered by minimum wage legislation as the changing composition of the labor force moved workers from manufacturing, where about 95 per cent of the employed were covered, to services, where only about 17 per cent were covered. The Kennedy administration moved not only to raise the minimum wage, but also to extend coverage to about 8,000,000 additional workers.

Accelerated Technological Change

"Automation" accentuated the importance of not only the distribution of increased productivity gains, as reflected in the annual improvement factor, but also the time-honored problem of technological unemployment. In the context of rapid growth this problem is more easily handled, but when growth slows, as it did in the later 1950's, all the difficulties of re-employment and retraining are magnified. On the other hand, the guarantee of maximum employment, the absence of severe depressions, and the existence of unemployment insurance tended to decrease to some extent the human problems associated with displacement, dispel the fear of automatic techniques, and limit the practice of inflating the number of workers required to do a job.

During the 116-day steel strike of 1959 over the issues of first wages and then union participation in the establishment of work rules, the small Kaiser Steel Corporation had broken ranks and signed a separate agreement which acknowledged that the impact of technological change was a matter of joint interest. The contract set up a joint labor-management committee to deal with automation in relation to the job and to "settle problems in these areas by mutual agreement." It also set up a precedent-breaking tripartite committee of experts, including one-third representation from outside labor or management, to "develop a long-range plan for the equitable sharing of economic progress."

The steel industry was not alone in being affected by newer approaches to technological displacement. Longshoring was undergoing one of the most rapid technological revolutions of any industry in the entire economy in recent times. At the decade's end this industry shattered precedent with an agreement that provided for payment by the employers' Pacific Maritime Association of $5 million annually for five years into a fund to supplement wage payments for work opportunities lost by increased mechanization. All presently registered longshoremen and clerks (minus normal labor attrition) were to be covered. In effect, therefore, the contract assured an annual wage for the existing labor force and acknowledged a partial property right of the worker in his job.[11] The practice of endowing the job with certain property rights appears to have made considerable headway during the decade.

The Growth Rate

It became abundantly clear during the decade that labor as a whole had acquired an enormous stake in a high growth rate. It was noted by most informed persons, not the least of whom was President Kennedy's Secretary of Labor Goldberg, that the slow growth rate in the years 1956–60 aggravated the problems of reabsorption of both the technologically displaced and the annual increments to the labor force. If the technologically displaced held the spotlight in the 1950's, both they and the new entrants in the labor force would increasingly press for expanded employment opportunities in the 1960's.

During the 1950's the low birth rate of the depression years operated to hold down the annual additions to the labor force. But the 1960's would require even more reductions in the standard retirement age, more increases in the military forces, more enrollment in higher educational institutions, and other measures

11. William Gomberg, "The Job as Property," *The Nation*, November 26, 1960, p. 411.

to arrest the flood destined to swamp the labor markets in that decade.

The Public Interest in Private Decisions

It has been indicated frequently in the preceding discussion that the 1950's stood out as a decade in which what were formerly often thought to be private matters took on a public complexion. This process clearly occurred in the case of both union policy and labor-management relations.

The 1950's was a cold-war decade. The nation's military posture presupposed a continuous flow of goods and services from all corners of the economy to the military establishment. As in the past American employers rarely used or needed to use the lockout, but rather could readily maneuver labor into employing its "ultimate weapon," the strike. Big labor was therefore in the unenviable position of taking actions that seemed to undermine the nation's preparedness. A continuous national-emergency aspect was added to the long-established national health, safety, and interest principle. This imparted to labor's actions a heightened public character such as had become increasingly attached to the private decisions of all large organizations. (The national emergency provisions of the Taft-Hartley Act of 1947 were invoked seventeen times by the President in the years 1947–59.)

Consequently, the right to strike went the way of other traditionally private rights and more and more came to be hedged around with governmental restrictions and interventions. The government became the invisible participant on the negotiating committees at the very outset of every major industrial dispute —indeed, at the time of filing an intent to open negotiations.

Intervention at the Federal level was implemented by two major pieces of legislation, the Labor-Management Relations (Taft-Hartley) Act of 1947, and the Labor-Management Reporting and Disclosure (Landrum-Griffin) Act of 1959.

The passage of the Taft-Hartley Act may be interpreted as marking the termination of the short life span of what Joseph Schumpeter called the "labourist capitalism" of the New Deal period. The Act provided the basic legislative framework for labor-management relations in the 1950's. Its content was essentially restrictive with respect to union organization and liberal with respect to the latitude of the individual worker, whether union, nonunion, or anti-union. It also emphasized the rights of the public in connection with industrial disputes, placing special restrictions on strikes that might be viewed as creating a national emergency or imperiling national health or safety. The procedure for dealing with such disputes allowed for a Federal injunction to arrest the proposed or actual stoppage. This would be followed by a sixty-day "cooling off" period marked by the intervention of the Federal Mediation and Conciliation Service; a fifteen-day period of voting on the employer's final offer; and a five-day period for the National Labor Relations Board (NLRB), which administered the act, to certify the voting results. The injunction might then be lifted. If the dispute were still not settled, the President could report to Congress with recommendations for appropriate action.

The Taft-Hartley Act prohibited the closed shop (under which an employer may hire only union members and retain only union members in good standing), a time-honored labor union objective; however, the union shop (all employees must become union members within a specified time) was not prohibited. (The act originally prohibited the union shop unless a majority of all employees in the *bargaining unit*—to be determined by the NLRB—voted for it. However, workers favored the union shop in such an overwhelming proportion of the elections that the provision was later repealed.) Most secondary boycotts and jurisdictional strikes were prohibited. Many "unfair labor practices" were prohibited. A sixty-day notice was required of intent to change or terminate a union agreement.

Every union official was required by the Taft-Hartley Act to file an affidavit certifying that he was not affiliated with the Communist Party or a supporter of any subversive group.

The Taft-Hartley Act was accompanied by a wave of restrictive state laws, including the so-called "right-to-work" laws tending to favor the nonunion worker. By the end of the 1950's there were right-to-work laws in eighteen states (chiefly agricultural states). Many states had adopted the "cooling off" principle. About one third prohibited sitdown, sympathy, or jurisdictional strikes; restricted picketing; and required filing of union financial statements and other reports similar to the Taft-Hartley requirements. One potentially significant reaction to the legal attack on the union shop in states having right-to-work laws was the formation, largely through union initiative, of "agency shops" in such states. Under this arrangement, nonunion workers in plants where union-membership requirements were prohibited might be represented by the union. For such representation and for administration of the contract with management, nonmembers paid to the union in lieu of dues an agency fee, or "union-service charge," usually through the check-off plan of collection by the employer.

It is significant for understanding the legal context of industrial relations in the 1950's that the assertion of the public interest in labor unions expressed in the Taft-Hartley Act was coupled with the launching of a purposely restrictive regulatory policy, which set the tone for government intervention in the ensuing decade. Associated therewith was a reduction in the legal status of unions, for the Taft-Hartley Act brought about the demise of the common-law conception that a labor union was a private voluntary association of individuals the actions of whose members were rarely subject to court review.[12]

The history of labor legislation in the decade closed with the passage of the Landrum-Griffin Act. The environmental background for this law was prepared in substantial part during the years 1957–59 by the publicity attendant upon the hearings before a special Senate committee, under John L. McClellan of Arkansas, empowered to investigate corruption and other "improper activities" in the labor and management fields.

Although the Landrum-Griffin Act strengthened many of the provisions of the Taft-Hartley Act, it was on the whole not as inhibitive of union latitude as the latter. The main impact of the new law was to embroil the Secretary of Labor, the Federal courts, and the NLRB ever more deeply in the internal affairs of the unions. The central theme of the act was the laudatory one of protecting the individual union member vis-à-vis the organization and its officers. Internal democracy and adequate financial reporting were to be assured through government action. The technicalities involved in the implementation of the act could multiply litigation, investigation, examination, negotiation, and supervisory activity to heretofore undreamed-of proportions. However, Labor Secretary Arthur Goldberg reported that for fiscal 1960–61, of 5,800 alleged violations, actual violations numbered 1,915, of which 98 per cent were "corrected voluntarily," a modest 33 cases having required legal action.

With the Landrum-Griffin Act, labor unions became quasi-public organizations. The process went far beyond governmental intrusion into the framework of collective bargaining. It is true that government participation did not, even with the 1959 act, develop to the point that it did in some leading European coun-

12. See in this connection L. Reed Tripp, *Labor Problems and Processes* (New York: Harper, 1961), p. 240.

tries, but it did proceed to an advanced stage in terms of American traditions.

The Labor Movement

Union Membership

The period of great growth in union membership occurred prior to the 1950's. There were two great waves of union organization, the first during the New Deal and the second during World War II. Thereafter, as Chart XIII shows, the trend of

Chart XIII. Labor Union Membership

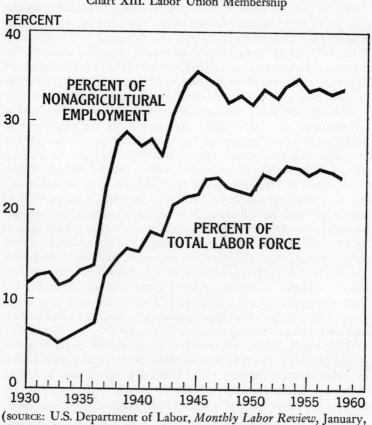

(SOURCE: U.S. Department of Labor, *Monthly Labor Review*, January, 1960, p. 4.)

union membership was roughly stationary, particularly with respect to the strategic percentage of nonagricultural employment. Union members accounted for about one third of this category and about one fourth of the total labor force. The number fluctuated around 14.3 million from 1945 to 1950. The Korean War period was again one of increased union membership, although the rise was moderate, reaching approximately 17 million in 1953. Thereafter the total was changed but little, except for a decline from 1956 to 1958 amounting to about 575,000 (Canadian members excluded). The greater part of this was accounted for by AFL-CIO attrition of some 400,000. About two in every three manufacturing production workers in continental United States were union members in the late 1950's, almost one half of whom lived in four states—New York, California, Ohio, and Illinois. The AFL membership in all areas was 7,143,000 in 1950, and the CIO about 5,000,000. By the time of the merger in December, 1955, the combined membership was over 16,000,000. The merger attracted a number of formerly unaffiliated unions to the new organization; however, expulsion of the Teamsters (the nation's largest union), the Bakery Workers, and the Laundry Workers by the December, 1957, AFL-CIO convention reduced the membership by about 1,600,000. Independent or unaffiliated union members in 1958 totaled rather more than 3,000,000, including the 1957 expellees, the railroad brotherhoods, and the remnants of the eleven unions charged with Communist domination, which at the time of their expulsion in 1949 and 1950 had about 875,000 members. It was evident that after mid-decade the AFL-CIO merely marked time and failed to organize the unorganized.

Failure to meet this latter challenge, the issue which twenty years earlier had been the chief inspiration for the birth of the CIO, involved more than lack of organization among the growing white-collar strata in both public and private employment. It extended to women, only about one in seven in the labor force having become union members in 1958. It extended also to Negroes, with respect to whom racial discrimination within the labor movement had become so serious that the Negro American Labor Council was founded in May, 1959, with the object of ending the union color bar. A. Philip Randolph, president of the Brotherhood of Sleeping Car Porters and a vice president of the AFL-CIO, was chosen to lead the new council.[13]

13. U.S. Bureau of Labor Statistics, *Monthly Labor Review*, January, 1961, p. 23.

The Merger

Many new forces came together in the decade following World War II to make the formation of a loosely merged labor organization highly desirable. The first influence was the Taft-Hartley Act: since this act brought all unions under what was felt to be an attack, its passage tended to solidify labor against the common enemy. Furthermore, the act's provisions stressing the employees' right to choose no union at all and prohibiting certain kinds of jurisdictional strikes attacked the AFL's hoary principle of exclusive jurisdiction. Labor had much to gain, given the new interventionist threat from government, by trying to convert jurisdictional conflicts into an internal union affair. This desideratum was the more imperative because by 1947 the two unions were less and less devoted to bringing new members into their organizations and concentrating more and more on weaning away the already organized from their existing union affiliation—a deadly type of indoor sport that could only weaken both branches of labor's house to the advantage of alien parties. It was widely and increasingly realized within and without labor's ranks that labor's civil war contributed to its vulnerability and loss of public favor.

The decline of the CIO after the end of the war had placed it in a dangerous position relative to the moderately growing AFL. Whereas the AFL had less than 1,000,000 more members than the CIO in 1945, by 1951, after the expulsion of the eleven unions for being Communist-dominated, the AFL had 2,250,000 more members. If fusion were to come on favorable terms, so the CIO unions reasoned, " 'twere well it were done quickly." As it turned out, they read the handwriting on the wall correctly, for on the eve of the merger the AFL was more than twice the size of the CIO. At the same time, the elimination of the most radical unions from the CIO removed precisely those elements most critical of the AFL leadership and also anathema to that leadership.

Certainly the industrial vs. craft union form of the internecine conflict, which had originally contributed so heavily to the schism in labor's ranks during the 1930's, no longer existed in the same sharp form. In the earlier period this conflict was largely an expression of the dispute over whether or not to organize the unorganized workers; in the 1950's, it centered largely around the argument over which particular union was to exercise jurisdiction over already organized workers—a distinctly lower-level type of controversy which itself attested to the existence of bureaucracy and stagnation. Also, since 1930 the AFL had moved more in the industrial union direction, with its plantwide units and the proliferation of Federally chartered locals. The merged organization made a bow to the craft vs. industrial issue, in its original form now worn thin, by setting up an industrial union department. The dissipation of the old issues was facilitated by the withdrawal of Lewis' mineworkers, the death of some of the older leaders such as William Green and Philip Murray, and the general mellowing of traditional hostilities.

Finally, both organizations had grown more alike in their acceptance of the old AFL principles of business unionism, the traditional philosophy of voluntarism, the goal of stability and quietude in labor-management relations (as reflected, for example, in the long-term contract), and the emphasis on administration and updating of collective bargaining agreements in already organized industries where union recognition was no longer at issue.

The merger itself was preceded by the famous no-raiding agreement between the two in 1953. This compact in effect provided for the nominal abandonment of the principle of exclusive jurisdiction and its replacement by the principle of an "established bargaining relationship." [14] However, neither the pre-merger agreement nor the merger itself solved the very knotty problems of jurisdictional rivalry. Indeed, their continuation attested to the truce-like nature of the loose merger itself. It was inevitable that failure to drive outward to organize the unorganized would involve a turning inward to build little empires at one another's expense.

There can be no doubt that winning the unorganized in the 1950's was made extremely difficult by the Taft-Hartley Act, hostile state laws and courts, hostile local authorities in the South and in rural areas, hostile employers (not all of whom were in unorganized industries), the indifference of women workers, the growth of tertiary employment with its attendant high organizing costs, and the reversal of the long-term trend toward skill dilution that had characterized the pre-automation era. Working against odds had in the past been a source of strength and inspiration for the cause of organization. But now, in the face of similar odds, deficiencies in union leadership had to bear major responsibility for organizational stagnation.

14. E. B. McNatt, "The Merged AFL-CIO Federation: Current Issues, Problems, and Prospects," *Current Economic Comment*, May, 1959, p. 22.

Corruption

As in most large organizations, in labor's leadership were elements that succumbed to bureaucracy and the material enticements afforded by the affluent society. Salaries and expense accounts that would make large corporation executives envious, though all too prevalent, were insufficient to prevent the appearance of graft, bribery, acceptance of loans or gifts from employers, wastage and embezzlement of union funds, and other forms of corrupt behavior. One of the first reactions of the AFL-CIO was to establish an Ethical Practices Committee. This committee, like so many of the organizational and policy moves of the unions during the decade, was a response to criticism from without; for a subcommittee of the Senate Committee on Labor and Public Welfare under Senator Paul Douglas had already in 1955 begun to probe into the alleged misuse of union-administered health and pension funds.

The unions' subsequent legislative proposals in the burgeoning welfare and pension field seem to have been most scrupulous though, interestingly enough, rather a failure for too considerable a period. In addition to moving internally through the Ethical Practices Committee, they pushed for Congressional action to assist in policing the administration of welfare and pension funds from the outside. (They had much to gain and little to lose, so far as pensions were concerned, for only a small percentage of the pension funds were administered entirely by unions or jointly with employers.) The Welfare and Pension Plans Disclosure Act of 1958, which went into effect January 1, 1959, was largely the result of AFL-CIO initiative, although the work of the Douglas committee and the public support of President Eisenhower and Labor Secretary James Mitchell contributed in no small measure. Many employers and the National Association of Manufacturers had asked in vain that employer-administered funds be exempt, on the usual privacy-of-accounts grounds. The Act of 1958, although a step forward, left much to be desired. For example, the required reports (the Labor Secretary's forms were *optional*) did not need to enumerate the specific items in the union's investment portfolio, and the Labor Department was not given enforcement power. Also, court decisions blocked unions from suing on behalf of employees, leaving it up to the individual covered worker to institute court proceedings.

Other steps taken by the AFL-CIO included adoption of six "codes of ethical practices" by the 1957 convention, applicable to the operation of union welfare funds, general union accounting practices, publicity of financial management for members, and the whole area of internal democracy. Contemporaneously the UAW convention acted on an earlier recommendation of Walter Reuther by setting up its impressive Public Review Board. This group of outsiders, consisting originally of three clergymen of differing faiths, a Negro judge, a Canadian magistrate, a university chancellor, and an economics professor, was appointed by the UAW itself and was designed primarily to protect the interests of the individual unionist or subordinate union body. The Board was empowered to make final and binding decisions regarding appeals from rulings of the international executive board in cases involving alleged violation of an appellant's rights as a union member and in other cases relating to violations of the AFL-CIO ethical practices code.

This drive to clean house, intensified by the fire directed against union internal management by the McClellan Committee, led to the aforementioned expulsions of December, 1957. However, none of these concessions forestalled the passage of the Labor-Management Reporting and Disclosure Act in 1959, which the AFL-CIO Executive Council characterized as the labor movement's "most severe setback in more than a decade."

Strikes

Early in the 1959 steel strike, Labor Secretary James Mitchell asked Professor E. Robert Livernash of Harvard University to make a study to determine why the steel industry was "continually plagued by strikes" and to make corrective recommendations. Professor Livernash's January, 1961, report concluded that:

(1) Experimentation with estimates of what steel production might have been had there been no strike (any of the five between 1946 and 1959) leads to the judgment that the probability of net loss (in production) over a period of about 1 year is small.

(2) Steel inventory unquestionably provided a significant cushion in past steel strikes. Since this inventory was in turn supplemented by the finished goods inventories in user industries, it is clear that final purchases of such goods were amply protected.

(3) Economic data do not indicate any serious general effects stemming from the strikes. Substitute materials and imported steel may have strengthened their positions. The extent of secondary unemployment due to steel strikes is believed to have some exaggeration.

(4) If it were possible to abstract steel from the collective bargaining environment of the postwar years, it is very doubtful whether

wage and other settlement terms in the economy would have been much modified. Steel appears much more to have been conforming to, rather than establishing, major wage trends in the economy.

(5) The exaggerated interpretation of the national emergency dimension of steel strikes and resulting Government intervention have tended to reduce the compulsions for avoiding strikes relative to the pressures for ending them. Partial operation in the interest of national defense should be given far more serious attention than it has in the past. If defense officials felt that a steel strike involved a threat to national security, it might be practical to keep open or reopen plants producing critical items. Under most circumstances, it is doubtful if this would require operation of more than a small fraction of the industry's capacity.

(6) The imposition of neutrals, as distinct from a situation in which parties voluntarily seek the assistance of neutrals, appears more likely to intensify conflict than to aid in the resolution of issues. In collective bargaining in steel, intervention has itself been a source of conflict.[15]

These excerpts obviously do not provide a strike history of the 1950's. However, the experience in the steel industry, in which strikes were particularly frequent, is an archetype of collective bargaining and work stoppage experience. Besides, the steel industry was important by virtue of its public prominence, its alleged role in inflation (belittled in the Livernash report), its presumed influence in pattern-setting, its wide use as an index of the economy's ability to compete with foreign producers, and its supposedly strategic position in the nation's defense potential.

Of strikes in general, during the 13 years 1947–59 there were 53,000 recorded work stoppages, of which 268 involved 10,000 or more workers. All strike idleness over the 13-year period took about one third of 1 per cent of the available working time of all workers in nonagricultural establishments (exclusive of government), or roughly 1 day a year for each worker. Major stoppages (involving 10,000 or more workers) were concentrated in a few industries and therefore in a few states. Of the 268 such stoppages, 173 involved the issue of wages, hours, and supplementary benefits; 20 involved union organization, wages, hours and supplementary benefits; 8 involved straight questions of union organization; 55 involved other working conditions; and 12 involved interunion or intraunion matters, including only 3 jurisdictional issues.[16]

15. *Monthly Labor Review*, February, 1961.

16. Joseph W. Bloch and Julian Malnak, "The Dimensions of Major Work Stoppages," *Monthly Labor Review*, April, 1961, pp. 336, 337, 342.

The State of the Unions

The labor movement in the 1950's secured for labor perhaps as much as, perhaps slightly more than, its conventional share of the social dividend. In the sphere of real take-home earnings it contributed to a 16 per cent rise. Labor's level of living rose moderately along with the growth of the economy. In the areas of technological displacement and other types of unemployment it relied perhaps too heavily on the hopes engendered by the Employment Act and the social security laws, inherited from earlier decades. The acquisition of "a little more" on each economic front was labor's chief gain. The achievement of a loose kind of unity between the CIO and the AFL was also a gain.

In the areas of securing internal democracy, minimizing bureaucracy, and eliminating jurisdictional conflict, progress was modest at best. In organizing the unorganized the failure was so great as to approach the edge of catastrophe.

In the political action sphere, labor was weak and on the defensive, though not by any means entirely ineffectual. By the decade's end labor had not even secured representation on the Federal Reserve Board. As for the broader political and legislative areas, labor tried to "roll with the punches" but by 1959 could be judged the victim of a technical knockout.

More important, perhaps because more subtle, the labor movement began to ossify in the 1950's. In the words of Professor Neil Chamberlain:

if one were to single out the most telling "personality" weakness of the unions, it would be their passion for respectability. The goal most ardently sought by union leaders generally . . . is to be accepted by their communities as good middle-class citizens. . . .

Respectability of one's personal conduct is an objective which most of us seek and which we would defend as a goal to be pursued—by union leaders no less than by business or governmental leaders. But respectability of one's ideas is another thing. To achieve that generally requires conformance to the status quo: the rebel is not respectable.

The historic function of unionism is as a reform agency within society . . . as a modifier of existing institutional arrangements. . . . Social acceptance is something denied leaders of the labor movement, if they perform the role for which they have been cast.[17]

17. Neil W. Chamberlain, "Organized Labor: A Diminishing Force?" reprinted from *Challenge,* Institute of Economic Affairs, New York University, January, 1960, p. 16.

An even more subtle influence may have been at work. In connection with its proper support of a rational national defense effort, organized labor's involvement in the millions of jobs in the military and military-related industries in manufacturing may have led it to embrace certain spurious notions regarding the meaning of "national unity." Even in wartime, as history and pressure-group behavior has amply shown, no group in a parochial society extends its cooperation without retaining its critical posture and furthering what it believes to be its rightful economic and political status. The nature and direction of organized labor's resistance to its political emasculation by hostile legislation and other restrictive measures suggest that its rebel role was seriously compromised.

Farm Policy

Economic Trends

The problems of institutional adaptation to relative economic abundance were neither unique nor restricted to the agricultural sector—agriculture was merely an over-publicized example. It is true, however, that the more atomistic structure of a great part of the farm sector, with its attendant inability of firms to act, as in oligopolies, according to the dictates of recognized mutual interdependence, made the private organization of effective restriction and bargaining schemes impossible in most cases. Added to this there was, and still is, the sluggishness of outward resource mobility stemming from the specialized nature of farm resources, a sluggishness that was reinforced by too slow growth rates in the nonfarm sector. On top of these factors there was the public program, supported of course by the farm interest itself, designed to guarantee a "fair" rate of return on investment. The nonfarm population began to accept in principle at least as early as the 1920's the substitution of governmentally organized cartel-type planning in place of the ruthless expulsion of resources from agriculture that would occur under the unfettered functioning of the private market mechanism.

After World War II the proposition that it was the province of government to underwrite commercial agriculture through price guarantees was fully accepted in American public life. This acceptance was of course part of the growing acquiescence in the practice (though by no means yet the principle everywhere) of governmental quasi-planning. Farm policy in the 1950's, as elsewhere in the sphere of government intervention, was the little more vs. the little less.

Public intervention and resource immobilities prevented neither the exit of farmers nor the quiet prohibition of entry from partially rectifying the pressure of excess capacity upon demand. However, productivity increases and chronic pressure of production on the market continued throughout the post-Korean years.

One of the more "unfortunate" aspects of the problem in the 1950's was the technological explosion in agriculture. Not only did the long-run curve for agricultural productivity take a sharp upturn, but the curve was steeper than that for the nonfarm sector. The comparative rates for the 1950's are shown in Table 8-3. Output per man-hour worked in agriculture rose more than

TABLE 8-3

Indexes of Real Product Per Man-Hour, Agriculture and
Nonagricultural Industries, 1949–60
(1947–49 = 100)

Year	Total	Agriculture	Nonagricultural industries		
			Total	Manu-facturing	Non-manufacturing
1949	103.1	102.2	103.3	102.6	103.9
1950	110.4	116.2	108.8	109.5	108.4
1951	113.2	114.5	110.6	111.2	110.0
1952	115.7	124.5	112.0	113.0	111.3
1953	120.4	138.6	115.1	118.3	112.8
1954	122.6	148.3	116.9	117.4	116.7
1955	128.0	153.5	121.9	125.6	120.0
1956	128.3	156.4	121.5	127.1	118.7
1957	133.0	166.7	125.2	127.7	124.1
1958	136.3	186.9	127.4	na	na
1959	142.3	185.4	133.1	na	na
1960 (prel.)	145.5	195.8	135.7	na	na

SOURCE: *Statistical Abstract*, 1961, p. 217, Table 291.

6 per cent per year over the decade, which in the annals of productivity increase is nothing short of phenomenal. Farm physical output rose one fourth between 1950 and 1959, but farm employment fell from 7.5 million to 5.2 million.

The technological advances were concentrated in the spheres of mechanization, materials-handling, management, electrification, and the use of chemicals. A 50 per cent increase in the application of plant nutrients was registered over the decade, and chemicals were used extensively against insects, diseases, and weeds; moreover, chemical additives were developed to ripen fields uniformly and to fatten livestock with less feed input. The chief R & D sources for these advances were the agricultural extension workers of the land-grant college agricultural experiment stations.

The inadequacy of the existing methods of dealing with the problem of abundance became increasingly clear as surpluses of price-supported commodities piled up through the waning years of the decade. The enormous surpluses, to which the fabulous productivity increments contributed so heavily, prompted the compilers of the Joint Economic Committee *Staff Report on Employment, Growth, and Price Levels* to propose in 1959 that the emphasis in agricultural research "be shifted away from increasing output toward increasing the use of farm products." [18]

The proposal was perfectly reasonable within the framework of an implicit emphasis on the demand side of the market. The income elasticity of demand for farm products is quite low (about .2 at best, with respect to per capita real disposable income increases), and farmers for decades had been producing as though it were much higher. The 1950's were no exception to that behavior pattern.

A partial view of the changing status of agriculture may be gained from examination of Chart XIV, reproduced from the January, 1961, *Economic Report of the President*. Observation may be supplemented by reference to Chart I also.

Farm Programs and Their Scope

The chief farm policy issues during the decade were the percentage of parity at which support prices should be set, the extent to which production controls should be applied, and the methods for disposal of surpluses. Behind the controversy over these three concrete issues lay the more general debate concerning the presumed encroachment of government on allegedly free markets. It is appropriate to refer to the encroachment as "presumed" because of the typically overwhelming support given to such government "interferences" by farmer referendums. And it is equally appropriate to refer to most markets for farm products as only "allegedly free," since the classical meaning of a free market requires many buyers and sellers, full knowledge of market conditions by all marketers, homogeneity of product, resource mobility, and enterprise profit maximization—conditions which have not generally obtained in farm product markets since at least the late nineteenth-century Agrarian Revolt.

Application of the major farm programs hardly extended be-

18. *Eckstein Report*, p. xxx.

Chart XIV. Indicators of Agricultural Conditions

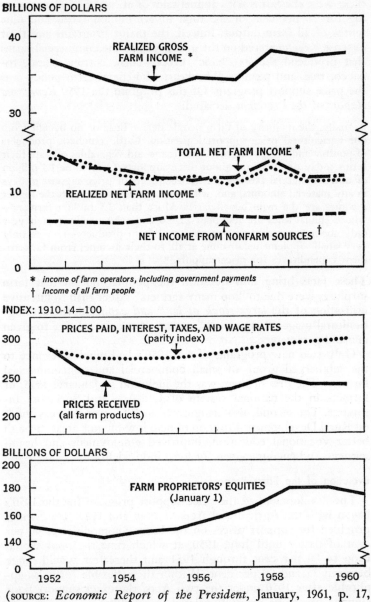

BILLIONS OF DOLLARS

REALIZED GROSS FARM INCOME *

TOTAL NET FARM INCOME *

REALIZED NET FARM INCOME *

NET INCOME FROM NONFARM SOURCES †

* income of farm operators, including government payments
† income of all farm people

INDEX: 1910-14=100

PRICES PAID, INTEREST, TAXES, AND WAGE RATES
(parity index)

PRICES RECEIVED
(all farm products)

BILLIONS OF DOLLARS

FARM PROPRIETORS' EQUITIES
(January 1)

(SOURCE: *Economic Report of the President*, January, 1961, p. 17, Chart 8.)

yond the 2.1 million commercial farms. Defined in 1959 terms, these were the farms with annual sales of at least $2,500, accounting for 56 per cent of the total of 3.7 million farms and nine tenths of all farm output. Indeed, the major programs and their expense were centered on the group within the commercial farms that produced the six "basic" crops—corn, cotton, wheat, tobacco, rice, and peanuts. The heart of Federal farm policy was the price support program. Of this program the 1959 *Economic Report of the President* declared:

Actually, the majority of farm people derive little or no benefit from our agricultural price support legislation. Cattle ranchers, producers of poultry and eggs, and growers of fruits and vegetables operate their farms today practically without price supports. Only some 1.5 million of our commercial farmers are the recipients of price support outlays in any material amounts, and, within this group, those with the higher incomes are the main beneficiaries. More than 2.5 million farmers—whose annual sales are less than $2,500 and who produce each year only about 9 per cent of our marketed farm products—receive only very small supplements, or none at all, to their incomes from Government expenditures for price support.[19]

These facts bring into question the popular notion that farm surpluses were due to "too many farmers" rather than to intensive utilization of the *large stock of land and capital* devoted to agricultural usage. "Large stock" means, of course, relative to given demand parameters.

Only two new programs of the 1950's had much relevance to the submerged group of small commercial and noncommercial farmers. The first of these was the inclusion in January, 1955, of farmers in the national system of Old-Age and Survivors Insurance. The second, also inaugurated in 1955, was the very modest Rural Development Program to help low-income areas through better vocational education, improved employment and health services, and encouragement of local industrialization.

Evolution of the Farm Program

The development of the price support program for the 1950's began with the Agricultural Acts of 1948 and 1949. The former provided for support prices on the basic commodities at 90 per cent of parity until July, 1950, at which time the floor would drop to 80 per cent through 1951 and thereafter would range between 75 and 90 per cent. Within these flexible formulas applicable after 1950 under the two Acts, the exact support floor allowed was to be inversely related to supply.

19. *Economic Report of the President*, January, 1959, p. 57.

The 1949 Act also introduced a "modernized" parity formula that retained the old 1910–14 base for the index of all farm parity prices but computed the index for each product from its average farm price in the ten most recent years. This new formula brought the parity index for each commodity more into line with contemporary intercommodity price relationships. The old parity formula had overvalued cotton, corn, wheat, and peanuts and had undervalued livestock and livestock products, among others.

The combination in 1949 of a Democratic Congress, an economic slump, a sharp drop in exports, and a fall in the parity ratio had several immediate repercussions on the farm program: these included application of the modernized parity formula to raise specific parity floors, inclusion of farm wages in the prices-paid index, extension of the 90 per cent commitment for the 1949–50 crop year through the harvest of 1950 for all basic crops, revival of acreage restrictions, and postponement of application of flexible support prices until 1952. The Democrats thus again revealed their partiality for high support prices and production "planning." High and rigid price supports remained the *de facto* policy until 1955, however, despite the advent of the Eisenhower administration in 1953.

The Korean War reversed the growth of carryovers; and the 90 per cent support prices, in the context of nonfarm price inflation, became a supply stimulus. Nevertheless, the Defense Production Act of 1950 forbade setting a price ceiling on any farm product below either parity or the highest price prevailing in the month preceding the war. Price supports at 90 per cent on the basics were made mandatory through 1954.

While President Truman's Agriculture Secretary, Charles Brannan, was in office he had repeatedly but vainly called for Congressional approval of his support plan for nonstorable products. The government had typically suffered substantial annual spoilage losses on such commodities. Under Brannan's proposal, labeled socialistic at the time, the nonstorables would move to consumers in larger quantities at market prices and the government would make "production payments"—direct subsidies—to farm producers to the extent of the discrepancy between the market price and the support price.

Only in the case of wool was the idea ever consistently put into operation. The Brannan plan for wool was acceptable because Congress viewed wool as a strategic commodity not produced in sufficient quantity to meet domestic demand.

The Korean War merely interrupted the flow of abundance, and production was additionally stimulated by the Act of July

17, 1952, extending 90 per cent price supports on the basics through 1954–55. There were also increases in the support prices of several nonbasics. (The nonbasic products under mandatory price supports were dairy products, wool, mohair, tung nuts, sugar beets, and sugarcane. Nonbasics under nonmandatory support included soybeans, cottonseed, oats, barley, dry beans, flaxseed, sorghum grain, and rye.) Commodity Credit Corporation (CCC) "investment," in the form of carryover inventory and loans extended, rose from $1.4 billion as of June 30, 1952, to $3.5 billion a year later. The government scrambled for additional storage space in the mothball merchant fleet, even though it had been able to dispose of almost all of its quota of 253 million bushels of wheat at $1.80 per bushel under the International Wheat Agreement. Nearly half of the total CCC investment was in wheat. Thereafter, the total CCC investment rose each year through 1956, when it stood at $8.3 billion.

The resurgence of surpluses, in the context of 90 per cent price supports and a sharp drop in exports during 1952–53, coincided with the advent of the Eisenhower administration; so did the vote of 87.2 per cent of the 415,000 wheat growers in favor of production quotas and price supports at 90 per cent of parity in August, 1953. The first annual *Economic Report* of the new President, coming shortly after 93.2 per cent of 478,133 voting cotton farmers had followed in the footsteps of the wheat growers, admitted, no doubt with chronic reluctance, that "farmers will need the continued assistance of Government." [20]

The *Report* added, however, that major crops had been priced out of important domestic and foreign markets by "high and rigid price supports." The tussle over differences in degree with the Democrats was thus joined, as the *Report* continued, with the ominous declaration that "undesirable consequences are inevitable if present rigid price-support policies are continued indefinitely." [21] The President praised the Acts of 1948 and 1949 for substituting the principle of flexible for rigid price supports and urged reduction of the frequency and extent of acreage allotments as a device for output restriction.[22]

The Agricultural Act of 1954 accordingly provided for flexible supports ranging from 82.5 to 90 per cent for the basics in 1955 and from 75 to 90 per cent thereafter. It was not found possible to escape per farm acreage allotments, however; and in addition the Administration was constrained to operate within the

20. *Ibid.*, January, 1954, p. 54.
21. *Ibid.*, p. 90.
22. *Ibid.*, p. 94.

limits set by older laws *requiring a minimum total acreage planted* for the important crops (e.g., 55 million in the case of wheat).

A further constraint was indicated by the wheat growers' vote in June, 1955, which recorded for the fifth straight year an overwhelming majority in favor of marketing quotas—potent evidence that "individualistic" farmers continued to reject the "free market" alternative. Lex Kelly, an official in the pro-Republican American Farm Bureau Federation, reported from Kansas at the time of the 1955 referendum that "there was lots of talk about voting down controls all along. But the referendum time came nearer and reality struck them right in the face, farmers just changed sides." [23] The time-honored business policy of government "interference to help" was still very much alive.

Surplus Disposal Problems

A solution to the growing problem of surplus disposal was supposed to be found without competitive encroachment on the "private" farm sector. School lunch programs and distributions to the armed services, however effectively they might have conformed to such general constraint, were of course completely inadequate to the disposal task. A food stamp plan for public welfare recipients was considered both dole-like and somewhat in violation of the competitive encroachment criterion. The mass outflow of international charity marking the early postwar years was by then felt to be needless (except possibly for the less developed countries). Consequently a new program of foreign quasigifts was inaugurated in the 1954 Agricultural Trade Development and Assistance Act (PL 480). It is noteworthy that PL 480 was viewed at the time as a *temporary* expedient to liquidate the accumulated stocks inherited from the preceding period of 90 per cent folly. Actually, PL 480 became the chief permanent channel for disposal of surpluses abroad.

A unique feature was added to the surplus inventory in the 1954 Act by designating part of it "set-aside" stock, with the objective of insulating it "from regular domestic and foreign markets." [24] The set-aside was not to be treated as part of the carryover for calculating price supports. It was this spirited-away portion of the carryover that was to be disposed of through the various charitable and disaster and foreign aid channels.

Things went badly during the two years following the 1954 legislation. Farm technology continued its phenomenal advance. Cotton and other crops were large. Commercial exports drifted

23. *The Wall Street Journal*, June 27, 1955, p. 1.
24. *Economic Report of the President*, January 1954, p. 94.

steadily downward. Livestock prices dropped sharply in the fall of 1955. Farm prices fell in December, 1955, to their lowest point since the Korean peak in February, 1951. Net farm income declined. It had to be admitted that efforts to stabilize farm income had not been very successful in rehabilitating that sector of the private market. Government activities on a broad scale, substantial public expenditures, and a somewhat more flexible scale of price supports had failed to obviate a condition in which support levels were "frequently the most important single factor in determining the prices prevailing in a number of commodity markets." [25]

The need for a new twist to the unsuccessful program of restriction was consequently felt by both farm leaders and the Administration. Accordingly, although the Agricultural Act of 1956 continued flexible support prices, a slightly different tack was taken in the accompanying Soil Bank Act. The latter instituted two varieties of output reduction planning—the year-to-year *acreage reserve*, providing payments for the basics equal to the support price times average per acre yield for each acre of the full allotment not planted; and the *conservation reserve*, under which farmers would be paid under long-term contracts (1) an annual rent for transferring cropland to specified conservation uses and (2) reimbursements for initial and maintenance costs of approved conservation practices on land so transferred.

In pursuance of Agriculture Secretary Ezra Taft Benson's recommendation to Congress, the acreage reserve program was discontinued after 1958 on the basis of its acknowledged failure to contain the forces of rising productivity and favorable weather. The conservation reserve feature, which applied not merely to allotment crops but to all crops, was retained. Participation under this program rose to 28.7 million acres (the inferior-quality ones, of course) including entire farms in many cases, and involved 306,000 farms in 1960.

The setting for the Agricultural Act of 1958 was no more propitious than was the 1954 setting for a "return to free enterprise." The Committee for Economic Development had pronounced the following sober judgment in December, 1957: "Public policy in 25 years and despite unstinting outlays has not succeeded in solving even one of the three basic agricultural difficulties: overproduction, instability of farm income, and chronic poverty of some farmers." [26] Utilized excess capacity, i.e., excess capacity in

25. *Ibid.*, January, 1957, p. 15.
26. *Toward a Realistic Farm Program*, December, 1957, p. 16.

the form of produced output, was apparently still more attention-getting than the plain idle capacity widely existing elsewhere in the economy.

However, it was true that increases in farm output were confined largely to the non-price-supported crops. Also, both net Federal budget expenditures for price stabilization (mostly for wheat, corn, and cotton) and CCC inventories drifted slightly downward after fiscal 1956. It was therefore possible to continue the downwardly flexible support policy. Furthermore, provision was made for the discontinuance of acreage allotments in corn, an action subsequently vindicated through a growers' referendum. The latter was the only referendum in the basic crops, however, that during the last years of the decade failed to approve marketing quotas (and the acreage allotments by which the quotas were applied to individual farms).[27]

The years were ticking off, however, and the failure of programs involving mere nuances in the old policies was patent as the decade approached its close. The experience of agriculture had shown that the Employment Act was no panacea for the solution of chronic imbalances accompanying economic change. It had proved impossible to avoid not only the obvious unhappy results of untamed abundance, but also the many adverse side effects of the price support program and the disposal of surpluses. Among these side effects were the encouragement of excessive production and per-acre yield in price-supported crops, stimulus of larger output of unsupported crops in the diverted acres, freezing of inefficient patterns of production among farms and farm regions, inflation of farmland prices, loss of foreign markets and induced expansion of competitive foreign production to a greater degree than otherwise because of high United States farm product prices, stimulus to the development of synthetic fiber substitutes, and hostility of some foreign countries adversely affected by indiscriminate disposal of surpluses abroad. Perhaps more important, the policy of output restriction slowed the rate of output growth in the economy as a whole. The agricultural sector was one of the slow growers in output, and a declining activity so far as employment was concerned.

The prospects for a more rational solution were still dim in early 1960 as the Congress became, in the apt words of William Blair, "locked in the annual struggle over the problem of surplus production." [28]

27. *Report of the Secretary of Agriculture*, 1960, p. 68.
28. *New York Times*, February 14, 1960, p. 6 E.

9 | America's Role in World Economy

General Features of the Balance of Payments

As shown in Chapter 1, United States foreign economic policy was shaped in vital respects by Soviet policy and by concern over potential Soviet influence in advanced as well as in less developed countries. The economic awakening of the less developed countries also exerted an influence of its own on United States foreign economic relations. The United States found it necessary as leader of the non-Communist world to bolster the internal economies and international liquidity position of Western Europe and Japan. Similarly, in the cold war competition for the economic and political allegiance of the emerging, less developed countries, it became increasingly necessary to plan the nation's trade, aid, and loan policies with respect to the presumed needs of such countries. The nation's balance of payments in the 1950's clearly reflected the strain of these foreign economic policies on the United States economy.

Certain American policies after World War II were designed to build up the internal economies of other, often competing, nations, in order to augment their holdings of gold and dollar reserves, and to liberalize United States import restrictions. These policies abroad had to develop side by side with powerful, traditional, neomercantilist pressures pushing in an opposite direction. What emerged on balance was usually some sort of compromise between the two sets of influences. Only with respect to military aid and to private foreign capital export (Chapter 6) was there overwhelming general agreement.

With the achievement of proximate international equilibrium after mid-decade, and with the strengthened competitive and reserve position of Western Europe toward the end of the decade, there began to develop in the United States stronger sentiment, expressed in policy, for traditional emphases on export stimuli, import barriers, conservation of United States resources (a goal inconsistent with import barriers), reduction of non-military aid to developed countries, and greater participation by Western Europe in both military and non-military international programs.

The evolution of these relations is reflected in the balance of payments (Table 9-1, and supporting Table 9-2). The prominent overall features of the record were the consistently positive balance on both the trade and the current account as a whole, the large totals for United States government payments abroad, the rising net outflow of private long-term capital, the deficits in the United States payments balance every year except that of the Suez Crisis (1957), and the settlement of the deficits through the accumulation of foreign holdings of gold and dollar assets (lines 12–16 of Table 9-1).

As has been previously mentioned, a breakdown of line 3 would show a net inflow of investment income, rising over the decade and rather larger for the whole period than the private net capital outflow—indicating, according to the somewhat obsolete traditional criterion, the mature international creditor status of the United States. Matching investment income with capital outflow involves resort to the economist's favorite indoor sport of relating items in the balance of payments to one another. There is no way of escaping this, however, if one is to make any sense out of events.

Division of the decade into the two periods 1951–57 and 1958–60 is designed to highlight the latter period as one of so-called "deterioration." [1] The question whether this period was episodic or lasting absorbed much attention during the decade's waning years. For example, the "Averages" columns for the two periods, when read along lines 13 and 14, show by sharp contrast the gold drain and the jump in foreign dollar holdings occurring from 1958 through 1960. From the viewpoint of one sector of the rest of the world, these latter developments appeared as an increase in gold reserves and dollar holdings (i.e., on the part of Continental Western Europe, the United Kingdom, and Japan, to

1. See Roy L. Reierson, "The United States Balance of Payments," *Staff Report*, Bankers Trust Company of New York, August, 1961.

TABLE 9-1
United States Balance of Payments, 1951–60 (in millions of dollars)

Line no.		Averages			1951	1952	1953	1954	1955	1956	1957	1958	1959	1960
		1951–1960	1951–1957	1958–1960										
	Current account													
1	Balance °	4,686	4,749	4,542	4,534	3,757	2,355	3,849	4,304	6,166	8,273	4,962	2,490	6,173
2	Trade balance °	3,155	3,224	2,996	2,921	2,481	1,291	2,445	2,753	4,575	6,099	3,312	988	4,687
3	Income on services and investments, net	1,531	1,525	1,546	1,613	1,276	1,064	1,404	1,551	1,591	2,174	1,650	1,502	1,486
	U.S. Government payments abroad													
4	Total °°	−5,053	−4,805	−5,631	−4,461	−4,337	−4,590	−4,157	−5,034	−5,317	−5,739	−5,999	−5,095	−5,798
5	Military expenditures	−2,688	−2,473	−3,190	−1,270	−1,957	−2,535	−2,603	−2,823	−2,955	−3,165	−3,412	−3,109	−3,048
6	Grants	−1,862	−1,961	−1,630	−3,035	−1,960	−1,837	−1,647	−1,901	−1,733	−1,616	−1,616	−1,633	−1,641
7	Loans, net †	−503	−371	−811	−156	−420	−218	93	−310	−629	−958	−971	−353	−1,109
8	*Private long-term capital, net*	−1,444	−1,134	−2,168	−783	−923	−320	−740	−674	−1,932	−2,556	−2,514	−1,743	−2,247
9	*Private short-term U.S. capital, net*	−334	−235	−565	−103	−94	167	−635	−191	−528	−258	−306	−77	−1,312
10	Errors and omissions	354	468	87	470	505	296	167	446	643	748	380	528	−648
11	U.S. payments balance	−1,791	−957	−3,735	−343	−1,092	−2,102	−1,516	−1,149	−968	468	−3,477	−3,897	−3,832
	Settlement of U.S. payments balance													
12	With foreign official institutions	1,397	658	3,123	−12	671	2,218	1,554	864	222	−913	3,088	2,487	3,795
13	Gold sales or purchases (+) or (−)	487	−5	1,569	−53	−379	1,161	298	41	−306	−798	2,275	731	1,702

14	Dollar assets, increase or decrease (+) or (−)	930	663	1,553	41	1,050	1,057	1,256	823	528	−115	811	1,756	2,093
15	With foreign banks	273	197	449	488	44	−69	19	410	429	60	47	1,159	141
16	With foreign private parties	121	102	164	−133	377	−47	−57	−125	317	385	344	251	−104
	Memorandum items													
17	Current account, Government payments abroad and net private long-term capital (lines 1, 4 and 8)	−1,811	−1,191	−3,257	−710	−1,503	−2,565	−1,048	−1,404	−1,083	−22	−3,551	−4,348	−1,872
18	Private short-term capital flows, excluding "official" (lines 9, 10, 15 and 16)	413	533	134	722	832	347	−506	540	861	935	465	1,861	−1,923

Notes.—*For details, see appropriate supporting table (Table 9-2 for trade).

**Excludes military transfers under grants.

†Excludes subscription of $1,375 million to the International Monetary Fund in 1959.

SOURCE: U.S. Department of Commerce, Federal Reserve Board, National Foreign Trade Council, Inc., and Bankers Trust Co. of New York.

TABLE 9-2

United States Trade Balance, 1951–60 *
(Supporting Table 9-1, line 2)
(In millions of dollars)

	Averages			1951	1952	1953	1954	1955	1956	1957	1958	1959	1960
	1951–1960	1951–1957	1958–1960										
Trade balance	3,155	3,224	2,996	2,921	2,481	1,291	2,445	2,753	4,575	6,099	3,312	988	4,687
Merchandise exports	15,552	14,796	17,318	14,123	13,319	12,281	12,799	14,280	17,379	19,390	16,263	16,282	19,409
Merchandise imports	12,397	11,572	14,322	11,202	10,838	10,990	10,354	11,527	12,804	13,291	12,951	15,294	14,722

Note.— Excludes military transfers under grants.
SOURCE: U.S. Department of Commerce, Bankers Trust Co. of New York.

select the strategic countries) from $18.5 billion in 1957 to $27.3 billion in September, 1960.[2] This sector of the rest of the world, unlike Latin America and other primary product exporters, which *lost* reserves, seemed willing to forego more imports in order to accumulate these reserves.

The division into two periods also reveals that in the later period the overall deficit in the payments balance (line 11) averaged annually about four times that for the period 1951–57. The situation had changed drastically from that obtaining during the years just after World War II and in the early 1950's. At that time the United States had deliberately contributed to the reconstitution of Europe's reserve position and had in general accepted the necessity for the rest of the world to limit purchases and maintain controls over imports and payments, just as it had acceded to the devaluations in 1949 and 1950. Indeed, it had also acted positively with its huge foreign grants and credits, some tariff reductions and customs simplifications, and much encouragement of the outflow of private capital during those earlier years. The United States had thus helped provide the developed countries of the world with the liquidity they needed to expand and regularize world trade.

By continuing to submit to a chronic deficit throughout almost the whole decade, the United States helped make possible a growth in world holdings of gold and dollars that managed to keep pace with the roughly 100 per cent rise in aggregate world imports. Not that merely keeping pace was considered satisfactory: factors such as persistent structural disequilibrium, a large and abrupt increase in the need for foreign exchange, international transfers of short-term money for quick speculative gains, and the recognition that there was an overall deficiency as long as any major country might experience reserve deficiency, prompted the advocacy of a number of plans for expanding the total volume of reserves. One such was the plan of Professor Robert Triffin for converting the International Monetary Fund into an international central bank, empowered to hold deposits and create credit.[3] Triffin's proposal was designed to assure that the requisite future growth of total reserves would not be composed so overwhelmingly of dollar and sterling currencies as obtained in the late

2. *Economic Report of the President*, January, 1961, p. 213, Table C-76.
3. Triffin's plan was only one of a number. See "International Payments Imbalances," *Report* of the Subcommittee on International Exchange and Payments, Joint Economic Committee, 87th Cong., 1st sess., Washington, D.C., U.S. Government Printing Office, 1961.

1950's.

It should not be concluded that the great improvement in the reserve position of the wealthy countries, particularly during the last half of the decade, was almost entirely due to United States policy or entirely at the expense of the dollar. As the 1959 *Economic Report* of the President stated:

The large increases in the gold and dollar holdings of the industrially advanced countries—Western Europe, Canada, and Japan—resulted in considerable part from the strains in the foreign trade and payments of the less developed countries and of certain others which are also exporters of primary products . . .[4]

However, by continuing to experience very large deficits after 1957, the United States had helped to expose itself to a condition at the end of the decade in which the total volume of dollar claims against it closely approached the level of its gold reserves—$16.8 billion vs. $18.7 billion respectively.

A glance at the trade balance account (Table 9-2) will show that it was not chiefly the import volume that, in the aggregate, from 1951 through 1955, implemented the policy goal of building world reserves, reducing trade barriers, etc. The big jump in imports had already occurred between 1949 and 1951. The jump from 1949 to 1950 was in both quantity and value; it was stimulated by devaluations abroad and by the Korean War. But the further rise of about $2 billion from 1950 to 1951, again due to the war, was all attributable to price increases; the quantity index actually fell 3 percentage points.

The dollar import magnitudes in Table 9-2 for 1951 through 1953 conceal a moderate quantity index rise from 165 to 182 (1923–25 base). This quantity index fell in 1954 to 169. The stable 1951–53 dollar magnitudes thus reflect the post-1951 import price declines. The mild 1954 drop was of course due to the recession. Within the total and in value terms, United States imports from the less developed countries fell from 1951 through 1953 (because of the collapse of the raw materials price boom in 1951, together with the cessation of the United States buildup of foreign materials inventories) but rose in other areas. Imports from Europe by value thus ran counter to the aggregate pattern, rising from $925 million in the year of mass devaluations, 1949, to $2.3 billion in 1953—a real contribution to the forthcoming easement of Europe's reserve problem. Western Europe's position in the American market continued to improve after mid-decade,

4. *Economic Report of the President*, January, 1959, p. 129.

both absolutely and relatively. The improvement was closely connected with the change in United States import composition toward more finished manufactures.

The stability of imports from 1951 through 1954 was associated with a declining ratio of imports to gross private product, whereas thereafter they were a rising proportion. But that was not all. Merchandise imports increased at a faster rate than merchandise exports in the latter years of the decade, rising 23 per cent in 1958–60 as compared with 1951–57, while exports rose 17 per cent. Associated therewith was a falling United States share of world exports of manufactures, although in the aggregate the United States maintained its relative position as an exporter. The importance of United States merchandise trade in world trade and relative to GNP is shown in Chart XV. Comparison with a "normal" year in an earlier era is facilitated by the inclusion of 1928 ratios in the chart. The constancy of the United States position in world trade and the declining role of trade in GNP are striking. However, it should be noted that trade relative to gross private product in 1960, a more meaningful comparison, approached the 1928 ratio rather closely.

Exports for 1956 were exceptionally high, chiefly because of new reductions in tariff barriers abroad and adverse crop conditions in Europe, and for 1957 because of the windfall to United States foreign sales (especially petroleum) resulting from closure of the Suez Canal. This partly episodic series of events generated some late illusions about the adequacy of the United States trade balance, thus adding to the shock effect of the drop in that balance in 1958 and 1959.

The proportionately greater rise in imports toward the end of the decade might have been considered appropriate for a mature international creditor and a nation professing free trade principles. However, the specter of an import balance on merchandise account caused great alarm because of the chronic and rapidly rising overall payments deficit, the new threat of foreign competition in the home market and abroad, the narrowing of the technological gap between the United States and other industrial countries, the slowed rate of domestic economic growth, the reinforcements of some of these trends by widening price differentials, the persistence elsewhere of some restrictions against United States products, the large outflow of gold and dollars, and the recognition that foreign aid programs would probably continue to be very large.

Chart XV. U.S. Merchandise Exports and Imports, 1928–1960
(Billions of dollars)

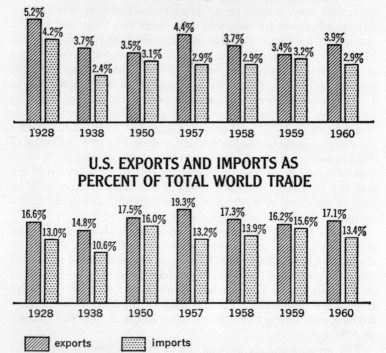

U.S. EXPORTS AND IMPORTS AS PERCENT OF U.S. TOTAL PRODUCT (GNP)

5.2% 4.2% 3.7% 2.4% 3.5% 3.1% 4.4% 2.9% 3.7% 2.9% 3.4% 3.2% 3.9% 2.9%

1928   1938   1950   1957   1958   1959   1960

U.S. EXPORTS AND IMPORTS AS PERCENT OF TOTAL WORLD TRADE

16.6% 13.0% 14.8% 10.6% 17.5% 16.0% 19.3% 13.2% 17.3% 13.9% 16.2% 15.6% 17.1% 13.4%

1928   1938   1950   1957   1958   1959   1960

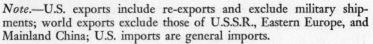

exports   imports

Note.—U.S. exports include re-exports and exclude military shipments; world exports exclude those of U.S.S.R., Eastern Europe, and Mainland China; U.S. imports are general imports.

(SOURCE: Conference on Economic Progress.)

Underwriting the Balance of Payments

The thesis that the 1950's ushered in the era of the (partly planned, partly unintentional) "underwritten economy" is supported by a closer examination of both the balance of payments and the nation's foreign economic policy during the decade.

An appreciation of the magnitude of the more or less direct and primary public underwriting in the sphere of the balance of payments may be approximated by ascertaining the annual supply of goods and dollars by the government to foreigners. A calculation of this sum for 1959 is presented in Table 9-3. The total revealed is substantial but difficult to relate to other magnitudes in such a way as to express the extent to which it effectively underpinned the economy and the balance of payments. Items 1 and 5 of the table may reasonably be construed as direct support to the private sector, like government domestic purchases of goods and services. The other items may be viewed largely as underpinning

TABLE 9-3

Estimated Supply of Goods and Dollars by the U.S. Government to Foreign Countries, 1959

Item	$ millions
1. Military transfers of goods and services under grants	1,988
2. Military expenditures of U.S. government abroad	3,090
3. Net non-military unilateral transfers to foreign countries	1,839
4. U.S. government net long-term capital outflow	358
5. Shipments of U.S. surplus farm products abroad under Public Law 480	927
	8,202

to exports. The most that can be said regarding this latter relationship is that, although almost all the gold and dollars thus transferred even as late as 1959 went to raise reserves, total United States exports would nevertheless have been substantially lower if such public transfers had not been forthcoming to satisfy liquidity demands.

It is in this sense that the United States public programs underwrote exports. In much the same sense the proposition was advanced in Chapter 1 that without the public programs (and the private capital outflow) the United States would in all probability have experienced a negative balance on merchandise account. In this connection it is noteworthy that when the private capital outflow was low in the first half of the decade, the public non-military grant and loan program was large; and later, as the private capital outflow rose, the public non-military program (especially in Europe) tapered off somewhat (lines 6 and 7 compared with line 8 of Table 9-1).

One of the secondary and direct means of government support to the private sector in the international sphere took the form of export encouragement through loans of the Export-Import Bank of Washington (Eximbank), a government agency. Eximbank loans financed United States commodity exports designed to help develop raw material sources abroad, to serve American private industrial and military strategic needs, and to provide in some cases "dollar exchange credits" permitting United States exporters and banks to collect overdue accounts.

The Eximbank was established in 1934 under the Reconstruction Finance Corporation to mitigate depression by stimulating exports, and it continued to apply this same neomercantilist principle after World War II. In the 1950's it adapted its lending in part to meet defense needs and in part to counter the action of similar competing institutions abroad. The bank made loans in dollars, subject to the requirements that the proceeds be spent in the United States and repayment be made in dollars. It extended some short-term but primarily long-term funds into risk zones slightly beyond those ventured by private bankers.

As an arm of the United States government, the bank's loans to domestic firms and to foreign firms and governments represented a kind of bilateralism that in general violated the nation's proposed policy of support for unregulated multilateral trade. In so doing, Eximbank was frequently criticized for competing with the International Bank for Reconstruction and Development. The elements of contrast in these two institutions reflected very well the characteristic postwar pursuit by the United States of both nationalist and international foreign economic policies.

As of the close of the fiscal year 1960, Eximbank had disbursed $4.3 billion in loans since the beginning of 1950. Its lending capacity was $7 billion, and its uncommitted loan balance was over $2 billion. The outstanding balance was $3.2 billion, of which $1.5 billion was in Latin America, the largest debtor area, and $1.1 billion in Europe.

Another secondary form of direct government support to the private sector, operating through the balance of international payments, involved underwriting the private capital outflow. It was clearly recognized that private capital export performed the dual role of providing funds to be spent on United States goods and of strengthening foreign reserves. Government policy in this area was concentrated in the direct investment guaranty program, administered initially (from its inception in 1948 through 1951) by the Economic Cooperation Administration (ECA), as part of the famous European Recovery Program (ERP), or "Marshall Plan," and during the latter part of the decade by the International

Cooperation Administration (ICA).[5]

The guaranty program was a nonactuarial plan designed to encourage investment abroad through public assurance of currency convertibility and through strictly construed protection against expropriation—the greatest institutional inhibitor of private foreign investment in the contemporary world. The program seems to have been given priority by the United States government over alternative forms of stimuli, such as tax deferral or partial or complete tax relief.

Bipartisan support in the Congress for public encouragement of private foreign investment in less developed countries was continuous after the inclusion in President Truman's 1949 "bold, new" Point Four Program (the fourth major point of his inaugural address) of technical assistance and "guaranties to the investor" in such countries. Investment underwriting in accordance with the plan contained the stipulation that the recipient country sign the bilateral investment guaranty agreement.

The program was slow to fulfill Administrator William C. Foster's goal of reducing the government's load in building up less developed countries, however. By the end of 1951 there were only 37 contracts covering investments and profits totaling merely $33.5 million. Two years later there were only 53 contracts for $41.2 million, with pending applications totaling $69.2 million. Moreover, *only four of the bilateral guaranty agreements were with countries outside Europe*. The chief barrier to expansion of the program in non-European areas appears to have been the decade-long resistance of the Senate to liberalization of the rigorous legal definition of expropriation.

The Mutual Security Act of 1956 made a number of improvements in the program that contributed to a considerable expansion beginning in 1958. However, the attempted emphasis on investment in less developed countries failed, for in 1959 over three fourths of the guaranties issued up to that time covered investments in Western Europe. (It was surprising how many of these insured against expropriation.) This misallocation relative to policy intent led to an amendment to the Mutual Security Act in 1959 that restricted future guaranties to investments in less developed areas.

5. This discussion of investment guaranties relies much upon M. von N. Whitman, *The United States Investment Guaranty Program and Private Foreign Investment*, Princeton Studies in International Finance, No. 9 (Princeton: Princeton University Press, 1959).

The newly important role of the program by the end of the decade as a stimulus to private investment was shown by the fact that in mid-1959 almost $450 million in guaranties had been issued and pending applications totaled almost $1 billion.

Governmentally underwritten agricultural exports carried domestic support policies for that sector into the international sphere. Here again, support for the domestic private sector (including, to some extent, the taxpayer) was combined with foreign aid. The extent of support was substantial. Aside from a moderate flow of exports moving under short-term credits extended by the Commodity Credit Corporation and the Eximbank, sales of government-owned commodities below domestic market prices, and export payments in cash or kind, the chief government programs accounted for 34 per cent by value of all agricultural exports in the years 1955–60. The largest single category of such support-and-aid consisted of sales for foreign currencies, particularly the "soft"—not readily convertible into dollars—currencies of less developed countries, under Title I of Public Law 480, the Trade Development and Assistance Act of 1954.

The Foreign Aid Program

The government's foreign aid program in the 1950's was an active expression of America's new sensitivity to the rest of the world. Although generally emphasizing military assistance to Western Europe, the program went through a number of changes. During the first years after World War II, aid was largely in the form of loans, the chief purposes of which were relief, rehabilitation, and reconstruction in Europe. The unprecedented total of almost $18 billion of such non-military aid was rendered in net grants and credits to Western Europe and its dependent areas from 1946 through 1950.

Following a period of emergency measures, such as assistance through the United Nations Relief and Rehabilitation Administration (ending in 1947) and large loans to Britain and France, the ERP, or Marshall Plan, was instituted as a terminal recovery project during the years 1948 through 1951. The program was designed primarily to keep Western and Southern Europe in the non-Communist sphere, chiefly through grants to be administered by the ECA and through the collaborative efforts of the simultaneously established Organization for European Economic Cooperation (OEEC). The recovery goal was spelled out to encompass reduction in the dollar shortage, increase in output and productivity, restoration and expansion of intra-European multilateral trade (to be facilitated by the European Payments Union's important guarantee of OEEC currency interconvertibility), elimination of trade barriers, expansion of exports to non-European areas, and inflation control. American aid under the program totaled about $12 billion (partly overlapping the aforementioned $18 billion) up to mid-1951.

The onset of the Korean War in June, 1950, changed the character of the foreign aid programs, although grants continued to predominate. Military assistance, allocated geographically according to military-strategic aims, dominated the programs thenceforth as civilian assistance declined. The conversion was administratively implemented by the absorption of ECA into the new Mutual Security Administration in late 1951. Net foreign grants, credits, and short-term assistance had totaled $38 billion from July, 1945, through December, 1952, of which only about $6 billion consisted of military grants, most of which was transferred in 1951 and 1952. But under the new orientation in foreign aid, from 1953 through 1960, of a total of $41 billion expended, almost $24 billion were explicitly for military purposes (Table 9–1, lines 4 and 5).

The reduction of aid to Western Europe to a minimal flow after the recovery phase of ERP was rather effectively carried out so far as non-military assistance was concerned. Military grants to that area, however, still accounted for over 40 per cent of the total of such grants in 1959. For one thing, the United States continued to pay the great bulk of the expenses for the North Atlantic Treaty Organization (NATO).

The geographical distribution of the non-military grants shifted near the end of the decade toward the less economically developed, militarily strategic areas—and wisely so, for the reserve position of this group had become desperate, and its developmental requirements had burgeoned. Western Europe, which had itself for some years been embarked upon foreign aid programs, got only $177,000,000 out of $1,641,000,000 of net new grants in 1959. The decline in public civilian aid was more than compensated, however, by an increase in the private and quasi-private capital outflow to Western Europe. In a sense this decline in public aid to Europe represented a partial fulfillment of the "trade, not aid" goal that had been much advocated since 1953 in both Europe and the United States.

During most of the decade foreign aid, both military and civilian, was characterized by a haphazard, stopgap approach, with minimal attention both to rational programming at home and to articulation with the long-run developmental needs of the foreign recipients. These characteristics, a prime expression of the "Soviet effect" referred to in Chapter 1, shaped the amount of aid, its duration in any particular case, and the geographical distribution of the funds. The program was also largely unilateral on the part of the United States, despite the fact that other advanced countries had similar programs. Indeed, funds were often dispensed without any serious attempt at coordination with other appropriate American agencies or agencies in which the United States was a participant, such as the Eximbank and the IBRD. Even collaboration between the State and Treasury Departments on these programs was sporadic. Some consistency, however, was achieved through a loose coordinating body known as the National Advisory Council on International Monetary and Financial Problems.[6]

It was the objective of American foreign economic policy through the decade to terminate public foreign aid and encourage trade and private capital export as a substitute. Only toward the end of the decade did the government begin to face up to the prospect that it would be called upon to make a large and continuing contribution to the growth of the more backward economies. What and how much would be done about it remained one of the unresolved challenges as the decade came to a close.

Import Policy

The history of United States tariff policy in the 1950's was on the whole one of partially successful efforts toward the reduction of such barriers. The Eisenhower administration generally took a more liberal position than the Congress (regardless of the party in control), but was itself continually forced by the influence of special interests acting through the Congress to compromise or back down on its recommendations.

After World War II, United States policy aimed at tariff reductions, simplification of customs formalities (the "invisible tariff"), and the removal of import quotas here and abroad. However, tariff policy in general tended to sanction reductions only if associated with the prospect of export increases. When tariff concessions were made, they were usually handled on a commodity-by-commodity basis. Across-the-board cuts—eminently more indicative of serious intent—were atypical. Also, import restric-

6. See Olin S. Pugh, *The Export-Import Bank of Washington,* University of South Carolina, Bureau of Business and Economic Research, June, 1957, pp. 45–47.

tions were generally considered to be the sole means of protection for the adversely affected business and labor groups. It was a fortunate circumstance, therefore, that the modest liberalization efforts were buttressed by real tariff reductions stemming from a combination of rising prices and the predominance in the tariff structure of specific (an amount of money per unit) rather than ad valorem (a percentage of the price of the imported item) duties.

The arena for part of the struggle over import policy was the international organization set up in accordance with the 1947 General Agreement on Tariffs and Trade (GATT). All the major trading nations outside the Communist bloc came to participate in the negotiations conducted at the periodic meetings of this provisional forum, with the United States usually facing the other signatories acting more or less as a group.

"The greatest immediate domestic threat to our foreign policy is to be found in the determination of a large number of Republicans and a few Democrats to amend the Trade Agreements Act so as to permit the Congress to nullify in future trade agreements tariff concessions made by the Executive," wrote Sumner Welles with prophetic insight in 1947.[7] American affiliation with GATT was through the executive department on the basis of the powers implied in the 1934 Trade Agreements Act, and the absence of Congressional ratification was often used as a club against the Administration's modest liberalization proposals. Also, the withholding of Congressional approval of the 1955 proposal to create a permanent executive body for GATT, to be called the Organization for Trade Cooperation, reflected that body's rising resistance to further liberalization in the late 1950's. This Congressional rejection scuttled the proposal.

GATT had committed its signatories to the principles of nondiscriminatory, or most-favored-nation, tariffs (the negotiated rate with a given country could be no higher than the lowest tariff on similar goods originating in any country) and removal of quantitative restrictions on imports (e.g., quotas and licenses). The latter was greatly vitiated, however, by "escape clauses" allowing exceptions (1) for balance-of-payments difficulties and, at American urging, (2) for implementing restrictive domestic production or marketing programs.

American liberalization efforts during the decade were usually harassed by a Congress set upon tightening just such escape

7. Sumner Welles, "Pressure Groups and Foreign Policy," *Atlantic Monthly*, November, 1947.

clauses in its own laws. For example, in connection with the renewal of the Trade Agreements Act in 1951,[8] Congress reinserted the "peril point" provision (no duty may be reduced if it would threaten serious injury to a domestic "industry") and added an escape clause allowing restoration of a tariff if its previous reduction had caused injury. The escape clause had to be included in all future trade agreements and inserted into those currently in force. These moves provided a grim and disillusioning background for the "trade, not aid" slogan. The 1955 renewal introduced an additional reason for escape based on impairment of national security, a provision much strengthened in the 1958 Trade Agreements Extension Act. The latter renewal measure, on the other hand, moved timidly in a counterdirection with an unprecedented four-year extension and some added tariff-acting authority granted the President.[9]

The resistance to liberalization as the decade waned was clearly anticipated in the January, 1954, report of a bipartisan Commission on Foreign Economic Policy (Randall Commission) which, after pointing to extensive tariff reductions already made, added ominously:

Now, we find ourselves facing demands for further opening of our markets at a time when our commercial exports are in approximate balance with the highest level of imports ever reached, while the world as a whole has considerably rebuilt its holdings of gold and dollar reserves. . . .

We are fully aware of the arguments for free trade. It is sufficient to say that, in our opinion, free trade is not possible under the conditions facing the United States today . . .[10]

A glance at the ratio of duties paid to value of dutiable imports, shown in Table 9–4, suggests that the year of the Randall Commission report was indeed the end of tariff reduction for the 1950's.

To be sure, there is more to import policy than is shown in the table, and there is more to the tariff record than simple averages. Nevertheless, the data are pertinent and suggestive.

The decline in the per cent of duty-free imports, a striking

8. These extensions of the Trade Agreements Acts, of which there were eleven in all, were based on the original New Deal Reciprocal Trade Agreements Act of 1934.

9. See M. E. Kreinin, "The Trade Agreements Extension Act of 1958," *Current Economic Comment*, February, 1959.

10. Commission on Foreign Economic Policy, *Report to the President and the Congress*, 83rd Cong., 2nd sess., House Doc. No. 290, January 23, 1954, pp. 43–44.

feature of the record in the 1950's, reflects primarily the rise in the share of fabricated imports, which were largely dutiable. Raw materials, to the great advantage of the less developed countries and domestic manufacturers, are mostly duty-free.

The data indicate that the greatest periods of liberalization, so far as the tariff is concerned, were 1936–40 and 1946–50. The United States in 1950 was not any longer, relative to its past

TABLE 9-4

Duties on Imports Entered for Consumption, Annual Averages and Ratios for Selected Periods, 1931–50, and Annual Averages, 1950–59

Yearly average or year	Amount of duties ($ millions)	Per cent of imports duty free, by value	Ratio of duties paid to value of dutiable imports	Duties per capita (dollars)
1931–35	314.5	63.1	50.02	2.46
1936–40	365.2	60.5	37.87	2.76
1941–45	379.7	66.0	32.13	2.72
1946–50	439.5	58.4	16.03	2.94
1950	522.3	54.5	13.14	3.38
1951	591.3	55.4	12.26	3.76
1952	570.1	58.2	12.69	3.56
1953	584.4	54.9	12.03	3.59
1954	529.1	55.3	11.57	3.20
1955	633.3	53.2	11.95	3.76
1956	709.7	49.8	11.30	4.14
1957	746.0	46.6	10.79	4.28
1958	820.7	41.9	11.09	4.63
1959	1,052.0	38.8	11.47	5.84

SOURCE: *Statistical Abstract*, 1961, p. 898.

history, a high tariff country. But during the ensuing decade the progress of tariff reduction seems to have been arrested, despite such mincing countermeasures as those already mentioned and others like the Customs Simplifications Act of 1956. The arresting of the secular decline may be said to reflect the rising strength of protectionist influences as the decade unfolded.

Tariff policy in the 1950's was still strongly influenced by the neomercantilistic bias that exports are good and imports bad. The persistence of these notions and their policy complements, not only with respect to the tariff but also in such things as Buy-American regulations and insistence upon a 50 per cent use of American-flag vessels for foreign aid goods, despite the absence of severe depression, and the existence of a dollar shortage throughout the greater part of the decade, calls for explanation. That explanation could probably be found in sectoral and industry excess capacity, the failure to deal rationally with resource immobilities, distrust of the Employment Act and of further government intervention generally, and the inordinate influence of particular vested interests on the democratic process.

International Monetary and Financial Machinery

To contribute to the establishment of unregulated multilateral trade and capital flows, the United States joined forty-three other countries at Bretton Woods, New Hampshire, in 1944 to set up the largely American-designed International Monetary Fund (IMF) and the International Bank for Reconstruction and Development (IBRD). The participants hoped to avoid through the IMF the drastic fluctuations in exchange rates that had followed World War I and the competitive currency devaluations of the 1930's. They hoped also, through the IBRD, to help meet the postwar need for long-term investment funds in Europe and the less developed countries.

The IMF was in operation by 1947, committed to deal only with its non-Communist member governments and their central banks. Its resources of $8 billion came from the gold and currency subscriptions, or quotas, of its members. (Britain's John Maynard Keynes had wanted a clearing union with $25 billion of assets.) A country's quota (of which the gold portion was the lower of either ¼ of its total quota or 10 per cent of its total gold and dollar holdings) was based on its national income, share of world trade, and related criteria. The total quota also determined voting power and drawing limits from the Fund's resources. The United States quota rose along with other members' during the 1950's and stood at $4,125,000,000 out of a total of $14,851,000,000 in 1961.

The Fund aimed at maintenance of exchange stability within a 1 per cent range of deviation relative to the dollar and at protection for members against *temporary* deficiencies in reserves. During the early phase of IMF history the latter usually meant making dollars available. A sort of escape clause allowed for agreed-upon exchange rate adjustments to correct "fundamental disequilibrium." All this was highly salutary from the standpoint of United States private traders and investors, as well as others.

The Fund agreement prophetically provided for a five-year transitional period beginning in 1947, during which time members were permitted to deviate from their permanent obligations as

Fund adherents. In view of the fundamental international disequilibria that obtained from 1947 to the mid-1950's, perhaps it was well for the IMF that net drawings were only $758 million through 1949 and *negative for the six years thereafter*.

What Brian Tew has called "the awakening of the Fund" came only in December, 1956, when, at the onset of the Suez crisis, Britain drew $561,000,000 from the IMF (and also borrowed $500,000,000 from the Eximbank). From that date through 1959, when renewed American interest in the almost depleted Fund was crystallized in an additional subscription of $1,375,000,000, gross drawings totaled $2,200,000,000 and net drawings $1,000,000,000. As was the case with American foreign aid, this increase was associated with a shift away from Europe toward the less developed countries.

In the breach the IMF had been completely inadequate to the task of achieving multilateral convertibility of currencies. But *after* the OEEC had set up the European Payments Union (1950–58) to eliminate trade barriers and establish the machinery for foreign exchange clearing among European countries, *after* Europe had brought its inflation under control, *after* ten of the OEEC countries had made their currencies convertible with the dollar in 1958, *after* European countries and a number of others had rebuilt their competitive positions in world markets, *after* "the chronic disequilibrium of the post-war years was at last coming to an end, so that a regime of world-wide multilateral settlement was now not only practicable but viable without recourse to additional trade restrictions" [11]—then the Fund could perhaps come into its own. And after all, defenders of the Fund's original charter might have argued, wasn't that the kind of placid, near-equilibrium world for which the IMF's temporary adjustment powers had been intended many years before? In the early 1960's, proposals such as Robert Triffin's for a more adequate international reserve system attested to the developing doubt that IMF could cope with a serious international liquidity crisis.

The role of the IBRD was perhaps a somewhat more influential one. As an intergovernmental development institution under American hegemony, the IBRD made some supplemental contribution during the later 1950's to the flow of quasi-private long-term funds (largely dollars) to less developed areas. It furnished

11. Brian Tew, *The International Monetary Fund: Its Present Role and Future Prospects*, Essays in International Finance, No. 36, Princeton University, Department of Economics, International Finance Section, March, 1961, p. 18.

technical assistance as well as direct loans against government guarantees.

IBRD resources came about equally from the sale of its own bonds in the principal world markets and from members' subscriptions. Membership was identical with that of the IMF. With the funds thus provided, the "World Bank" contributed to the internationalization of foreign lending through joint loan participation with the Bank by private institutional lenders in different nations.

The World Bank lent only as much as could reasonably be expected to be repaid, and only for specific, carefully scrutinized projects. Loans could be extended to finance payments for imports related to specific projects, involving very largely power or transport construction rather than fabricating facilities. Loans for government-owned manufacturing enterprises were precluded. Although repayment in inconvertible currencies was acceptable (and in this regard the IBRD differed from Eximbank), the loan policy of President Eugene Black and the Board of Governors was generally conservative. No equity capital was provided. Charges on the Bank's loan funds averaged between 4 and 6 per cent.

Although the IBRD's general goals tended to place it in competition with the Eximbank, it differed in that it was international (though not as international as the United Nations) and therefore avoided the stigma of bilateralism. Also, the funds it extended could be spent freely where the best price could be obtained. Furthermore, its loans were ostensibly commercial rather than political. The American stake in the World Bank was therefore contingent upon a general stimulation of the less developed countries' contribution to world trade rather than upon immediate American trade.

Loan disbursements by the IBRD during the early 1950's were inconsequential, but in fiscal 1954 they reached a modest $304 million. After dropping slightly in the next two years, they rose to $500 million in fiscal 1958 and to $583 million in fiscal 1959 and fell slightly to $544 million in fiscal 1960. Although these totals were noteworthy, they were quite inadequate to approach the long-term capital needs of the less developed nations.

Traditional banker conservatism, implemented by rather substantial interest and commission charges by the IBRD, together with the loan capital limitation and the virtual exclusion of manufacturing enterprise, prompted the establishment in 1956 of the affiliated International Finance Corporation. IFC was a feeble attempt to liberalize loan policy through authorization to lend "in association with private investors" to private enterprises in less developed countries. It originally could not invest in capital stock. Interest rates on its miniscule total of $45 million of investments as of September, 1960, averaged 7 per cent.

The IFC had not approached by 1960 even the very modest start made by its exclusively American, also liberalized, counterpart, the Development Loan Fund. The DLF (established 1957) was an offshoot of the Eximbank and represented a similar attempt to escape banker conservatism in the form of loans repayable in foreign currencies and on easy terms.

The pattern of thus attempting, however timorously, to create more liberal United States and international lending institutions addressed to the needs of less developed countries reflected a somewhat enlarged though belated recognition of those needs. The final action at the decade's end, proliferating the already long list of such institutions, was the establishment in September, 1960, on United States recommendation, of still another IBRD affiliate. The International Development Association was to "provide capital on more liberal terms of repayment" and to "help finance a wider range of projects" than the IBRD or the IFD. The plethora of organizations was equaled only by the insufficiency of resources devoted to the purpose.

Paradoxes of Foreign Policy

Review of American foreign policy in the 1950's has revealed a persistent conflict between historic mercantilistic drives and a new sensitivity to the economic needs of other nations. Morality and utopian notions of selflessness aside, it is difficult not to see the mercantilistic considerations in every major aspect of policy. When the Inter-American Development Bank was set up in 1960 and a new aid program for Latin America was concomitantly announced, it could not be denied that United States export industries would be benefited. Similarly, the government decided in 1959 to "tie" to American exports the loans made by the DLF.

There can be no doubt that the chronic payments deficits of the 1950's, their sharp rise in the ending years, and the revived competitive threat from abroad, including even the Soviets, intensified the neomercantilist pressures on United States foreign economic policy. Proposed solutions leaned heavily toward the increase-of-exports approach. Domestic farm price supports were criticized for blocking the translation of rising farm productivity into more competitive prices on the world markets. A renewed drive was called for by the Committee for Economic Development against world-wide barriers to trade in agricultural products —a policy in which, the CED readily acknowledged, the United States had "acquiesced and indeed taken the lead." [12] The increase-of-exports solution was also brought to bear upon wage rigidities and labor organization. Related thereto were widely advanced recommendations for stepping up industrial productivity through increased R & D effort and tax concessions to stimulate investment.

Even anti-inflationary monetary policy and "fiscal responsibility" (i.e., the classical precepts) came in for their share of the common task of raising exports. Devaluation was considered too extreme a measure as the decade closed, although the point was widely bruited about that the 1949 devaluations by other countries had been excessive.

On the import side, the policy of slowdown in the trend of tariff reduction and the strengthening of escape devices helped the mercantilist scissors cut another inch or two into the free trade White Paper.

In the sphere of foreign aid the policy was similarly mixed. On the one hand, it was urged that the rate at which foreigners were gaining reserves be slowed down. Proposals in this spirit ranged from reducing the American contribution to NATO to a sharp cut in total aid. On the other hand, the Soviet effect and the direct clamor for aid on the part of the less developed powers possessed an insistence that was not easily denied. Some groups felt that the "discipline of the balance of payments" was not relevant to the determination of the scale of foreign assistance of any important type.

Accompanying the steps toward multilateralism during the decade there had been a striking growth of regionalism in both the Communist and non-Communist world trading communities. Most notable among the regional associations were the European Common Market (West Germany, France, Italy, and the Benelux countries), and the European Free Trade Association (Britain, Switzerland, Sweden, Norway, Denmark, Austria, and Portugal). In Latin America and Asia, nations were slowly moving toward the creation of similar regional associations as the decade ended. Major purposes of these organizations were the elimination of trade barriers among the members and the establishment of trade

12. "National Objectives and the Balance of Payments Problem," *Statement on National Policy*, CED, February, 1960, p. 26. A number of other points made in this summary of policy conflicts are drawn from the same *Statement*.

preferences in favor of constituents and against outside trading bodies. A vital unsettled question for the United States, as well as for the world, raised by this movement was whether the regional associations would become fortresses of protectionism or a step toward planned world multilateralism. The immediate question raised in the United States with respect to the European Common Market emphasized, as usual, its presumed threat to American export markets and the large American private investments in that region.

10 | Investment, Growth, and Public Policy

The Shrinkage of Plant and Equipment Investment

Unlikely Hypotheses

Because the rate of economic growth was a focus of national policy in the 1950's, experts carefully examined the role of the major output and spending streams as determinants of the growth rate. This emphasis on spending streams resulted from the observation that supply factors apparently placed no constraints on economic expansion, at least on the aggregate level.

Historically, private investment, especially P & E investment, has performed a highly strategic function in the growth process. Along with other determinants of growth, investment created income and employment, increased productivity, and raised productive capacity. Yet in the 1950's, aggregate private P & E investment apparently failed to exhibit its historic dynamism.

To the question why private P & E investment did not average a higher rate, it was suggested earlier (Chapter 5) that too low a rate of profit could have been at the most a minor part of the answer. Despite the sharp contrast in growth rates during the two halves of the 1950's, the ratio of gross profits after taxes to corporate net worth showed no trend during the course of the decade. This is remarkable in view of the slowed growth of aggregate demand after mid-decade. Moreover, it is pertinent to recall that the rate of profit after taxes relative to invested capital in the 1950's compared favorably with the more virile 1920's.

That the high interest rate policy of the Eisenhower administration could not have perceptibly depressed P & E investment was certainly evident in the large corporate sector, even including the public utilities, whose comparatively high investment record in the 1950's suggested an investment demand schedule that was interest-inelastic. (However, as acknowledged in Chapter 5, there may have been some dampening effect on small enterprise investment.)

Nor was corporate cash flow a block to high level investment commitments. Indeed, internally generated funds, flowing in higher proportion to national income than was the case in the 1920's, provided a major source for the large outflow of private foreign investment during the decade.

It is most doubtful that high and rising money wages inhibited investment. The weight of evidence, in manufacturing at least, points to a sharp rise in per unit salary costs, a moderate rise in per unit employment costs, and a moderate decline in per unit wage costs after 1953.

Furthermore, rising wages apparently did not induce the substitution of capital for labor. Such substitution is usually believed to occur, *ceteris paribus*, when price ratios move against labor and toward capital. But the prices of both capital goods and labor rose during the 1950's, as the two price trends moved fairly closely together.

Some have argued that decline in the rate of population growth leads to a drop in investment opportunities. The connection is tenuous at best, and this is especially true with respect to the time lag between the two. However, the population factor in the 1950's must have been favorable, if anything; it certainly could not have been a depressant.

Plausible Hypotheses

So much for the factors which presumably were not the primary retarding influences on the rate of private nonagricultural P & E investment. There are, on the other hand, a number of possible factors which could largely explain the retardation.

It was indicated in Chapter 3 and elsewhere that P & E investment in the 1950's continued a secular pattern toward being absolutely more capital-saving, i.e., toward a reduction in real investment outlay per unit of output capacity. At the same time, investment continued to be absolutely labor-saving: it reduced the labor required to produce a standard unit of output. This is merely to say that investment continued to contribute to the historical increase in man-hour productivity. A concomitant development, also extending far back in history, was of course a decline in the amount of production labor required per dollar of real fixed investment put in place and operated at normal capacity. Put briefly, these three developments entailed a fall in the capital-output (K/Q) ratio, the labor-output (L/Q) ratio, and the labor-capital (L/K) ratio. It has been pointed out that these changes were wrought in part by a shift within total P & E investment in favor of equipment relative to plant.

Both a rationale and a comparative empirical test for these investment characteristics have recently been provided in a careful study of the slow growing Belgian economy in the postwar period by A. Lamfalussy.[1] Professor Lamfalussy's "defensive investment," which he found to obtain widely in stagnating Belgian markets, has many, though not all, of the aforementioned characteristics of P & E investment in the American case. Defensive investment is featured by the reorganization of existing facilities and heavy reliance on innovations embodied in equipment rather than plant, the goals being to conserve funds, lower costs in the interest of survival rather than expansion, raise labor productivity through increased capital intensiveness, and, where the price elasticity of demand is deemed low, to minimize the enlargement of capacity.

All this as applied to the American case in the late 1950's would add up to the proposition that a given constant dollar of P & E investment would probably, despite the intent of many investment decision-makers, add ever more to capacity. By thus reducing the amount of investment spending associated with a given increment to output capacity (not actual output), both initial income and potential super-multiplier income totals would be so much less. Hence any tendency for income to lag behind the expansion of capacity would be aggravated. The operation of such a tendency may have inhibited the growth of P & E investment and income in the 1950's.

The additional labor-saving feature of P & E investment, a by-no-means new characteristic, meant of course that to provide a full and rising volume of employment, investment would have had to be that much larger. Hence, private P & E investment had an added responsibility to compensate through greater employment for the rising labor productivity it brought about. At the

1. A. Lamfalussy, *Investment and Growth in Mature Economies* (London: Macmillan, and New York: St. Martin's, 1961).

same time its largely "defensive" character in the later years made for a lesser ability to stimulate the income increases necessary to fulfill this responsibility.

The dilemma associated with these peculiar features of fixed investment in an advanced business system may well be what Professor Samuelson had in mind when he suggested the possibility that contemporary wealthy economies could reach such a state that they would be unable to induce a deepening of capital (more capital per unit of output).[2] Most studies have shown that capital deepening as a general phenomenon ended around the second decade of this century.

Domar-Harrod Growth Models

We know from the Domar-Harrod formulae that aggregate output or income at constant prices must rise in proportion to the growth of productive capacity if full employment is to be sustained. The rate of growth of productive capacity is equal to the marginal net savings ratio, s, times the incremental output-capital ratio, $\Delta Y/I$. The symbol s stands for $\Delta S/\Delta Y$, the symbol Y stands for total income (output), and I (which equals ΔK) represents net investment. Total savings is, of course, S. The requirement for sustained growth is, then,

$$\Delta Y/Y = s \cdot \Delta Y/I$$

The Domar-Harrod models of the required rate of income (spending) growth operate with additions to *capacity* based on offsets to "net" savings increments at constant prices. The latter are usually defined as gross savings minus depreciation. However, some part of depreciation is represented in the financing of increments to output capacity. This portion is embodied in both "modernization" investment and any capacity-raising replacement investment, types of largely autonomous outlays whose scope secularly increased with the rise in the nation's stock of capital and the relative augmentation in its equipment component. Such portion must be added to the traditional "net" savings to get the true total of net savings, i.e., the total that needs to be matched by capacity-raising net P & E investment.

In the present state of knowledge there is no way to determine exactly what part of depreciation and obsolescence allowances should be added in to get true net savings as here conceived. Let us assume, however, that true net savings averaged about 6 per

2. Paul A. Samuelson, *Economics*, 5th edn. (New York: McGraw-Hill, 1961), pp. 810–811.

cent of GNP and that the average ratio equaled the marginal ratio, s.

What of the remaining term on the right-hand side of the above equation for sustained growth, the incremental output-capital ratio, $\Delta Y/I$? Capital-saving innovations and the nation's changing product mix by the 1950's had continued to raise both the average Y/I (our Q/K, except that K is stock of capital and I is a representative addition to stock) and the incremental $\Delta Y/I$ to ever higher levels. The secular tendency for the equipment element to rise in importance relative to structures also tended to increase $\Delta Y/I$. (Since the accelerator is the inverse of the same ratio, its efficacy as a stimulant to investment when spending rose had accordingly been reduced.) This was the end product of decades of capital "shallowing."

Kuznets shows that the actual output-fixed capital ratio averaged about .63 in the regulated industries in 1950 and that the actual ratio of value added to fixed capital in all manufacturing in 1948 was 1.37. For the interval 1923–52 the ratio of changes in net national product to changes in net capital stock averaged two thirds.[3] The January, 1952, *Economic Report of the President* showed a ratio of business output to private stock of capital of approximately 55 per cent.[4] Since 1955 was a good year, this ratio for the actual relationship is probably not far below the true output-capital ratio so calculated. For manufacturing in that year, about 90 per cent of capacity was utilized. Hence, 55 per cent may be considered a floor for the ratio. Since the average ratio relates to the entire stock, and the incremental to new additions with up-to-date fixed capital goods, the $\Delta Y/I$ ratio will be higher than the average. Therefore, the Kuznets ratio of two thirds for the incremental seems reasonable.

Combining the values applicable to the right-hand side of the growth-rate equation, we see that the required growth rate in the 1950's was

$$\Delta Y/Y = .06 \times .67$$
$$= 4.02 \text{ per cent per year.}$$

Unless these estimated values for s and $\Delta Y/I$ are in error, they emphasize that the 2.5 per cent annual growth rate of real in-

---

3. Simon Kuznets, *Capital in the American Economy*, National Bureau of Economic Research (Princeton: Princeton University Press, 1961), p. 217, Table 33; p. 209, Table 30; p. 85, Table 7. We use the inverse of Kuznets' ratios.

4. *Economic Report of the President*, January, 1952, p. 55, Chart 3.

come in the later 1950's was notably below the required rate. Actually to achieve such a rate it would be necessary to reject the contemporary emphasis on raising saving and P & E investment in favor of bolstering alternative channels of demand. In an economy with such a high $\Delta Y/I$, private and social consumption (in the form of welfare or waste) must be highly correlated with the required income gains if the added capacity associated with even modest net investment is to be economically justified.

A second complex of relationships that may have inhibited the volume of P & E investment spending involved the alleged conservative and bureaucratic nature of the corporate hierarchy and the monopolistic character of markets. But whether or not the executives of large nonfinancial corporations, and of the financial intermediaries that provide so much of their external financing, are unduly "security conscious" is a largely unexplored matter. More exploration has taken place with respect to the effect on investment of the reinforcement of entrenched monopoly positions, but the results are inconclusive. This does not mean that possible adverse effects of monopoly on investment should not be entertained, particularly certain aspects of the relationship. For example, one important aspect of the reinforcement of entrenched monopoly positions is the exploitation of the seventeen-year patent privilege, to which brief reference was made in Chapter 7. This and other monopolistic aspects of contemporary markets have, it is generally agreed among industrial organization theorists, tended to block the entry of "new firms" and "new men" so dear to the heart of Joseph Schumpeter. It seems certainly true that some inhibition of investment is a concomitant of inhibited entry,[5] and inhibited entry is found in most markets today. But quantification is next to impossible.

A third partial explanation of the sluggish investment performance, advanced in Chapter 4, was found in the moderately greater proportionate expansion of the service industries (including government). As an explanation, the crucial related proposition was that the K/Q ratio was lower in the service lines than in the commodity-producing industries (with the notable exception of the public utilities). Hence, for any given increase in output in these activities a comparatively low amount of investment would be required.

5. See in this connection P. Hennipman, "Monopoly: Impediment or Stimulus to Economic Progress?" in E. H. Chamberlin (ed.), *Monopoly and Competition and Their Regulation* (London: Macmillan, and New York: St. Martin's, 1961), esp. pp. 432–434.

A fourth partial explanation could perhaps be found in the rate of growth of consumption (and government purchases), which may well have placed a ceiling on investment growth. Since the average annual rate of growth of total consumption was only 3.4 per cent, and in the important nondurables only 2.7 per cent, investment could have been held down by a consumer spending limit. This point cannot be passed over without some further attention.

The proposition was advanced in Chapter 4 that a greater proportion of private P & E investment than formerly is in contemporary conditions *induced* investment. The proposition implies that so-called "autonomous investment," or "investment for further investment" (Fellner), or "enterprise investment" (Lamfalussy)—all of which express executive investment motivation of a swashbuckling, non-security-conscious type that is more or less independent of imminent consumer spending—has become, for whatever reasons, a declining phenomenon. The editors of *Fortune*, writing as far back as April, 1940, could well have had such an hypothesis in mind when they declared, "The central economic problem is not . . . a revival in 'investment' in the old sense of the word. The central economic problem is simply the conversion of a high potential power to consume into an actual power to consume: a wider distribution of progress. . . . In the consumer lies the frontier. . . ." [6]

Investment is ultimately a "derived" demand. Such has always been the case. What seems to have gone out of the investment flow is that autonomous, capital-deepening portion that "built ahead of demand" and raised demand along with it. Hence, given the earlier noted characteristics of the capital goods flow together with the possible inhibiting influences of monopolistic elements and security-conscious executive motivation, *the moderate rate of growth of consumer and government spending may well have been the decisive factor in investment retardation.* If current sales and the rate of capacity utilization were, besides profitability, the chief independent variables of the investment function, such an hypothesis would stand up well under empirical scrutiny, although the latter years of the period under study are admittedly all too brief a basis for a firm conclusion. In this connection it will be recalled that commercial capital equipment

6. Cited in *Factors Affecting Volume and Stability of Private Investment*, U.S. Joint Committee on the Economic Report, Senate Document No. 232, 81st Cong., 2nd sess. (Washington, D.C., U.S. Government Printing Office, 1950), p. 31.

output, geared closely as it was to household consumption and the spread of metropolitan areas, continued to expand in the late 1950's long after the industrial equipment index had almost approached its zenith—possibly a kind of old-fashioned capital-widening phenomenon.

An additional candidate among the possible retarding influences on real investment was mergers and acquisitions. As pointed out in Chapter 7, such moves in many cases were no doubt substitutes for the creation of more productive capacity. The influence of this factor was probably minor, however.

Finally, it has often been reasoned that foreign competition, by depressing sales of domestically produced goods, can inhibit domestic investment. It is possible that this, as well as the export pattern, could have been a marginal factor operating against a higher domestic investment rate in the late 1950's, although it must have been minor, as Chart XV suggests.

Investment, the Public Budgets, and Consumer Spending

Perhaps some combination of the six possible explanations enumerated above would suffice to account for the inadequate performance of private P & E investment. Certainly some, if not all, of these forces were operative. However, at least one additional matter commands attention, if only because of the continuing controversy surrounding it both in the 1950's and in preceding decades. This matter is the relationship of "big government," actual and normative, to the workings of the private investment mechanism.

In the contemporary capitalistic world, even many who do not consider themselves proponents of crude *laissez faire* have insisted that large government budgets represent an encroachment on the private market system. The degree of encroachment, if such is the proper term, may be represented handily by the fact that in the United States, Federal civilian expenditures, including transfer payments, amounted to 3.0 per cent of GNP in 1929 and 7.5 per cent in 1955. (Military expenditures are typically viewed either as not an encroachment or as an acceptable encroachment.)

To those persons whose viewpoint is identified with the "unfettered" (but governmentally assisted) private investment mechanism, the encroachment process has typically been deemed a depressant with respect to its presumed action on that mechanism. Criticism was leveled against the extension of regulatory authority over business, the growing *civilian* component of the *Federal* budget, and the way the latter was financed. Within the civilian component of the Federal budget, welfare expenditures, representing the so-called "welfare state," were the chief target. As to the methods of financing, the criticism was distinctly classical, being directed against deficits and any taxes on the sources of savings.

The size, character, and growth of the central government budget, and the presumed adverse incidence of its associated tax progressiveness on private investment, were and are political issues in every major advanced business economy. The business community continued in the 1950's, no less than in earlier decades, to forecast the withering away of private investment incentives should the encroachment process persist.

There is no analytical technique available to test the empirical validity of these propositions. There is no way to determine whether the extremely moderate augmentation of the Federal civilian government sector in the 1950's operated to "choke off growth and strangle the private enterprise system," as Mr. Robert C. Tyson, Chairman of United States Steel's Finance Committee unhesitantly asserted in June, 1961.[7] Keynesian and other reformers answered, as they had traditionally answered, that such augmentation was the only long-run alternative to rather complete replacement of that system, replacement in all probability by some form of socialism. To this the conservative retort, as traditionally advanced, was that government encroachment opened the door to socialism. Indeed, the contestants approached matters in much the same way they had approached them in the days of the New Deal, although the emotional index was notably lower.

Economists of the Schumpeter persuasion, who had forgotten the dark days of the early 1930's and who took positions similar to that of Mr. Tyson, were too obsessed with the progressiveness (however mild) of the effective Federal tax structure to appreciate the strong regressive features of that structure—features that were sufficiently inimical to consumption to commend themselves to those enamored of the classical pro-savings approach. The same group also tended to overlook the sales boost provided by government expenditures to the leading firms in most of the important growth industries as well as in the lagging sectors.

As for government regulation, most of it, as shown for example in connection with the new labor regulation of the 1950's, was by no means always, or necessarily for the most part, inimical to the wishes of business. Nor was this the first time in twentieth-

7. *The U.S. Steel Quarterly*, August, 1961, p. 5. Federal non-defense expenditures, excluding transfer payments, as percentage of GNP *fell* slightly between 1950 and 1960. Federal civilian employment, however, rose slightly.

century American economic history that more regulation resulted from pressures originating in the business community.

The case for a balanced appraisal of the impact of expanding government on private enterprise incentive is reinforced by consideration of the way in which the so-called miracle of West German postwar expansion was misused on this side of the water as an argument for "free enterprise." The high rate of economic growth in West Germany during the 1950's was explained by the minimum-government advocates as largely due to the unfettered operation of the private investment mechanism (all government purchases averaged over one third of GNP, whereas in the United States this averaged about one fourth).

As is well known by the informed, nothing could be much farther from the truth. The West German "miracle" was possible only because of a large civilian government budget, including what would be considered from an American perspective sizable welfare components; a small military budget; substantial United States public foreign aid in the early years; extremely liberal and selective tax exemptions by the German Federal government; selective investment aids; export subsidies; accelerated depreciation; government loans at notably less than market interest to selected private enterprises and industries; selective government expenditures and tax concessions, including unique tax incentives for residential construction; active government labor recruitment and allocation; a nationalized industry sector much larger than in the United States; and a generally more advanced level of central government planning.[8] To think that it was this program, together with the famous currency reform, that was widely heralded as "the restoration of free markets"! Many were deceived, perhaps, by some decartelization and the selling off of some nationalized properties. Actually, the West German pattern resembled in many respects the state capitalism of Japan in its era of rapid development before World War I. Nor was it by any means a new pattern even to Germany, whose drive to maturity was inaugurated under the "socialistic" Bismarck.

A neomercantilist investment program of the German type, if added onto the much larger United States military budget (about 10 per cent of GNP), would involve in the case of the United States a reduction of the average consumption ratio from two thirds to about 55 per cent. There is certainly some question,

8. See in this connection the discussion "Lessons from the West German 'Miracle'" by K. W. Roskamp in *Challenge*, Institute of Economic Affairs, New York University, July, 1961, pp. 10–14.

aside from whether it would be economically sustainable, as to whether such a reduction would be politically acceptable in the democratic American climate. In the context of the American social balance as represented by the economic history of the 1950's, it appears that the private investment mechanism will have to function in the foreseeable future without benefit of special measures by the state to shift very substantially the allocation of resources toward relatively more investment and less consumption.

In the last half of the 1950's the United States had *both* insufficient (as a spending stimulant) P & E investment *and* excess capacity. Assuming for a moment that government spending and net exports had been neutral in their effects during that period, it is doubtful that a rate of investment increase *moderately* greater than the actual rate would have been enough, through multiplier effects, to raise consumption spending sufficiently to justify itself, i.e., to provide sustained full-capacity utilization of the expanded capital goods plant. A rate of increase sufficient to accomplish this—one containing plenty of capital widening, investment for further investment, etc.,—would have had to be *very substantially* greater than the actual rate.

The significance of this latter judgment lies not so much in the inevitable cyclical disproportionality between output capacity and demand that would ensue. More importantly, it lies in the fact that the politically feasible prescriptions advanced during the late 1950's ostensibly to bolster private investment—such as softer Treasury depreciation policies, somewhat lower corporate income taxes, and more moderate union wage demands—would alone have been much too mild a dose of the classical medicine to do the job. And harsher and more harshly applied remedies undoubtedly were and are no longer politically feasible.

An illustration of the remedies thought feasible by an outstanding enlightened conservative may be found in the proposals of Professor Arthur F. Burns, first Chairman of the Council of Economic Advisers under President Eisenhower. In connection with a controversy between President Kennedy's Council and himself over appropriate growth and related policies, Professor Burns suggested, in order to achieve a higher rate of economic growth, giving "no less attention to the reduction of governmental obstacles to growth than we give to the devising of new governmental stimuli to growth": liberalization of the tax rules governing depreciation; reduction of the tax rates applicable to the higher personal incomes; alternatively, imposition of a low but broadly based Federal excise tax; inauguration of an extensive worker-training program; exertion of greater effort by colleges of business administration to improve small business efficiency; elimination of featherbedding by labor and business executives; extension of unemployment insurance coverage and benefits; and amendment of the Employment Act to include a commitment to maintain reasonable stability of the consumer price level.[9] Unless such proposals be viewed as an "opening wedge," they are clearly insufficient to the task confronting private investment in a program placing chief reliance on such investment to achieve a substantially higher rate of growth. (The lack of realism in such an attempted solution has already been discussed.) In this connection, it is significant that Professor Burns apparently wished to cover himself, for he promptly added that he would be reasonably satisfied "if it turns out that we fail to achieve all the improvement we seek," to "do no worse than in the 1950's. . . ." [10]

If, on the other hand, one were not satisfied, as many were not, with the performance of the 1950's, the feasible and adequate prescriptions would presumably lie in other directions. Those directions have already been suggested at various points tracing the history of the decade. One very important channel is increased social consumption through expansion of what Galbraith has termed the "starved public sector." Another is inauguration of a large and sustained program of gifts in the form of goods and services to less developed countries. A third is increased private consumption on the part of the low-income population. With regard to the last named, the analogy with the 1920's is again appropriate. Writing of that decade in his *Controlling Factors in Economic Development*, Harold Moulton declared, "A larger relative flow of funds through consumptive channels would have led to a larger utilization of existing productive capacity and also to a more rapid growth of plant and equipment. . . ." [11] There is little need to emphasize these policy alternatives further. In the 1950's, the government succeeded in putting a floor under consumption, but fiscal policy was insufficient to raise to satisfactory heights the ceiling on the rate of growth of consumption. Hence, a more vigorous policy of underwriting consumption, without relaxing its investment underwriting, might have been much better than the actual, attempted emphasis on budget reduction and

9. See *The Morgan Guaranty Survey*, Morgan Guaranty Trust Company of New York, August, 1961, pp. 11–12.

10. *Ibid.*, p. 12.

11. (Washington: Brookings Institution, 1949.) Cited in *Factors Affecting the Volume and Stability of Private Investment*, *op. cit.*, p. 31.

budget balancing.

In the American economy of the 1950's, the Federal tax system, the generally effective program of minimizing the budget, and the commitment to the annually balanced budget converted the Federal budget into a force for dampening growth during the last half of the decade. Most of the burden of growth inducement by government was therefore shifted to the state and local jurisdictions. The latter, with their regressive tax systems, were ill equipped for the task of spurring growth through the stimulation of consumption. Whatever expansionary effects came from this quarter may be attributed largely to steady increase associated with modest deficits.

If a policy that restricts private and collective consumption poses danger to economic stability, and also to the democratic philosophy, then the best alternative for stimulating greater growth and more investment may well be a positive and vigorous policy designed to raise the rate of growth of consumer spending, including housing as part of consumption rather than investment, and to supplement it with more social consumption and foreign grants.[12]

The techniques for accomplishing these aims, techniques employing the principle of inducement and underwriting rather than rigid controls, are generally well known and need no elaboration here. Suffice it to say that consumption would be stimulated from the tax aspect only through a reduction of the regressivity dominating the state and local structure and strongly penetrating the Federal. As for the budgets as a whole, if they are to be balanced as they grow, *they will have to grow all the faster because of the balancing.*

A growth rate of GNP of 4 to 5 per cent per annum might generate more inflationary pressures than the sluggish growth of the late 1950's. This danger will have to be faced if the goal of rapid growth is determinedly pursued.

12. A recent growth model, structured in terms of privately and publicly financed mass consumer durable asset formation, developed by H. T. Oshima ("Consumer Asset Formation and the Future of Capitalism," *Economic Journal*, March, 1961, pp. 20–35), places such an emphasis on even firmer ground than was heretofore the case.

Index